I0605354

ON THE GROUND

My Life as a Foreign Correspondent

BRIAN STEWART

PUBLISHED BY SIMON & SCHUSTER

New York Amsterdam/Antwerp London
Toronto Sydney/Melbourne New Delhi

A Division of Simon & Schuster, LLC
166 King Street East, Suite 300
Toronto, Ontario M5A 1J3

For more than 100 years, Simon & Schuster has championed authors and the stories they create. By respecting the copyright of an author's intellectual property, you enable Simon & Schuster and the author to continue publishing exceptional books for years to come. We thank you for supporting the author's copyright by purchasing an authorized edition of this book.

No amount of this book may be reproduced or stored in any format, nor may it be uploaded to any website, database, language-learning model, or other repository, retrieval, or artificial intelligence system without express permission. All rights reserved. Inquiries may be directed to Simon & Schuster, 1230 Avenue of the Americas, New York, NY 10020 or permissions@simonandschuster.com.

Copyright © 2025 by Brian Stewart

All photos appear courtesy of the author.

All rights reserved, including the right to reproduce this book or portions thereof in any form whatsoever. For information, address Simon & Schuster Canada Subsidiary Rights Department, 166 King Street East, Suite 300, Toronto, Ontario M5A 1J3, Canada.

This Simon & Schuster Canada edition September 2025

SIMON & SCHUSTER CANADA and colophon are registered trademarks of Simon & Schuster, LLC

Simon & Schuster strongly believes in freedom of expression and stands against censorship in all its forms. For more information, visit BooksBelong.com.

For information about special discounts for bulk purchases, please contact Simon & Schuster Special Sales at 1-800-268-3216 or CustomerService@simonandschuster.ca.

Interior design by Carly Loman

Manufactured in the United States of America

1 3 5 7 9 10 8 6 4 2

Library and Archives Canada Cataloguing in Publication

Title: On the ground : my life as a foreign correspondent / by Brian Stewart.
Names: Stewart, Brian (Journalist), author.
Description: Simon & Schuster Canada edition. | Includes bibliographical references and index.
Identifiers: Canadiana (print) 20250112396 | Canadiana (ebook) 2025011240X | ISBN 9781668052150 (hardcover) | ISBN 9781668052167 (EPUB)
Subjects: LCSH: Stewart, Brian (Journalist) | LCSH: Foreign correspondents—Canada—Biography. | LCSH: Television journalists—Canada—Biography. | LCGFT: Autobiographies.
Classification: LCC PN4913.S758 A3 2025 | DDC 070.4/332092—dc23

ISBN 978-1-6680-5215-0
ISBN 978-1-6680-5216-7 (ebook)

For Tina and Katie . . .
And in memory of my parents

Contents

1

The Child in the Ethiopian Famine

Across the north of Ethiopia runs the great massif of highlands and mountains that, rising to four thousand metres, form the fabled Roof of Africa. Everything about the land appears stark, remote, dramatic, and timeless. Life exists, precariously, across sun-seared plateaus and atop flat buttes, the jagged gorges in deep shadows and the isolated terraces dotted with the grass-roofed huts of subsistence farms. I have returned to this land many times over four decades to cover human struggles for survival and humanitarian efforts to save lives. My connection there is precious to me because no other story ever affected me so deeply.

The reason I first flew into Ethiopia for CBC TV in the fall of 1984 was to investigate alarming rumours of a giant famine advancing across the northern highlands—not just widespread hunger but a full-force famine that could kill millions of the world's most vulnerable people. True famines are rare, arising not just from drought and harvest failures but from the combination of major calamities in severely misgoverned lands and involving failed rains, insect infestations, soil overuse, environmental collapse, extreme poverty, and some form of war as well. When such a famine occurs, oppressive governments not only try to hide it but may even collude in promoting it to curb the growth of troublesome populations.

Several times during my first reporting from the famine epicentre in northern Ethiopia that year, I made a point of visiting one particular relief centre early in the mornings: the St. Vincent de Paul Clinic, which sat isolated on a flat, burnt-out plain outside Makelle, the capital of Tigray province. A line of dull-green eucalyptus trees along its side broke up the monotone browns and greys of the surrounding fields, giving it an oasis-like air from a distance. It was anything but calm when you reached the gates. The clinic lay on the path of one of the largest mass famine migrations and was daily overwhelmed by refugees seeking help. Still more would arrive through the night and quietly line up waiting for the gate to open.

The clinic was run by the Catholic order of Sisters of Charity, who had operated the mission among the poorest of Tigray regions since the 1920s. Because it was situated on a road leading into Makelle, it took some of the first brunt of the migration as increasing waves of starving and sick people trekked down from the farms in the highlands. The Sisters, both Ethiopian and foreign, offered what medical aid they could for the sickest and helped families bury the dead with dignity. They understood that a score of diseases, from meningitis to typhoid and pneumonia, were surging among people so malnourished that a cold could be fatal.

The individual stories told by the refugees increased fears that an apocalypse was building: however bad it was here, far worse realities were spreading in the trackless hinterland. Once families had exhausted everything they owned, they left with only a small pouch of grain to trek over barren and bitterly cold ground for days, past human and animal corpses. Through the terrors of the night they huddled together to sleep, only to find more dead around them in the morning. Most feared were the hyenas shrieking in the dark, attracted by the smell of death. Whole villages tended to leave together, so if one died, there would be others to bury them. Sometimes they walked for weeks, passing through ghost villages depopulated in the panic. Death was everywhere, the stench overwhelming; a common sight was mothers still carrying a dead child in their arms, reluctant to leave it behind to such horrors.

When my CBC news team and I arrived at the clinic around nine one morning, we were already emotionally battered after a week covering the hardest-hit region and still had weeks to go on just our first assignment here. With me was my hard-driving, tireless producer Tony Burman, who had fought Ethiopia's bureaucracy for months just to get us here; our lanky and brilliant cameraman Phillipe Billard, experienced in filming crises of every kind but shaken now by what his lens captured; and sound technician John Axelson, a last minute addition to the team, fitted in well despite brutal circumstances.

We weren't surprised to find that the crowd already covered the entire stony courtyard or that both the staff and the refugees looked exhausted. A modest stone-and-concrete administrative building stood in the centre, surrounded by a few corrugated iron huts used as temporary shelters. A nurse nodded when we asked to record interviews, so, half crouching, I started down a line of parents and infants slumped along the main wall. Several had already lost one child, and their eyes pleaded as they held other sick infants.

Almost immediately I noticed a short, lean man in the customary shawl who was trying to comfort a girl about three years old who looked barely conscious. She seemed to be the most serious case there, and I kept glancing their way as I continued my interviews. Suddenly, the child slumped into a heap on the pavement. I called to a nearby nurse, and she rushed forward, picked up the girl, and raced her inside to an examination room. The father ran after them and we followed, camera rolling.

As we entered, the girl lay on a table. I was struck by her face as her glazed eyes appeared locked on something far in the distance and her rasping breath slowed. In my emotional state I saw her face as a tragic symbol of Ethiopia's countless children denied hope, robbed of life, beseeching the distant world for justice. A tired-eyed Irish sister said softly: "The child will die very soon—she has pneumonia and is very malnourished. She will die here, maybe within fifteen minutes. There isn't anything we can do at this point."

We left to allow her to die with whatever dignity the situation could provide. Stumbling outside into the glaring light, we learned she would be buried later that afternoon in a grave being dug for the most recent dead. We drove away, not speaking much, and almost by rote continued on through the day collecting scenes of other relief operations swamped by huddled masses of the sick and dying on grounds with no hygiene, little food or shelter, and fading hope. How could we show an individual tragedy among this sea of desperation? I began mentally scripting the news item that would focus on the child's death, the searing power of that tragic face and those last breaths.

We would need the burial scene for our report, so around 5 p.m. we drove back to the clinic. We were finally talking freely among ourselves about how emotionally upsetting that scene with the child had been, so painful to witness the end of her life. Someone seemed to speak for all of us when he said angrily that her agony drove home just how bloody hellish, unjust, and utterly depressing was everything we saw here: "Bodies after bodies of children, just bundles. Bloody hell, where's the aid?" I hoped that viewers would identify with her and see how real people, not just vague images, were being destroyed by a famine the world could stop if it had the will.

As we pulled into the courtyard, there was a bustle of activity and the shock of seeing real smiles on faces. One of the Ethiopian staff ran up, saying, "You must come!" We scrambled out and followed her toward a small crowd of people who were also smiling and clustering around the same Irish nun, who held a bundle in her arms. I approached—it was the girl, awake, alive, safe. "Sister, I see we had a little bit of luck today," I stammered. She smiled more: "Yes, we felt a surprise pulse and we gave her one last shot and rehydration, and she will survive."

She was still very sick, so the nuns would keep her in the clinic for as long as she needed to recover. The father, standing nearby, appeared dazed by the sequence of events, from doom to deliverance. I asked her name and someone replied, Birhan (Light). Her last name was Woldu.

Ten days later, we returned to the clinic when we heard that Birhan was ready to be released. At the door of her shelter, the father emerged with the child standing beside him and her younger sister, Silas, in his arms. Birhan was shy of strangers, but it was a wonderful scene of survival that once more touched us all.

I finally had a brief chance to talk to the father, Woldu Menamano, who stood barely five feet tall and appeared all lean muscle and bone, so weather-beaten he seemed ageless (he was thirty-six). He had spent his life battling hardscrabble poverty through many droughts and at least two famines.

Any notion of pity, however, would have appalled him, for he was an immensely proud man who insisted that, in their remote highland village of Lahama, the family's conical, thatched, mud-and-dung-walled hut had been a loving home and a happy place when Birhan was born. Given any decent rain, he was skilled at growing crops on small plots and had built up holdings of two oxen, a donkey, and some goats. He had sold the best honey and yogourt around. In good seasons, when it rained, the highlands could be lush, but now there was only death.

Though he'd never been to school, Woldu was an intelligent and vivid talker. After three years of drought, he said, the crops didn't grow and the rivers were dry. His wife had died of an illness and, to feed his three daughters, he'd had to sell everything, even his farm implements and the cooking pots. They had only the clothes they stood in and a few handfuls of grain. How could he not flee? I have rarely heard a better personal description of why famine is different from other calamities.

Neighbours were "falling like leaves," he told me. "The village was starving." They all left together, and the days of trudging toward hoped-for help was like walking through a cemetery of unburied dead.

They had no shelter, so slept under one blanket on frigid ground, fearing hyenas in the dark and vultures circling overhead through the day. On a future trip I got a sense of that terror when I came across a dead woman half-eaten by hyenas, and a boy who'd fought himself free of one at the loss of much of his hand.

When they finally could stop near a small village close to Makelle, they slept outside on the ground with barely enough rations to survive. By then Birhan was so sick that Woldu feared she was dying. With no medical aid nearby, he wrapped her on his back and half-ran fifteen kilometres in a loping gait to the Catholic mission. When they arrived just before dark, it was so overcrowded they couldn't get in. He spent another night trying to keep Birhan warm.

In the morning, he finally got his place in the line inside. At some point strange-looking *firangi* (foreigners) with a camera machine came by. Then Birhan collapsed as if dead.

The misery in the northern highlands of Ethiopia had caused barely a ripple of interest in the outside world, much of which was enjoying prosperous times with bumper harvests and unprecedented stockpiles of grains. Some commentators were calling the eighties the "age of greed." Out of a population of forty-four million in Ethiopia, between six and seven million were soon at risk of starvation, and tens of thousands had already perished.

Although some private aid groups and government studies had warned for months of a steady drop in Ethiopia's food supplies, there was no international alarm about the coming catastrophe mainly because no television pictures of mass starvation had emerged to show just how devastating the human cost could be. Ethiopia's Marxist regime, the Derg (Committee), was determined to keep foreign news crews from poking into the scandal of mass deaths at a time when it was expensively celebrating ten years in power. The strongman leader, Mengistu Haile Mariam, knew that kind of revelation would feed growing insurrection in northern provinces. The solution? Simply ban travel permits to TV news teams, at least until after the September celebrations. Margaret Thatcher's Conservative government and Ronald Reagan's White House wanted nothing to do with the Derg, including any form of direct aid. Most Western nations took the cue and stayed clear.

I was then in my second year based in the CBC's London bureau as foreign correspondent, in the dream job of my youth. It was a vast beat: I was responsible for the United Kingdom (including Northern Ireland's unrest), much of Africa, and various conflicts in the Middle East, which meant a lot of time covering the civil war in Beirut. By June, Burman and I were picking up alarming accounts from our sources in NGOs and universities of a third straight year of drought across northern Ethiopia. Burman started lobbying the Ethiopian embassy to give us visas, using every Canada "nice guy" image he could think of. At the time, the Canadian passport had respect as a symbol of an internationalist middle broker.

In the world of TV foreign news, the 1980s were exhilarating—glamorous enough to be looked back on as a golden age. Well-staffed news bureaus had budgets to travel extensively, and reporters could spend enough time on location to understand and develop stories properly. The new satellite technology allowed us to feed items almost in real time from remote areas of the world, while video seemed "more live" than film for feeding out footage of wars and catastrophes directly into living rooms at home. For me, personally, I thrived on working in an endless vortex of crises and historic moments. But there was also a downside: for months on end, the reporters, producers, and crews lived on alert with suitcases packed, never knowing where we'd be next, leading to emotional exhaustion. Sure, between tough foreign assignments, the good life of covering peace talks or elections in capital cities and exotic countries made up for a lot of hellish postings, but the inner wear and tear could build up alarmingly over time.

One October morning when I was researching the history of

Ethiopia's past famines and wars, Burman raced into the office announcing yes, we had our bloody visas! We were the first TV network in the world to get the go-ahead. Soon after, we got news that the BBC also had entry, though for a much shorter period. Given the urgency of the story, we knew we were in a race to get as much material out as possible before, as we feared, the Derg would expel us.

Arriving in the capital, Addis Ababa, we scrambled to find relief agencies with planes willing to take us with them when they flew north on missions. We left within hours to fly to Makelle in northern Tigray, the hardest-hit province. Flying at twelve thousand feet, we could just make out thin black lines that trailed along the roads near sizable towns—a seemingly endless number of destitute refugees making their way toward distant relief camps through the grey countryside devoid of green.

Once on the ground, we ran into a situation barely operating above chaos. On any day as many as eighty thousand to one hundred thousand refugees were in Makelle alone in severe stages of malnutrition. There were no food riots—only a quiet despair. Many of the Orthodox Christians believed they were suffering heaven's punishment for past sins; others were too weak to move or too proud to make a fuss. Along many roads we saw what appeared to be slowly moving tides of humanity, sometimes almost crawling, masses decimated by cholera, pneumonia, dysentery, and flu. They would often appear out of a haze floating across the land from small fires and dust clouds. The smells of human waste, fires, sickness, and the rotting corpses of animals could be overwhelming. Most of the human dead were quickly buried, except in the countryside where famine victims often had neither the time nor the strength to inter those who died around them. On average, people who were already starving walked for two or three full days, parents leading or carrying several sick children, to reach a place where they might appeal for aid. At moments when burials were underway, mothers might weep and chant, but that was the only sound, apart from prayers and the wind.

Ethiopia's own Relief and Rehabilitation Commission staff were supported by small, overworked teams of foreigners from Oxfam, Save the Children, Catholic Relief Services, the International Committee of the Red Cross, and other NGOs. The hardiest had been struggling to run hunger relief and medical care for months, and I could find no hint of optimism among them. Instead, there was a seething rage over world indifference. For nurses, the hardest task was the morning triage as they went down rows of mothers or fathers holding a child, measuring the circumference of a tiny arm to pick out those still likely to survive. I approached a nurse with Médecins Sans Frontières (Doctors Without Borders) and asked what the world should do: "Send food! Food! Food!" she cried before backing off in apparent hysterics.

One nun, Sister Jean Harris, had spent weeks travelling through rebel lines to her outpost near Makelle, treating any in need she could find. She told me stories of diving into ditches or hiding under hedges with others to avoid strafing by government MiGs and attack helicopters. She had been working nonstop for months as the death toll rose, first into the hundreds, then thousands some days, within the region. What was changing, she said, were the numbers giving up: "They're tired, too tired to go on. First the fathers often die, then children, and only last do the mothers give out, for they feel the need to keep going for the rest."

When we were at a relief site, I would spent some of the time watching visuals that Billard was getting, pointing out details I wanted to write into the script. I also walked around the camp, talking to organizers, staff, and refugees. Like most correspondents, I wore a safari suit with big pockets to hold notebooks, pens, passport, media cards, and throat medicine, essential amid the dust. Burman kept it all moving, arranging ground transport, schedules, and the satellite news feeds he had to travel to Nairobi in neighbouring Kenya to use. At night, he and I plotted how best to record "the true picture," though we never knew what new scale of horrors the next day would bring.

"I remember that you and I had conversations where we asked, 'Are we really experiencing what we think we are experiencing?' because this is just incredible," Burman recalled years later. "My biggest worry was just how to get this story out. We were in the middle of nowhere, it seemed, and how could we portray something so vast that would make sense at home?" We felt we'd have one or two chances at best to wake Canadians up to the real tragedy of Ethiopia. Disaster stories normally have only a few days before audiences turn their attention elsewhere. I felt sure that CBC, which was run by serious people, would place the story at the top of the national news.

The script was up to me, and it would fail unless it firmly captured not just the depth of the catastrophe's misery but the urgent imperative for international action. I needed to get across that endless floodtide of humanity, so I wrote: "All across northern Ethiopia, famine is along each road, and at the gates of every town. By the hundreds of thousands, peasants are fleeing the worst drought in memory. Unknown thousands are dying along the way. It's feared close to a million could die within months unless the world responds with a massive relief effort. Relief agencies here are swamped; they've never seen starvation on this scale."

Much of the first report was shot when we flew to the desolate plateau of Korem, the most notorious of the relief camps. Some eighty thousand refugees crowded onto the site around a series of huts that could shelter not even a tenth that number. In the surrounding fields there was no water, no shelter, no sanitation. It was fiercely cold whenever the sun sank behind the hills, and the sound of coughing and retching remained constant. I added in one of my on-camera stand-ups that I was wearing three layers of clothing and was still very cold, while all around people shivered in one thin rag trying to get through the night.

In the nearby hills there was the threat that the insurgent Tigrayan People's Liberation Front, the largest of the anti-government guerrilla movements, was keen to kidnap foreign volunteers or media to get them to acknowledge their cause and famine needs, and then release them for propaganda value. The government guards thwarted their plans by locking foreigners into a cement-block "guesthouse" at night. I tried to sleep, but I kept hearing a ghostly moan through the shutters that I couldn't identify. When we were released at first light I realized that the sound had been coming from a long line of refugees who had huddled all night along the road, praying as they faced their likely end. When I mentioned the sound to the others, none had heard it. They had slept, and I worried that I might have been hallucinating. Years later I read a description by David Lamb, a former correspondent for the *Los Angeles Times* who also spent an icy night in Korem around the same time: "When all the valley is as still as death and the foreboding darkness seems eternal, the wailing begins, softly at first like the distant chant of ghosts. It is a high-pitched, eerie howl that slices through the night, gathering strength until it lingers and echoes over the mile-high valley—thousands of voices united in prayerful pleas for mercy and forgiveness."

For several hours after dawn, my team was alone among the refugees because the medical staff were even more carefully guarded in lockdown caution. Everywhere we looked were desperate people needing help to survive—mothers holding up half dead or actually dead children—and not one of us could do a thing to assist. It was a hideous feeling—all we could do was report, and we summoned all the energy we had to do just that.

When a handful of Médecins Sans Frontières doctors and nurses finally appeared, several were from Canada and looked stunned to see anyone from outside, particular from the CBC. One medic from Quebec approached with a caution: "Are you actually ready for this? You are about to experience things here that will change your lives forever." Burman answered, "Please show us all—everything—we have to show this to the world."

Touring the famine huts—we didn't know what else to call them because medical aid was so limited—we were immersed in scenes of bodies being tied and carried out for burial and scores of dead, mainly children. We were shaken by a terrible feeling that what we were seeing was only the beginning of something beyond our full understanding. Everything we saw suggested millions faced death (the Red Cross would soon warn of six to seven million at risk).

To me it seemed a dystopia set more in the future than the past, as though we were experiencing, as I wrote, "the world as it would look after a nuclear holocaust when all normal life was destroyed and swept away." In my on-camera conclusion, I expressed my fear that the world would not respond quickly enough despite this proof of catastrophe: "It is difficult to imagine anything more horrendous or pitiful than these camps, but within months things here could be ten times worse. That's the most frightening thing of all here—the fact that this may not be the height of a catastrophe but just the beginning of an even greater one."

Once our material taped, we had to get it to the satellite feed point in Nairobi. First, though, we had to edit it in Addis Ababa, where our London editor, Colin Dean, had flown in with his gear to set up an editing suite in a hotel. There we had food, showers, and laundry, but no rest for Burman or me as we edited our footage to get the impact we wanted in the four minutes we would get on *The National* at 10 p.m. We had only hours to put the pieces together. Dean had not been in the field with us, so it was his first look at famine. "Oh my God," he gasped. "Can we even show this? Will they allow it?"

When I sat down to write the script, it seemed to compose itself in a stream of consciousness unlike anything I'd known before. Rather than my usual obsessive rewriting, the sentences flowed onto the page, and I didn't change a word. As morning advanced, Burman started tapping his watch and pacing, impatient to carry the cassette through the airport and onto the fight to Nairobi. He faced the real threat that authorities might demand to screen the tape before he left and then seize it. In desperation he stuck it to his back with sticky tape to smuggle it past airport security. The tension was high because this iron-fisted regime might throw him into a prison cell, expel the rest of us, and confiscate all our equipment. We might even get the CBC permanently barred and ruin access for other networks. I was glad it was his task, not mine. Too sleep-deprived to think much, I wished him well and collapsed into my bed, hoping not to be awakened by security police.

Burman made it, and fifteen hours after our report was fed by satellite, I got a phone call from *The National*'s host, Peter Mansbridge, a friend since our days together at the Ottawa bureau. The November 1 newscast had just ended, and he rasped in obvious emotion, "Do you have any idea what kind of impact your report's having? People in the studio were in tears, and that's never happened before." Before hanging up he wished me luck, adding, "This report will follow you throughout your life."

In the weeks that followed, the BBC and CBC reports set off an unprecedented explosion of international empathy—shock waves reverberating wherever viewers saw the images. Within forty-eight hours our news story of Birhan Woldu's survival against all odds had the special impact I was hoping for: here was a symbol of hope in a devastated land, a light in that darkness. Her story affected not only Canadians but even more viewers across the United States, where the NBC network carried it. It spurred more interest in relief efforts.

Britain and Canada were the first nations to respond, but did so in strikingly different ways. In Britain there was an immediate public outcry, a mass movement spearheaded by show-business celebrities, musicians, and particularly the rock star and activist Bob Geldof, who began organizing performers on both sides of the Atlantic and across Europe to raise money. So many pledges poured in that he set up an organization called Band Aid to launch Live Aid by June 1985—the largest-ever famine relief concert. The Thatcher government, however, remained firmly aloof, as did the grain-rich European Common Market and most governments in the West.

In Canada, in sharp contrast, the government led the charge: the newly elected Progressive Conservative majority of Brian Mulroney immediately declared it would take the lead in demanding not just a Canadian but also a world response to the emergency. At 24 Sussex Drive, Mulroney and his family had watched our report and wept. Having been interested in foreign aid projects as a youth, Mulroney knew more about Africa than any Canadian leader before or since. First thing next morning he called Stephen Lewis, whom he had recently appointed ambassador to the United Nations, to ask if he'd seen CBC's report.

"Yes, Prime Minister, and I hope that you are about to ask me what I think you are going to ask me."

"Yes, I am," said the prime minister, and instructed Lewis to go before the General Assembly in New York and rouse the world to immediate action. Barely a day later, Lewis, a powerful orator, told the UN that the CBC report had been the most shocking news item he'd ever seen and demanded nothing less than "a Herculean effort on the part of all member nations" to confront the famine.

Meanwhile, Mulroney rallied Parliament and lobbied the United States, the United Kingdom, and other key allies to overcome their ideological hostility and save vast numbers of innocent lives. Our first report on November 1 "set off what can only be described as a political tsunami," Mulroney biographer Fen Osler Hampson wrote years later. The rush to aid Ethiopia swept the country, leaving no part untouched. The outpouring of empathy that united politicians and public remains unique in Canadian history: according to author Nassisse Solomon, everything changed the moment *The National* "aired a four-minute editorial on the devastating famine in Ethiopia by reporter Brian Stewart . . . between 1984 and 1985 the Ethiopian famine became a unifying national cause and 'clarion call' to international action for Canadians from coast to coast."

Within days of Canada rallying the General Assembly, the UN and the International Committee of the Red Cross launched what was then the greatest single humanitarian effort in history. It would expand into a drive to save not only as many as seven million Ethiopians but also to help care for twenty-two million people in danger from food crises across much of sub-Saharan Africa. TV's first searing images and brutally honest reports "shook the world in 1984/85," according to the official UN history. The depthless horror of such a truly mass starvation appeared more immediate on video than it would have on film, and was larger than anyone had imagined, so that the public uprising demanding humanitarian intervention built over the coming months, eventually triggering billions of dollars in aid relief and a historic rise in new humanitarian NGOs and volunteer causes across much of the world. Above all, the Ethiopian relief operations, the UN reported two years later, led to "the greatest single peacetime mobilization of the international community this century."

I was not surprised that Canada performed well when the empathy stakes were high. Canada's record of involved internationalism had been growing since the late 1950s, giving it in some diplomatic circles the title of the "Samaritan state." Canadian diplomats, foreign aid officials, and private NGOs were highly respected internationally, and the CBC's foreign news coverage was valued more than it had ever been in peacetime before or since. There was cross-party agreement in many areas; even in the year before the famine, the Liberal government of Pierre Trudeau had supported Ethiopian anti-poverty programs, despite the regime's pariah status in the West.

Still in Ethiopia, we were encouraged by brief accounts of the remarkable response in Canada, but I had no time to take solace as we left Addis Ababa immediately to return to the famine lands to do more reports, including a documentary for *The Journal*, the current affairs portion of the news hour. Sadly, very little had improved in the relief camps. Stocks of food and medicine were even more stretched, and shelter, hygiene, and fuel were utterly inadequate for the mass movement of populations. Aid workers were exhausted, angry, and close to despair. When I asked a normally upbeat Irish priest how bad it was, he just glared at me, growling "Ahh—desperate! Desperate!" as he walked away.

My own mood was hardly better. An estimated one million tonnes of food, largely grain, would be needed from outside donors over twelve months, and that estimate seemed to be rising every week. But there were strong doubts anything close to that total would actually arrive, given logistical hurdles, the internal war, and general chaos. A great many people I was seeing every day would suffer an agonizing death, while even children who managed to survive might be mentally damaged by starvation.

I worried also about growing exhaustion in our small team—Burman, Billard, Axelson, and me—as the daily tragedies battered us all. I noticed more heavy silences among us as we kept our thoughts to ourselves, awash in personal emotions boiling below the surface. Even eating field rations roused feelings of guilt, and lack of sleep was a growing hazard. I noticed that my hands often shook as I tried to take notes.

"I too worried about illness because we were working what seemed to be twenty-hour days, and I don't think any of us got untroubled sleep at any point," Burman recalls. "I remember I got chills and started shaking so bad I thought, 'Oh God, this is going to knock me down'—but it didn't."

It seemed unlikely we wouldn't get sick. Disease was all around us and we all had coughs, which I didn't help by nervous chain-smoking. (I never lit up again after this trip.) Illness would spell doom, however, for given the visa hurdles, no replacement team could take our place. If I went down, Burman, who began his career as a reporter, could handle my role, and if he collapsed, I might at a pinch have taken over field producing duties. But neither Burman nor I could handle the sophisticated video camera if Billard got sick.

We were recording the biggest story in the world, the most important any of us would ever cover, yet by the third week of November we still seemed to be the only TV crew around. Apart from informing Canada, our reports and footage were also being shown on other world networks including CBS in the US. "I think what helped us through it," Burman recalled later, "was that inner knowledge that the situation was just so enormous, we had to hold it together and get the story out. I noticed too that we talked much less than normal. I think, frankly, we were reluctant to break into the inner space each of us needed to get through this."

We had little time to brood because the first conference of donor nations opened in Addis on November 8. Almost by the hour, Canada was emerging as the driving force behind the international rescue mission. Stephen Lewis was the leading spokesman for a small group of ambassadors demanding that the new UN Command Centre for Ethiopian Relief be set up in Addis rather than the traditional power boardrooms of New York and Geneva. Maurice Strong, known across the UN as "the man who got things done" and the first president of the Canadian International Development Agency, was appointed executive coordinator of the UN Office of Emergency Operations in Africa. He was, in effect, the supreme commander running a stupendously complex series of relief and rehabilitation operations involving several dozen nations and scores of arrangements with private relief groups.

The Canadian embassy in Addis was the most hard driving of the diplomatic bodies pushing for united action. Then came word from Ottawa that foreign minister Joe Clark would attend the conference—the first senior minister of any advanced Western nation to visit Ethiopia in a decade. His arrival had an electrifying effect on weary and demoralized relief aid agencies.

With his trademark can-do optimism, Clark immediately injected energy into the meetings at the Hilton Hotel. A quick study, seemingly tireless in any situation, he offered Mengistu's government a bridge to Western donor nations and assured NGOs that Canada was fully committed to the emergency. The mood shifted noticeably: participants vowed that difficulties would be overcome, logistical problems were given priority, and relations with the steely Ethiopian regime improved. Clark's delegation even met with Mengistu to discuss ways to coordinate foreign and domestic aid efforts.

Clark was not given access to the north—too insecure—so just before leaving he asked Burman if he could see our report and field tapes, which he had missed while travelling. We crammed his team into our bedroom/edit suite and began the screening. Everyone was shaken, and Clark along with several in his entourage broke down in tears. As I interviewed him later, he struggled with his emotions and could now fully grasp why Canada had been so shaken by the coverage. Our story of the screening, together with his interview, resonated powerfully at home. On the tarmac a reporter asked Clark why governments had suddenly sprung into action after doing nothing for so long. "Television," he replied.

Later that night, as I packed my travel bag, I again worried about the inner injuries, the psychic scar tissue, I was accumulating. Why was it so many people wept and talked openly of their reaction to these scenes, but I had not? I couldn't even cry in private for all the worn-out mothers and dying children I had seen. I recalled a line from Dante's *Inferno*: "I could not weep, so much of stone had I become within / They wept."

It would take two more extended visits into Ethiopia before, one night in a small country guest house, my swelling memories of sorrows witnessed in this land finally brought tears that seemed unstoppable through much of a very dark night.

By the third and fourth weeks of November I could at last see that an international relief effort was getting underway and even resistant powers were starting to come around. But I knew that getting food and medicine to those on the ground would be a logistical nightmare. Ethiopia was short of everything—food, medicine, transport, spare parts, even peace. Enormous, the size of France and Spain combined, with eighty ethnic groups in a population of forty-four million, it was a transportation nightmare. Relief convoys would have to range from sweltering tropical forest areas in the south to a distant and largely denuded north, where four regions—Eritrea, Tigray, Gonder, and Wallo—were taking the brunt of the famine. The country had few roads, railways, ports, or airports, and in the north most people got around as they had for millennia, by foot and by donkey. How could the million tonnes of food needed to feed the vast numbers under severe threat of starvation be delivered? There wasn't even enough storage for such a flow—I knew that already one of the earliest Canadian shipments of fifteen thousand tonnes of grain had spoiled at the unsheltered port before it could be loaded onto trucks.

Depressing as the obstacles were, however, I began to see as days passed that more lives were being saved. Standing in a relief camp, I'd sense the sudden excitement as someone spotted a dust cloud on the horizon, followed by a small convoy of relief trucks on a hillside dirt road. When one of the long-haulers pulled in, it would be swiftly unloaded and the food immediately cooked for families huddled on the ground. Grain was also distributed in pails to refugees packed outside the overcrowded camp.

I also saw more relief flights overhead heading into Makelle's airport. The Addis operation put together an early fleet of twenty fixed-wing aircraft and thirty helicopters that crossed the chilliest Cold War lines—Hercules transport planes from Britain, larger air carriers from the United States and the USSR, helicopters from Poland in the Warsaw Pact. In my second tour a few months later, as pressure on governments to aid Ethiopia soared still higher, the air fleet grew into an armada of seventy-five relief aircraft of all sizes, many capable of flying into small airstrips.

As the situation got more desperate, the UN Command Centre in Addis considered the possibility of airdrops—shoving bags of food out of planes to land in a drop zone below. A majority of experts thought they were too expensive and wasteful because many bags would break on landing, but proponents countered that the spillage would soon be scooped up by eager waiting hands. Almost overnight the plan was implemented, and soon we taped the first mercy drops as dozens of bags tumbled from the sky above. They saved an estimated two hundred thousand more lives.

As if famine wasn't grim enough, we found dark new elements to the story to try and unravel. There were rumours, but little visible evidence, that the Mengistu government was forcibly resettling vast numbers of the famine refugees from the northern highlands to the tropical lowlands in the south. Some aid workers were expelled for damning it as ethnic cleansing—a way to remove Tigrayans and weaken the local Tigrayan People's Liberation Front rebel army. Some four hundred thousand were flown south in the first wave. It was all done away from foreign observers, especially the media.

One morning as we were about to set out for another shoot, an unmarked van with two army officers inside pulled up beside us. "Get in," the closer officer ordered. My time covering conflicts in Latin America and Beirut had left me jittery about rides with strangers, including army officers. Journalists too often never came back from such mystery rides. "Just get in," the second officer commanded. "There is something you should see." Warily we clambered into the van and were sped out of Makelle. Quite soon, however, we pulled up in a back part of the airport, away from the civilian terminal. Nearby a giant Soviet Antonov cargo plane sat with its back ramp down to receive a long line of weary-looking Tigrayans. They were being forcefully escorted by armed guards who looked like government militia. They did not seem to notice us.

"Be quick," one of the officers snapped and motioned Billard to get his camera out. Within forty seconds he had footage of the rumoured resettlement operation in action—the only outside media to ever capture this shadowy operation. It now seemed clear that the officers wanted to alert the outside world to the forced movement. Who they were we never learned, for we were soon back on the same sidewalk we'd been snatched from and they vanished down the road. For the next three years this same forty seconds of CBC tape was replayed every time a network reported the forced removal of hundreds of thousands of northerners from their homeland.

Once we had completed our first assignment in Ethiopia, we went straight on to the famine zones in nearby Sudan and Mozambique before wrapping up our travels toward the end of 1984. When I finally boarded the plane to England from Johannesburg, I was a wreck. I passed out and remember nothing of the flight or much of the first four days in London, which I spent in bed with a fever. Today, many employers would be quick to offer psychological counselling, but that thought was still alien to news organizations, and to most foreign correspondents as well.

When I finally got to the London office, I found that staff had put up a touching welcome-back sign for us. I was so overwhelmed I couldn't speak. I withdrew into myself: people suggested I had the new "Ethiopia syndrome," the tidal waves of emotion experienced by those wound too tight in the field who were disorientated by the luxuries and calm at home. The nicer the compliments I received, the more pleasant the dinner party with old friends, the crappier I felt. I had flashbacks to those starving families along the roads as we drove past. I felt guilt, no matter how much I donated to aid organizations, for not having done something to help a particular individual or family. For weeks I had nightmares—strong ones of starving children and corpses piled in mortuary tents. I also began to worry that our Ethiopia footage might establish a dangerous new reference point:

What if people would now react only to similar extreme images of horror, when it was already too late to save millions?

In London I was struck by a remarkable mood of empathy toward Ethiopia—millions of pounds were being raised, and expectations ran high for the coming summer's Live Aid concert. When I flew back to Canada for Christmas I found the sympathy was even stronger than in the United Kingdom. Strangers came up to ask me what they should do to help, and my dad's business friends called me up for advice—one even quit his lucrative job to go volunteer in the relief effort. In the first month after our November 1 broadcast, more than $28 million in today's currency had poured in from Canadians. The federal government set up matching funds to encourage giving but, within weeks, had to double its pledge.

The Mulroney/Clark effort continued behind the scenes as they worked the phones urging allies to put more effort into tackling the Africa-wide crisis. Another remarkable Canadian, David MacDonald, was appointed as the effective czar of the whole campaign, officially called Emergency Coordinators of Aid to Africa. A wiry, fast-talking former United Church minister, MacDonald had long been a charismatic pitchman for a form of humane internationalism that Canada now seemed determined to achieve. Doctors took sabbaticals to work in clinics; pilots arranged leaves to deliver supplies. The total donations and volunteer contributions will never be fully known, but, even with fifteen million fewer Canadians than now, over the next two years, $430 million in today's currency flowed in not only from the government but from farmers, steelworkers, schoolchildren, and others in every corner of the country. The country's musicians turned out a fundraising single whose title, "Tears Are Not Enough," exactly caught both the enthusiasm to help and the hard challenge to be faced.

The expression "global village," coined by Canadian Marshall McLuhan, was often used, and with reason: the largest amount per capita raised came from a group of Inuit in the Far North who had experienced their own famines in the past and now told the CBC, "We want to help." Word got around. Later, when I was talking to elders in an isolated rural village in Tigray, one of them told me through my interpreter, "We heard what your 'Eskimos' did and we want you to thank them for us. We will try to help them if they are ever in need."

People kept predicting that compassion fatigue would soon end the wave of caring, but it took far longer than anyone expected for Ethiopia and Africa to recede from Canadians' concerns. At the start of the second year, government pollster Allan Gregg found that the clear majority of Canadians "were more concerned about global problems of hunger and starvation than about domestic economic problems." Even as late as March 1986, he discovered that one-quarter of those polled held "world hunger and poverty as their second major issue of concern." The enormous success of Canadian efforts was likely unmatched for crisis management in peacetime, saving at least seven hundred thousand lives—a number suggested by international famine experts given Canada's share of the roughly six million saved overall. Close to a million lives were likely lost, although the exact number will never be known.

Back in Tigray in early February 1985, I asked if anyone knew where Birhan and her father were, but no one had time to search out a single family when millions of people were displaced. Moreover, the forced resettlement program was causing panic in the refugee camps as word spread that the government planned to move about a million more poor northerners from the infertile highlands down to the south, where the soil is rich. But the area is also malarial and unhealthy, a steaming-hot forested land quite unprepared to accept the number of people arriving there. Ultimately, up to sixty thousand were believed to have died of disease, many while trying to flee back home to the north.

Finding no trace of Birhan and her family, I feared I would never learn what happened to them—a thought that gnawed at me for years. Strangely, I did see a fleeting image of her that February. We had again brought in Colin Dean as our editor and, as before, he set up a rudimentary suite in his hotel room. He was normally a chatty, sunny-natured Londoner, but our material affected him and, by the time an item was edited, he was sometimes very emotional. Like me, unable to escape the horrific images we had seen, he had trouble sleeping.

One night I was irritated when he seemed to be pulling an unscheduled all-night session. The clattering of editing, along with rock music I couldn't identify, kept waking me up. First thing next morning, Dean called us in to see the video he had completed using our past footage as his homage to the victims. He hoped the CBC might find a slot somewhere to show it. When he flicked the switch, on came a short, intensely moving mix of tragic images set to the poignant music of the song "Drive" by the Cars. The most striking image, of Birhan's face in distress, appeared near the end, anchoring the mood and the message.

When it ended, Dean wiped tears from his eyes. I was mute, deeply touched by the power of the piece but completely pulverized. Would the CBC run it? It did not, for reasons I never discovered, and after we returned to London the video lay undisturbed on a shelf. Then, a couple of months later, the pop star and political activist Bob Geldof, busy organizing the giant Live Aid concert, agreed to an interview with the CBC. I was away, but my fill-in, Terry Milewski, and cameraman Phillipe Billard took the cassette along and pushed him to screen it. Back in Geldof's office, when he started the video, all activity stopped. As writer Oliver Harvey recounts in his book *Feed the World: Birhan Woldu and Live Aid*, David Bowie happened to be there and pronounced it "the most dramatic thing I've ever seen." He volunteered to drop one of his songs in the performance to make room for the tape. On July 15 it played to the seventy-five thousand people at Wembley Stadium and the simultaneous concert at the John F. Kennedy Stadium in Philadelphia—and to a TV audience estimated at 1.9 billion in 150 countries.

I was back at the family home in Toronto at the time, taking a rest from the Ethiopian coverage and spending time with my dad, who was getting on. I wasn't in the mood for a concert, but I did watch some of the live TV coverage. Suddenly I saw an emotional David Bowie walk to the mic to introduce "a video made by CBC television. The subject speaks for itself. Please—send your money in!" And there was Dean's creation. On a giant screen the first keyboard music swelled and the heart-wrenching images Billard had captured appeared. Just before it ended, I was confronted by the haunting face of Birhan—and now, so was the world.

The video had a historic impact. Geldof later revealed in Harvey's history of the event that Live Aid, despite an unprecedented global audience, was collecting much less than expected when Bowie walked out to announce the CBC tape. In Geldof's words: "The response for many in the stadium and at home was tears. For others it was action." The telephone pledge system broke down completely as a flood of calls poured in, raising over $300 million (in today's currency) within hours, and still more as funds also flowed to NGOs involved in African relief.

That Live Aid concert also changed the political climate, making humanitarian concerns a far higher priority in Western foreign policy. Almost overnight, politicians realized the galvanizing impact of such causes on modern voters. Shipments of emergency food and medical aid picked up substantially as well. Future British prime minister Tony Blair was one who felt the concert changed his life and eventually influenced his actions in politics and in power. Birhan, the video, and the whole Live Aid phenomenon had, Geldof insisted, stopped people in their tracks. "Cynicism and selfishness had been eliminated for a moment. It felt good. A lot of people had rediscovered something in themselves."

Birhan and her family could not have been more separated from the global TV phenomenon. Still barely surviving in a Tigray refugee camp, they knew nothing of Live Aid, and the world knew nothing of them—the stark image of her led many to believe she was dead. In fact, Birhan was not dead, though she came close to it often over the coming years. Her older sister Azmera died before the family found the bare shelter of a tent and received life-saving foreign aid rations.

Then new disaster struck. Their father, Woldu, who walked miles every day looking for sticks to sell as firewood, was picked up by government troops collecting people for the feared resettlement program. After two weeks of confinement on bare ground, the family were marched like cattle with other refugees into the belly of an Antonov cargo plane and flown to the steaming lowlands far to the south. They had no idea where they were and were given only a small plot, with a plough but no ox to pull it. Food was always scarce, sanitation almost nonexistent in the small village, and children were dying from cholera all around them. Woldu decided that, to save his family, they had to escape back home, on foot, while hiding all the way from armed government patrols. Arrest would mean being sent back or even prison for Woldu.

The journey of thirteen hundred kilometres took them two months, walking from dawn to dusk, sleeping in open fields or ditches, eating only handfuls of grain and wild herbs. Transport was impossible because Woldu had less than ten dollars in local birr. Birhan and Silas were too small to walk, so he carried them both, strapped to his shoulders. The oldest sister, Lemlem, aged eight, also walked, as did his second wife, Letebirhan, despite a chronic limp. Remarkably, they made it all the way back to their original village of Lahama.

They were home, but in a poor region of one of the poorest nations on earth, living in conditions little changed in a millennium. Woldu worked a small plot by hand and spun cotton on a half-broken loom.

It took him three years to acquire four goats, a plough ox, and ten beehives. There were no schools, and no one to teach even basic writing. By age five, a barefoot Birhan was herding goats in the mountains from sunrise to dusk, guarding against hyenas and foxes.

I returned to Ethiopia in 1988 after the CBC current affairs/documentary program *The Journal* asked me to do a series of in-depth specials on global issues. Tony Burman was to head the new unit. Over drinks, I suggested we try to find "that girl, Birhan." I had been haunted by thoughts of her and her family, feeling we had a responsibility to them because our coverage had made her a hugely influential symbol of Ethiopia's famine and roused the massive global relief response. We both felt a need to show there was hope for Ethiopia's recovery and life after catastrophe. Sure, I conceded, the chances of finding her were slim, but even if we failed, the effort itself would speak of the value of each single person in such a crisis. Burman needed no convincing. As I talked, he enthusiastically flipped over a napkin and began scribbling down myriad producer's tasks—logistics, visas, crew, budget, and dealing with the Derg. I knew he could sell the idea to *The Journal*'s dynamic chief, Mark Starowicz. We were going.

The odds of finding Birhan seemed poor. The population in northern Ethiopia was still battered by the aftermath of famine and internal wars. The Derg government was even more paranoid about foreigners poking around. Aid organizations would not help for fear of upsetting the Derg. We also knew that if we did find the family, our attention could be dangerous for them. The only solution was to involve the government in our quest, feeling that Canada's good standing in Ethiopia might provide vital protection for the family if we succeeded. In due course we got our permits for limited travel.

We figured we'd spend weeks chasing leads in relief centres and NGOs. Instead, we quickly got a vital breakthrough. Searching with the only names we had from our meeting at the Catholic mission in November 1984—Woldu, Birhan, and Silas—officials found them listed on recent records at an aid ration distribution point. We left in a scramble to catch a plane to Makelle, accompanied, inevitably, by Derg plainclothes agents.

On landing, we were put in a van and escorted under guard to the town of Ashegoda, ten minutes' drive outside the city. Before long, another van parked alongside. We learned later that, a day or two earlier, a government official had showed up at the Woldu family hut in Lahama and ordered Woldu and Birhan to come immediately to Kwiha, near Makelle. They were terrified, wondering if they would be punished for escaping resettlement and sent back to that hell. "What do you want with us?" Woldu asked, but the question went unanswered. They were held under guard overnight and given a handful of rations, as though they were prisoners. Then they were told to get into the back of a van and driven to Ashegoda.

At this point, the back door of our van was flung open and a young girl hopped in, followed by Woldu. "My God, it really *is* her!" Burman gasped. Birhan was remarkably calm and quiet. The Derg agents drove us to a small village where bags of grain were stacked beside a suspiciously comfortable hut that they described as "their home." They told us to conduct a brief interview there with Woldu, but he looked so mystified that I kept it short. I had brought a tightly wound roll of cash that I planned to slip to Woldu if Burman could distract the guards long enough. The tension was high. On cue, Burman sidetracked them with boisterous questions and cheerful slaps on shoulders, while I motioned to Woldu to join me inside the hut, just in time to slip him the money before another agent rushed in to watch us. We got some final shots of Birhan and Woldu walking up a hillside path.

I had already made plans not to lose touch again. It was clear the best escape route out of extreme poverty for children, especially girls, was education. I'd been impressed during my 1984 visit by a dynamic

Salesian monk, Father Bullo, who ran a prominent Don Bosco Technical Training Centre. Before leaving Makelle, I arranged with him to have me finance Birhan's education in a local primary school. Woldu agreed—Birhan would be the first in his family to attend school. The money I had given also enabled them to move into a safer small stone cottage in Kwiha, where life would be markedly better, close to schools, medical aid, and a market. This was the start of my ongoing connection to the family, which still endures.

Back in Canada, our documentary *Life after Death* centred on the struggle in Ethiopia to recover from famine and improve the lives of victims through long-term development programs. Just responding to crises was not the answer. Birhan's survival and chance of a better life underscored the message that others too must be given an escape from the endless succession of droughts, famines, and oppressive poverty that made life so perilous in areas like Tigray. The program was well received and helped spur still more public interest in overseas development. In 1991, when the Derg was overthrown, a new era of optimism followed.

As time passed, I had to search out Tigrayans in Toronto who planned visits to the Makelle area in order to send Woldu's family occasional support payments. I wrote letters to the family and, every few months, would get a reply that had been dictated. On one of my later trips, I got a lucky break. My efficient young driver-guide, Bisrat Mesfin, turned out to know the family and offered to help. He knew David Stables, a British aid official who had set up a new NGO, the African Children's Educational Trust (A-CET). He assured me they could handle my scholarships for Birhan and her siblings. They'd also guide her along the best future educational course.

During another visit in 1998 I sat with Woldu and his family in a series of meetings with educators. Birhan, now seventeen, loved school and had many new friends. Woldu still farmed on a plot in the countryside and had an ox for ploughing, a milk cow, and "the best honey in Ethiopia." Life was good. The family were profoundly religious, followers of the strict codes of the Ethiopian Orthodox Tewahedo Church. They had come to believe that Birhan had been saved by God for a purpose—to help the poorest and make sure that no one suffered from famine again. I worried that such a heavy responsibility imposed an unfair burden on her, but again I was struck by her composure. Nothing seemed to faze her, and her family roots were strong.

A few years later, when passing through London, I received a dinner invitation to the historic Reform Club. It came from Michael Buerk, the BBC's legendary foreign correspondent, who, along with our CBC team, had got out the first horrifying reports on Ethiopia's famine in 1984. I was surprised, but I figured he might want to discuss the upcoming twentieth anniversary of the famine.

Over dinner, Buerk laid out his plan to do a major documentary to commemorate this anniversary. He had closely followed our stories about Birhan and asked me to put him in touch with her so he could include the "upbeat" meaning of her survival in his feature. I felt uneasy: the BBC's vast audience would mean more glaring fame for her and the family. But it was not my choice; it was up to them. I gave him the African Children's Educational Trust as his best link to Birhan. Buerk said he would let me know how it turned out.

What he didn't tell me was that he'd worked out a deal with one of London's most super-hyped tabloids, the *Sun*, to do a three-part series on his return to Ethiopia and on finding the "lost" Birhan. He also was working on an even bigger deal with Bob Geldof, who was planning a second massive concert in aid of world hunger relief to mark the twentieth anniversary of Live Aid, and Buerk wanted to highlight the discovery of the "face of famine," Birhan. There would even be a book deal.

And so, the mighty intensity of British media swept through Birhan's life in 2005. Her educational advisors were dubious but saw benefits for a vital cause—education and development in Africa. The book deal would involve some payment to Birhan and the charity as well. Now in her early twenties, Birhan was also curious to see the outside world, if only briefly.

Buerk produced a documentary that appeared to discover Birhan, without mentioning that both she and her location were well known in Canada because of our extensive coverage. He and the *Sun* also ran three days of spectacular headlines on their "finding" of Birhan. They paid $5,000 to Birhan and A-CET and flew her to Addis to meet Geldof and Prime Minister Tony Blair, who was attending an international meeting on African debt relief. Birhan, a striking figure in traditional Tigrayan costume, took all meetings with the same aura of serenity. "Birhan, do you realize your image has been an inspiration to millions?" Blair whispered. "Yes," she replied, "I am aware of that and very grateful."

The spotlight could hardly get brighter: Birhan was flown to London and appeared on stage with superstar Madonna at the anniversary concert in front of 205,000 fans in Hyde Park and a global TV audience in the hundreds of millions. When Birhan walked on, the famous CBC footage of her near death flashed on a giant screen.

I watched the performance from my home, struggling to identify this poised young woman with the dying child I'd seen in the pit of a murderous famine. Geldof later noted in Harvey's account: "Who was the greatest star that day, Madonna or Birhan? For the world it was clear. Here was *our* miracle. Here was living proof that it was not futile to help. With one smile, Birhan defeated the cynics." Birhan flew back to Tigray, happy to continue her college studies—nursing and agricultural science—to best serve the farming poor of Tigray. That was her mission.

Almost immediately *The Oprah Winfrey Show*, the most-watched chat show in the world, asked Birhan and Bisrat Mesfin, now a prominent figure in NGO circles, to fly to a taping in Chicago. The organizers also tracked me down to join them. The theme they chose focused on the power of a few images of children in war and famine to change history. The studio audience gave Birhan a standing ovation the staff claimed was unique. TV pro though I was, I felt awkward, even nervous, on the famous yellow couch, but Birhan was not. She later told me Chicago was interesting, but she needed to hurry back to classes. Like everyone in Oprah's studio that day, I was presented with one of her famous gift bags on the way out. Her largesse was legendary, including giving away cars, so I was naturally curious. Mine contained women's pajamas, a woman's reading shawl, and the classic feminist book *The Good Earth*.

Birhan's trips were over, except for one. I had long promised her as a graduation present a vacation in Canada with my wife, Tina, and daughter, Katie. In August 2006 she came with her friend Rahel, and I ensured there would be no media. Birhan loved Toronto and was amazed by the abundance of water in Ontario, especially the flood roaring over Niagara Falls. Much of her life had been lived in droughts, and as we stood in our rain slickers on the boat below the falls, she said it seemed like "a second baptism."

When I retired from the CBC, I went back one last time to those former famine lands of Ethiopia to thrill at the sight of decent harvests, new roads, and a Makelle bustling with shops, internet cafés, new hotels, hospitals, schools, and a prominent university. All seven of the Woldu children had completed high school and were doing well. The family invited me to dinner, and I listened to more of the father's positive and often humorous take on life. Birhan was working with the A-CET educational trust to extend education into farm areas in the hinterlands. She also had a boyfriend she was soon to marry and spoke of their hopes together.

A few years later, Birhan had two daughters, but then many things went wrong. The marriage didn't work out, a business they had launched failed, and, in 2021, the central government joined with neighbouring Eritrea to crush Tigray, destroying decades of post-famine progress and killing an estimated six hundred thousand people—barely covered by Western media, but the highest death toll of any recent war in the world. The network of schools that A-CET had built up over decades was looted or destroyed, and Bisrat and Birhan struggled to keep classes going despite the war.

For over a year I had no contact with the family while all communication with the outside world was cut, but after many attempts I have recently reconnected with them. Birhan, now remarried, is still serene. Despite the horrors, her daughters are in one of the rare local schools that remain. She has few material goods but even more of a life mission—to help her Tigrayan people recover. She was heavily involved with Bisrat's local charity, which brings education to rural children, and also did field work with several aid projects in remote villages where suffering is most acute. She recently launched, with her husband Berhane Reda, a new organization (PIDO) to work with severely disadvantaged youth. Occasionally she writes to urge me not to worry. She is determined to survive—again.

Of all my foreign reporting experiences, Ethiopia is most often on my mind, with memories both painful and cherished. But to move my reflections on, I must first go back to the beginnings.

2

Radio Free Brian

The year 1956 stands out as a major turning point in history. Crammed with momentous happenings previously unimaginable, it completely altered the world by the time the year ended. The seismic shocks kept coming: a time of world revolt in politics and great-power relations even as the often bland popular tastes of the fifties were shaken into tumultuous creativity. It's been called the year the sixties began.

I was a fourteen-year-old Canadian living in Surrey, England, while my father was on a four-year business posting there. I was mesmerized by the TV, radio, and newspaper coverage of the upheaval around the globe, especially by those all-absorbing events people called "crises." I could hardly sleep with the excitement of it all, and my bedside radio crackled long into the night with accounts of nations clashing and mass movements of people rising to "fight for freedom."

In the United States, Martin Luther King Jr. was leading the historic Montgomery bus boycott—the spearhead of the antisegregation movement that would fundamentally change American political life and inspire the world. In the Soviet Union, Nikita Khrushchev denounced the tyranny of the late dictator Stalin in a speech that sent shockwaves across that vast country and sparked riots in Poland, turmoil in world communism, and a stunning armed rebellion in Hungary. So unbelievable it seemed, CIA director Allen Dulles speculated that Khrushchev had to be drunk when he spoke.

British prime minister Anthony Eden, meanwhile, was believed by many to have gone quite mad amid the wildest event of the year—the Suez Crisis. That fall, two Western empires in retreat, Britain and France, tried to reverse accelerating imperial decay by conspiring with Israel to boldly invade Egypt and force it to give up the vital Suez Canal. Egypt's leader, Gamal Abdel Nasser, had nationalized the canal in July. Thereafter, war fever ran high in England: as preparations for the assault built on one side, antiwar passions steadily grew in the press and in street demonstrations. The full invasion, in the first week of November, turned within hours into a madcap failure that sank any illusion of Britain's major-power influence on world events.

The domino effect, carrying enormous consequences for the world, ensured the rise of a radical new Arab nationalism across the Middle East and growing demands for the end of colonization in Africa. More immediately, the United States publicly condemned the Anglo-French action, and this falling-out among allies threatened a crisis run on the pound. Eden, broken in body and spirit, was chased from office amid scenes of near bedlam in the House of Commons.

Almost incredibly, the Anglo-French airborne and seaborne landings at the Mediterranean entrance to the Suez Canal occurred in the same two-week period in October-November that Moscow sent tanks and bombers to crush the Hungarian uprising in Budapest. Freedom fighters in the ancient European capital fought back in heroic but doomed street battles. Simultaneous to both military actions, Khrushchev, in support of Egypt, threatened nuclear rocket strikes on Paris and London until the invaders retreated. Throughout it all, the United Nations was struggling around the clock to put a lid on the raging firestorms.

It was a lot for my young teen's mind to keep up with, but I threw myself into the task. In Britain there were only two TV news channels, the BBC and ITN, and sitting before our small black-and-white

TV screen, I manually switched between them so often that my father nicknamed me Click-click. I nagged my parents to take me to a movie, any movie, so I could watch the accompanying grainy newsreel films from the battlefields and other areas of crisis.

I was able to follow these dramas closely because, although I attended a British boys' boarding school, Badingham College, I was one of the rare day boys. To fit the boarders' schedule, I had to endure long school days, from 8 a.m. to 6:30 p.m., with a lengthy sports period in the afternoon, but I was able to go home every evening because we lived only two blocks away. There I was free to watch TV, listen to BBC and shortwave radio, and read news magazines as well as the *Daily Telegraph* and the *Guardian*. I not only absorbed current affairs but transmitted the information between classes to my boarding friends, largely cut off as they were from the expanding swirl of events.

Soon I even got to boast of a new phenomenon—UN international peacekeeping—when the first ever blue-helmeted force was sent to Suez to separate the combatants and allow the invaders to withdraw with a modicum of decorum. This force was the brainchild of Canadian diplomat Lester Pearson and commanded by Canadian general E.L.M. "Tommy" Burns. "We Canadians are the very best at this kind of stuff," I trumpeted to all who would listen, without knowing much about it. I even confronted our gaunt and gloomy geography teacher, Mr. Butterton, with this Canadian masterstroke because he had once humiliated me in class by dismissing Canada as "that vast land in the west from which no worthwhile news ever comes." Discouragingly, my proud moment did not change his view.

Still, I continued as a sort of Radio Free Brian of the lunch and tea breaks. Whenever possible I also sabotaged Latin grammar classes by raising questions about "the situation with Suez, sir." Did we need more tanks? The teacher, a much-decorated tank commander from the Second World War, veteran of the battles at El Alamein in North Africa, could usually be counted on to drop the tedium of declension studies in favour of military speculation. For once my attention-deficit problems in class found a useful focus because my distraction now was news. I liked telling people "the latest," and it made me feel so alive.

One group I was especially intrigued by were the special reporters who popped up at the heart of upheaval and crisis to explain things. I marvelled at their poise and grasp of events of historic importance. I was envious. History was by far my favourite subject, and I wanted one of those few ringside seats to its making. I had no desire to fight in a war, but surely history needed witnesses? That November, when a teacher set an essay on future goals, I wrote: "When I grow up, I want to be a foreign correspondent."

I was born in Montreal in April 1942, right in the middle of one of the most tumultuous wartime years: four months after Pearl Harbor, and four months before the start of Germany's Stalingrad campaign and Canada's disaster at Dieppe. I seemed primed to live in eventful times.

I likely wouldn't have been born had my father, Charles Stewart, not had poor feet and a bad knee that ruled him out as combat material. Despite his parents being strong pacifists, he would have fought overseas if ordered, but he never pretended disappointment. My brother, David, arrived in 1939, the year the war started, and my sister, Heather, at the very end, in 1945. We children were part of the Silent Generation, growing up overshadowed by the tough and victorious older generation that had endured the Great Depression and won the war, while we were destined to benefit from postwar prosperity and future job opportunities.

Our parents met by chance at the height of the Depression in the bargain basement of Simpson's department store in Montreal, where he sold socks and she, an office stenographer, was shopping carefully on her seven-dollar weekly wage. They were a strikingly attractive couple, later known for their hospitality and wit, and her diaries confirm it was love at first sight. Yet their courtship barely survived a storm-wracked engagement in which her threats to ditch the ring—and him with it—kept the outcome in suspense for months. His piteous notes to her, often several a day, confirm this uncertainty. I suspect religious and cultural differences were at the heart of it, as was so often the case in Montreal at the time.

Dad had come to the city in 1936 from a comfortably well-off family of nine children raised in a large Victorian-style home of diligent Presbyterians in Seaforth, in rural southern Ontario. Their roots were largely Northern Irish. His father, Harry, always impeccably dressed and severe by nature, ran the region's largest clothing store; his mother, Matilda, enforced stern discipline at home. A decent middle-class income and large gardens, along with friendly local farmers, helped buttress the Stewarts through the worst of the Depression, but signs of its devastation were seen everywhere, especially in the trainloads of unemployed men riding through town in increasingly desperate searches for work and relief. The children all recalled a secure and even fun childhood within a small-town community where they were known everywhere as "them kids of Harry." When Dad left, he had little money, a modest education, but lots of confidence in merchandising as a future.

My mother, Mary Ellen O'Brien, had no fond memories of her childhood in Ireland, of which she rarely spoke. A Catholic, she was born out of wedlock in 1914 into abject poverty in a country village near Waterford, a few months before the outbreak of the First World War and not long before the Troubles, a time of rebellion and conflict, swept the south. Her father disappeared before her birth, at a time when single mothers were condemned by both their relatives and society as sinful, and their children lived aware of that disapproval. Her mother, also called Mary, struggled as a maid to raise her for five years in a stone cottage without running water but left her behind with a kindly grandfather and uncle when she sailed to Montreal to seek out better work and marriage. Abandoned for the second time, Mom worked part-time as a cowherd on local farms but also attended a trade school for girls. Her worst memories were of frequent armed conflicts in the early twenties.

The war for independence, followed by the civil war between Irish factions, kept local country life tense. The British fought to suppress the independence struggle in the south by sending in a notorious mercenary force of war vets known as the Black and Tans. They were much feared for their brutality: Mom related that after they raided her grandfather's cottage looking for rebels, they settled in, demanding that "the young girl" fetch well water for tea. In her mind, the Protestants and Northern Irish spelled hatred, terror, and trouble.

Mom carried this baggage with her when her mother eventually felt settled in Canada and sent a steamship ticket for her to join her and her husband. In 1928, at the age of fourteen, she sailed alone and arrived in Quebec with two dollars to her name and an address for her mother.

As a young woman, Mom rarely talked of her sad childhood, but her outwardly bubbly manner and considerable wit often covered up an anxious personality prone to bouts of depression. I believe the fears she had experienced lay behind many of the courtship storms. Catholic-Protestant tensions in Canada were still significant in the thirties, and she panicked when my father pressed her to visit his family in Seaforth who she thought might despise her for her religion and her background. Dad fought on, even vowing to join the Catholic Church and taking lessons from a priest to reassure her. When she did relent and meet the family, they greeted her with remarkable warmth—and so began a very successful marriage.

The early years together were austere, but Dad proved to be a major talent at all things related to merchandizing, rising over many postings from bargain basement salesman to president of the Simpson's Canada-wide chain of stores. They were both loving parents who supported all my ambitions to work in a very different and sometimes perilous world. I feel guilty now for showing little interest in Dad's career, although he keenly followed mine.

For our family, as for many in Canada, the postwar period was one of rising expectations and excitement. I remember open neighbourhoods filled with life and young playmates. There had been a bad time, we children heard, but it was now gone. My first memory was of my father polishing army boots for a victory event in 1945—"Bad man gone away," I think he said. People held block parties to greet returning vets and celebrated Canada's war record with parades and air displays, while victory gardens had a final flourish before new buildings took their place. After years of restrictions, consumer goods were finally available as home appliances multiplied and wooden toys magically turned into plastic ones. One night Dad woke us for a ride up Mont-Royal in the first car he owned to see the myriad lights of Montreal sparking below. Older children introduced us to games such as the warlike Bombs over Tokyo, where we dropped marbles into a circle in the sandbox. By the time I was five I was happily eavesdropping on adult conversations about amazing adventures far away, in ships at sea or in airplanes over distant countries called the "enemy," landing on a beach somewhere.

That year I also boarded a train with my family to Halifax, where Dad was to manage the local Simpson's store. It was my first great adventure, sleeping in compartments, eating with adults in a fine restaurant with white tablecloths and shining silverware, watching the vast countryside race by during the day and hearing it roar past at night. Life seemed to be expanding ever outward at a pace never experienced before.

I fell in love with Halifax right away. The neighbourhoods were leafy and homey, the parks welcoming, and we lived close to the Northwest Arm inlet, where we could often smell the ocean. We felt free to wander, and we could bicycle across the city with friends in a morning, go down to Bedford Basin, and look out over the vast natural harbour—the second largest in the world. The ships fascinated us—Canada's sea-grey warships (especially our aircraft carrier *Magnificent*), visiting naval vessels, sea-battered trading boats streaked with rust, tramp steamers and large freighters, and giant passenger ships, including the *Queen Elizabeth*, their decks crammed with curious people. There were also tugs, ferries, and coast-guard vessels coming and going—an engrossing vista that fed wanderlust in many of us.

That restlessness was everywhere. After the lean years, adults were as excited as their kids to travel, and jerky home movies captured the pace. Everyone seemed to take family car rides along the ocean or through Canada and down into the United States. Business trips resumed for my dad and other managers. Some said that Doris Day's 1945 hit "Sentimental Journey" was the first song to capture the dreamy restlessness in music so striking of the era, along with "Those Far Away Places," "Red Sails in the Sunset," and "Harbour Lights."

I started reading newspapers early, before I was nine, because I was devoted to the Montreal Canadiens in hockey and the Brooklyn Dodgers in baseball. I began scrapbooks on each team, cutting clippings and photos from our papers and any others I got hold of. I also noticed that baseball movies always showed men sitting in special booths, with a card inscribed "Press" in their hatbands. They apparently knew everyone and got into dressing rooms others could not enter. Lucky them, I thought, as the germ of an idea began slowly to form.

By the late forties I was hearing about troubled places called Gaza and Palestine, of an "emergency" in Malaya, and much about French soldiers fighting in Indochina, especially in a place oddly named the Red River Delta. China seemed to be in a war, something connected to a place called Formosa. Then in the summer of 1950 the war in Korea started, and some soldiers and airmen from Halifax went to serve there. For the next three years I followed the war in the papers, on radio, and in exciting newsreels. I also found there were big crises of other kinds to note, including the arrival of many immigrants fleeing disruptions in Europe as well as floods in the Netherlands, for which we raised money in class.

We also had drills at school for an atomic attack, the "dive under your desk if you see a sudden flash" routine that we simply took in stride. The one fear that affected parents and children alike was polio, which stalked our summers before the vaccine rolled out. At some point I saw a demonstration of the iron lung respirator, and the mere thought of that entombment freaked me out. We were cautioned to avoid water fountains and, for some reason, never to eat the tip of an ice-cream cone.

Our parents led a very social life in Halifax at a time when lunches, cocktail parties, and fundraising dinners figured highly in the lives of professionals and the so-called managerial class. Reciprocating these invitations ensured that the activity rarely flagged. Our second house, on Norwood Street, seemed to host a steady stream of gatherings of friends, visiting store buyers, shipping agents, and military representatives—usually ending in sentimental sing-songs. Children made a well-groomed, smiling appearance and answered simple questions about school or sports before they could retreat, in my case to my bedroom with books, magazines, and my radio.

In all, life for a preteen in Halifax in the early fifties was remarkably free. Neighbourhoods accepted games and sports wherever they broke out, and doors were often left unlocked. Summer camps and schools sought to drill us in proper love of country, loyalty to the monarchy, and respect for veterans. Discipline was stricter, however, and students were beaten fairly frequently on the hand with the notorious strap of thick leather. I got the strap only once and found it did not hurt much but was definitely embarrassing as schoolmates, including the girls, snickered at my plight. I had hoped they would think me heroic; they did not.

We were shattered one day when Dad came home and announced, softly, that he had been promoted. We were all going over to England for four years while he headed Simpson's large foreign-buying operation. It would be a grand life, he vainly tried to convince us, with a big house somewhere in the countryside, fun trips through Europe, and travel on a famous giant liner, the *Queen Mary*. The family bore up bravely, but for me, nothing could reduce the heartbreak of leaving so snug and friendly a life with all its certainties for the distant unknown.

The dreary movies and grainy news photos I had seen portrayed England as a bleak black-and-white world. Worst of all, it seemed a grim hell for schoolboys. I'd recently watched the film *Tom Brown's Schooldays*, in which younger boys appeared to be terrorized by canings and having their butts roasted over fireplaces. The thought of losing all my friends made me inconsolable, and I immediately fell sick for a week despite all efforts by my parents to dispel the gloom.

In the summer of 1954, we flew out of Halifax to Toronto, then boarded the train to New York. Before long, the adventure of well-heeled travel worked its magic. We were not wealthy, but Simpson's was generous and allowed us four days to enjoy New York before crossing the Atlantic. We stayed at the Roosevelt Hotel in central Manhattan, an experience somewhat ruined for my parents because it coincided with one of the major US Airborne Division post-Korean reunions—a raucous horde of many hundreds partying nonstop, hurling water bombs and thunder-flash crackers into the streets, and, horrifying to our mother, displaying their lady friends on the windowsills draped only in towels. Nervous hotel clerks swore they were helpless to restore decorum with such a crowd. I loved it all, but our blinds were drawn as firmly as the Iron Curtain.

I had dreamed of seeing my hero Jackie Robinson and the Dodgers at Ebbets Field, but they were travelling, so Dad took my brother and me to the old Polo Grounds instead to see the New York Giants superstar Willie Mays—Robinson's rival as a Black icon. I got my first view of nonwhite America as our taxi rolled through Harlem, which appeared to be throbbing with excitement and purpose and well-dressed people. I had no inkling that its solid Blackness was not the good-news story whites tried to stress: "They have everything here and it's all theirs—shops, restaurants, hotels, stores," our cabbie boasted. None of us imagined the upheavals that lay ahead.

The United States is always at a point of historic change, and

1954 was no exception, though the new beginnings underway were not easy for visitors to grasp. Just two months earlier, the Supreme Court in *Brown v. Board of Education of Topeka* had ruled that school segregation was illegal. The battle for civil rights that would rock America for a generation was on. In that same month the French lost Indochina, a fact I knew because I was much taken by the name Dien Bien Phu, the place where they were defeated in their last stand against Communist forces. I read in the papers that the country was now called Vietnam, with the North going Communist in opposition to the South, and a small number of US advisors being sent to the South to help fight off the "Reds." The new age was upon us, though we didn't realize it at the time.

Simpson's had booked our family into a three-room first-class suite on the legendary *Queen Mary*. We sailed off to England early in July during the last inning of the age of luxury liners. Within four years, airlines would begin to dominate intercontinental travel. The entire trip seemed like the grandest of movies as our rooms thronged with a farewell Champagne party. During the voyage we dressed formally on certain nights for the finest of dining, and we all enjoyed the movie theatre, gym, and shops. Along with the majesty of the ocean, all this novelty helped to ease the heartache of losing Halifax, my friends, and most of what I had valued up to that point. I knew from seeing poor immigrants and refugees arrive in Halifax from a Europe still recovering from war that other people had it much worse, so I shut up, gave my parents a break, and made my pampered peace. I would just have to make the best of whatever lay ahead. If I couldn't count on a stable life in one city lasting for long, I would learn to welcome change and adventures in all kinds of places.

After two years at Badingham College, my announcement that I intended to become a foreign correspondent was treated with bemusement by teachers and bafflement by school friends, who had picked up parental views that all news people tended to be grubby spivs in shabby mackintosh raincoats. Our austere but kindly Church of England headmaster and school owner, the black-gowned Rev. A.J. Wilkie, received my odd ambition with a baleful smile. In term reports he regularly wrote of my pleasing personality but bone-idle character.

The verdict on my sluggishness in class was widely shared by most of my instructors at a time when teacher comments were not minced. My portly and chain-smoking Irish house master and English teacher, John O'Brien, had a short fuse when it came to my "varying moods that left me capable of reaching the heights" but in the same composition sinking to "pure unadulterated rubbish." Even my favourite subject, history, brought condemnations. The master, ex-officer John Horne, a witty explainer of Britain's rich and stormy past, spotted indolence lurking behind my smiling enthusiasm for Anglo-Saxon fortifications or the voyages of Sir Francis Drake: "He has always tried to be as idle as possible," he snorted in one report to my parents, "and as a result his punishments have been many."

Fortunately, the college avoided the cruel discipline of caning and bullying then common in British boarding schools. Rev. Wilkie rejected that "savage" approach, preferring a gentler neo-Edwardian regime. Good manners were enforced, bullying tendencies were supressed, and no boy was ever thrashed. The usual punishment—detention—was served in the impressively stocked school library.

Although not top-rated academically or socially, Badingham, which kept class sizes as low as ten, provided a good education. The college itself had a dreamy, timeless appearance. Built as a private mansion in 1705 by the renowned "gentleman architect" William Talman in red brick and stone dressings, the main building was attractive if stolid. Some of the rooms boasted wall and ceiling murals of swirling clouds and saintly subjects by the French devotional painter Louis Laguerre. Set on thirty acres at the edge of Fetcham Park, the school's sweeping playing fields were bordered by stately trees. Rising beyond the rugger pitch was the eleventh-century Anglo-Saxon parish church largely constructed in Roman-era bricks. No doubt the college had atmosphere.

Everything about Badingham advertised a focus on creating modest gentlemen who would rise, at a respectable pace, to solid middle-class careers in business, medicine, the foreign service, or the military. There were only a handful of foreign students who were far more exotic—the sons of visiting businessmen or diplomats. I had no trouble fitting in, finding fellow students generally humorous and many of the masters agreeably excentric.

In reality, Badingham had elements of homey mediocrity and tiredness about it. An air of shabby gentility clung to the creaky floors and musty classrooms. I ate only lunch and tea there, so didn't mind the food, but it was so awful that, on one occasion, the boarders bravely staged a silent strike and refused to eat. Teachers, who sat at the head of tables, gave the rebels five minutes to feel the spirit of rebellion, then crushed them on cue from Wilkie with a firm and simple command: "Eat the food!"

Even with a relentless grind of compulsory sports every afternoon but Sundays, our teams were haphazardly trained by teachers and never seemed to defeat other schools at anything. Given the custom for winning sides to applaud losing opponents off the field, many of us didn't seem to mind much. During four years there, my only success was as high-jump champ at our own sports day. My trophy cup, barely ten centimetres high, still sits in my library.

Over time I came to understand how the oddly weary air of Badingham reflected British upper middle-class society as a whole in the mid-fifties. True, life was getting better, rationing had finally ended, and future prosperity seemed close at hand, but Britain was still a nation straining to retreat gracefully from its declining imperial status and the long-term wear of the grim thirties and the war years. Decreasing global power fed a rising resentment of America for its new superpower status, to the point where "Yanks Go Home" graffiti was not uncommon. Meanwhile, large numbers of Britons were emigrating abroad as many regarded the Suez shambles as a last straw.

In geography with Mr. Butterton, we had our own radar dome picking up signs of national decay. With each new warning of British doom carried by the Fleet Street press, a brief flash of contentment crossed his sour and bony face. He used his wall-sized maps to drive home the point that India and Pakistan were gone, other parts going, and rebellions in Malaya, Kenya, and Cyprus underway: "All too costly, don't you see? We can't afford it, never could—just not worth it." The actual morality of empire was never raised by him or anyone else, and it certainly didn't enter my head.

Across the hall in history, the proud imperialist Mr. Horne, who had served as a military engineer "blowing up things" in the Malayan conflict, was willing to concede decay only from the inside (gesturing around the room) rather than from without (pointing at the flag). He once startled us when he grabbed a broom and began sweeping the floor to demonstrate a new skill we all needed to acquire—and fast. "The way that hired help is becoming so hard to find now in England you'd all best learn how to sweep, iron, and tidy up a house, lads," he warned. "When I was young, I was taught to use a rifle. You will need to be as good with a broom as a gun." The mere thought of us house cleaning struck us as wildly risible.

The opposite poles taken by Butterton and Horne added to the excitement of the Suez Crisis. The students, and most of the teachers, were strongly patriotic, and we had been conditioned by popular movies to view war as an adventure. When we asked Mr. Horne his opinion on the outcome, he replied, "It will lead, hopefully, to our march on Cairo and the suicide of their leader, Gamal Abdel Nasser." In contrast, Butterton's sonorous voice dipped to denote a tragedy for all: "We will lose, I have no doubt, and it will cost a fortune. I see our bankruptcy ahead."

Butterton was to prove almost exactly right: Britain called off the slow-moving and vaguely directionless invasion when a run on the pound undercut Tory war hawks and destroyed Eden's leadership. It was a striking lesson about war fever leading to unpredicted disaster that guided some of my reporting decades later. People who were loudly calling for a full invasion only a month earlier now wondered where that idiot plan had come from.

Although indifferent at sports, Badingham fielded a serious compulsory cadet corp. It was conducted to prepare us for the two-year National Service that awaited all British males at age seventeen or eighteen, during a time when the Cold War made the chances of going to war somewhere rather high. We were drilled weekly by no-nonsense war veterans in the use of rifles and Bren light machine guns—which I was proud to be deemed strong enough to carry. I knew I'd avoid call-up because we would be returning to Canada, but I still found field manoeuvres interesting. Later in my career, this experience occasionally proved useful in reading a territory for threats.

I realized that, to be a witness to crisis events and especially war, I would need to study past actions seriously. Fortunately, the library had long shelves of illustrated volumes on Britain's numerous wars. I discovered the ten-volume *Illustrated History of World War Two*, which I read cover to cover. I also boned up on related subjects such as diplomacy, refugees, wartime economy—and to my horror, civilian suffering in all theatres of war and Nazi war crimes, including the Holocaust.

My parents looked askance at my obsession with military matters. Dad thought I would outgrow the topic as soon as I got back to Canada and resumed my interest in sports. My mother hated all conflict and grew tearful at the sight of me in my itchy cadet uniform because it reminded her of the terrors of her Irish youth. She did, however, share my fascination with news and history and encouraged both my bookworm and news-junkie tendencies.

Dad's dream job involved visiting department stores and factories all over Europe, even behind the Iron Curtain. He had to buy in bulk all manner of merchandise, from new fashions to furniture to glassware, for the chain of Simpson's stores across Canada. He had contacts in every capital, and on our holidays we often dropped in on galleries, department stores, and factories. During school holidays I got a fascinating look at a Europe fast recovering after the Marshall Plan era and entering a new period of prosperity, though still beset by the disruptions of war. Wherever we motored seemed always ready to explode in disputes. In Belgium we had to be careful not to run into miners' riots; crossing France we passed long army convoys carrying soldiers to duty across the Mediterranean in Algeria; and in Paris I saw buses filled with riot cops awaiting the next wild protest to put down. Dad had no such taste for tense times: once, walking up the Champs-Elysées, he ran into a massive demonstration marching forcefully toward distant riot police. Caught in the middle, the only escape he could see was to dive into a cinema, where he sat for two hours watching a movie in French—a language he did not understand.

In tense times and the more normal calm periods, we also enjoyed stays in expensive hotels and meals in fine restaurants. In Paris a contact led us to a large lunchtime theatre where a tiny but powerful women sang: Edith Piaf. It would be a decade before the name meant anything to me. Odd sights seemed the norm then. Once when my brother and I were walking late at night with Dad, he led us across the street to look in the window of the world-famous Maxim's Restaurant. He announced its unparalleled status rather proudly, having eaten there several times. We saw in the dim light of the vacant main room rows of tables draped in gleaming white cloth, and then, on the one nearest the window, we noticed a large rat siting on its haunches and casually looking up at us. "Well, Billy be damned," Dad muttered. "Is nothing sacred anymore?"

To me, something about this bizarre scene came to represent the mixed nature of the decade. Societies had one foot in the new prosperous world and another in the still bitter postwar aftermath as empires came jerkily to an end. At this rate, I figured, the next decade would be a great one in which to begin my career in the media.

My fascination with news may have been unusual, but my limited range of available interests was at least part of the reason. In the semi-rural town of Fetcham, Surrey, the new friends I made were all "sealed up" in Badingham or some other boarding school during the term. So was my sister, Heather, whose school was too far away to commute regularly. My brother, David, left Badingham early to pursue a business opportunity in Hamburg, Germany, leaving me alone with my parents in Bell House, Bell Lane—a large rented white dwelling, centuries old, rustic, ramshackle, and rumoured to be haunted.

We liked the place and its grounds, but on foggy or windy nights it developed some creepy atmospherics. My superstitious mother believed certain "visitations" were possible, and the ancient local farmer who dropped off eggs and vegetables had a habit of asking in a low whisper if we had "seen anything strange at night?" We had not. Still, a cleaning lady refused to enter one room off the kitchen—the same one my Jack Russell terrier slunk away from quivering and never once entered. I did not believe stories of visiting spirits, but neither did I wander the grounds in the fog. Within the house itself, some of the lights downstairs would suddenly switch back on by themselves during the night. On the staircase outside my room, I occasionally heard creaks like footsteps ascending, yet when I peeped out, no one was there.

In bed I would listen to my small radio long into the night—the BBC, Radio Moscow, Armed Forces Radio, and the mainly music private network Radio Luxembourg. On this channel early in 1956 I heard the announcer introduce for the first time a new sensation—"Elvis Presley, singing 'Heartbreak Hotel.'" In an instant I had a new music hero—and another newsflash to alert my school friends about, although we had no idea for weeks what he looked like.

I also heard about a revolution flaring across British theatre with the arrival, first, of *Waiting for Godot* and, later, the explosive *Look Back in Anger*, which captured an unprecedented mood of unrest among the "Angry Young Men" and foreshadowed a changing society.

My parents attended the second night's performance of *Godot* and came home shocked. At least Dad was, not by the two shabby tramps uttering bizarre dialogue he didn't understand but by the crass behaviour of audience members who stormed out, slamming seats and huffing "rubbish" as they went. "What's got into people nowadays?" he muttered in puzzlement.

In the summer of 1958 our time in Britain was over. I said farewell to another group of friends and, at sixteen, joined the family sailing to New York on our way to Dad's next promotion—in Toronto. This time we boarded the legendary *Île de France*, an art deco gem of a liner that was once the pride of France. Launched in 1927, it was now one of the last of the great liners and dripping with history.

The onboard restaurant was among the finest in the world, but the *Île* was almost as well known as the "rescue ship." It sailed slowly, compared to her class of ships, and at a stately enough pace to pick up scores of survivors in war and in peace. Her final rescue happened on our crossing, involving a half-day-long dash off course to pick up a Dutch sailor with a dangerous burst appendix aboard a small cargo ship. The incident caused great excitement among the passengers, but the crew carried out their duties calmy and casually: the stretcher was transferred across a short gap, the ships tooted each other in greeting, and off we sailed back on course. After our voyage, the grand ship completed just one more crossing and then, in true fifties style, was sold to buyers in Hong Kong to be blown up as a prop in a minor movie.

I can't say I fretted much about my future as we docked in Manhattan, but it did occur to me that, for all my big talk of becoming a foreign correspondent and for all my excited daydreams of bold adventures in pursuit of distant news, I hadn't the slightest clue how to go about it.

3

Toronto the Good and the Swinging Sixties

Arriving back in Canada, I knew that despite my ambitions to one day to cover the world, I first needed to rediscover my own country. After four years abroad, I felt at least half foreign. Was Canada really the big, boring place my teachers at Badingham College had dismissed? At a personal level, relatives marvelled at my pale, weedy British look and posh English accent—not an impression I welcomed.

My first impressions of Toronto were not encouraging. The city in the late fifties was touted as a leader in the new Canada, but it was difficult for a newcomer to read. The downtown core looked stodgy past rather than exciting future, with no skyscrapers and an uninspiring mishmash of sombre red-brick commercial and industrial buildings. An experienced traveller once compared our downtown in dead of winter to that of Novosibirsk, Siberia.

The official mindset was still predominantly late Victorian, old-school Protestant with a heavy Northern Irish flavour. The drinking age was twenty-one, and Sundays were intended for prayer. The curfew on the Sabbath meant that professional sports could begin only at 1:30 p.m., and at 6 p.m. players were abruptly yanked off the field and spectators sent home. "I may have missed something," a fan sneered on one occasion, "but did they set us a new bedtime as well?"

Alongside such negatives, there were admittedly some strengths. The lake when glimpsed across railway lines added sparkle, while residential areas were thickly treed and quietly pleasant. The breakneck expansion of planned new communities such as Don Mills held promise, and the economy was setting eye-popping growth records, spurred on by the postwar baby boom, a new consumer culture, and waves of immigration from Europe. Toronto's population of 1.5 million in 1959 was increasing at an unprecedented annual rate of 5.06 percent.

I was slow to detect signs of the new age that the city and country were entering, even though they were happening all around me. For my dad, who now managed all five Toronto-area Simpson's department stores, it was like hitting the Klondike at the height of the Gold Rush. "This place is going to boom like nothing this country has seen before," he told us over dinner in our new house. I was dubious, but within a few years a major US publication would hail Toronto as the "city that works," local headline writers would swoon over the "boom town on the lake," and major upheavals would shake politics, culture, and the arts. Toronto and Montreal were in keen competition, increasingly hailed for their modernist compatibility with the world.

However, I had more pressing interests than tracking the bold new dawn. I needed to make new friends and, above all, start dating. In England, Hollywood movies had brainwashed me into expecting to come home to fresh-faced girls at school, eager to attend dances, cheerful in a Debbie Reynolds fashion, and impressed by anything a boy had to say, especially if it involved a witticism. Such prospects brought a rare spring to my step, and the first dabs of Brylcreem to my hair.

My heart dropped, however, when I saw my new school—the famed and sombre Upper Canada College. Behind a wide Victorian front, in drab red brick with a central clock tower, and exclusively for boys, it struck me as Badingham times ten. It was less tolerant, though, as masters still administered canings to younger boys, some with great gusto. UCC's strict focus was on producing high-achieving elites in business, law, and government. Culturally, this emphasis on elitism tended to reflect the rather patrician Victorian Tory and protestant mindset of upper crust Toronto at that time.

My family was certainly not patrician, but my dad was saddened to hear I utterly hated UCC. I vowed I would do this one year but then either move to a "normal" school or take off overseas and survive on my own.

In fairness, my memory of UCC should not reflect on the school today, which has become more representative of the population. Its education standards are very high, and it has many impressive alumni. Unfortunately, my brief time there coincided with the year when, literally, the roof almost fell in.

On opening day, the headmaster told the assembled students that the main building roof might collapse. The core structure was decaying so rapidly that pipes were splitting and some doors would neither open nor close. We were quickly assured classes would continue inside the strange-looking wooden huts we had seen around the grounds. All I really saw of this famous institution in action took place in a series of portables around a construction site.

With its elite connections, the college had no trouble raising emergency repair funds. British friends even came to the rescue: Prince Philip visited to help fundraising, and Field Marshal Montgomery promised to dedicate new front doors. Meanwhile, I settled in, struggling with a different curriculum but enjoying history classes and essay writing. I played rugger, marched in the cadet corps in my smart navy-blue uniform and white gloves, and generally got along. One early friend, Michael Cassels, introduced me to a wide group of people and a stream of weekend parties. We found ourselves amid the first generation of teens that had money to spend, derived from allowances as well as weekend and summer jobs, giving us spending power and heightened independence. We could show off new clothes, records, portable radios, and occasionally cars, and, like instant experts, discuss amazing travel options.

The bestseller *Europe on $5 a Day* appeared in 1957, and we were soon buzzing with gossip about which youth hostel in Marseille was best, where drinks were easiest to get, and the ideal length for a Euro Rail pass. Wanderlust was all the rage, made more so by the arrival of foreign films in artful black and white—*La Dolce Vita* from Italy, the French New Wave, Bergman's Swedish productions, and even soulful patriotic war epics from Russia. In books, Ernest Hemingway's influence was still strong, in large part because his foreign locations rang so true and seductive to us.

For me, like many others, the major influence was Jack Kerouac's *On the Road*, which opened a new front in the youth movement—one anchored in North America but outside the consumer-dominated and money-making obsessions of the age. Suddenly new options in our world appeared that valued a pure love of freedom and lit new horizons. So, for a while, it seemed.

The culture was starting to move, but in which direction? In music, rock and roll dominated dance floors and car radios, but when we went out for an evening, still denied access to bars, we settled into new coffeehouses such as the Bohemian Embassy, where in a haze of cigarette smoke we drank rounds of coffees, ate sandwiches, and listened earnestly to folk songs, moody jazz, bongo drum solos, and poetry readings. Between the sets, long hours of conversation flowed about the ills of material-obsessed society, the fraudulence of advertisers, the need to help antisegregation efforts in the United States, and our own existential need to fight off US cultural hegemony—a theme an increasing number of Canadian writers and academics were warning about.

To be in the scene, at weekends we aimed for a modified beatnik look, with a dingy tweed jacket and black turtleneck. A knowledge of art films and underground poetry helped, especially that of Allen Ginsberg (Kerouac's friend!). His controversial "Howl" confirmed in its opening line that we were at last a "generation."

This was also a time when social rigidity was still fighting a solid rearguard action. In 1959, hours after the Grey Cup game in Toronto, I watched in amazement as a crowd of revellers, no more than two hundred in all, were scattered by police for being too noisy and rambunctious. The few who booed the police were hurled into a van. When more boos ensued, an elderly police sergeant, red-faced and sweating, screamed, "You're all a bunch of bloody bums! Go home or you'll go to jail!" The crowd believed him and left quietly. That same year at a party in Forest Hill I saw one man slap the face of another because he dared use the F-word in the presence of a woman. No one objected to this swift justice because such language in mixed company was then quite unthinkable. Yet the sixties were only months away.

Meanwhile, UCC had one more humiliating debacle to face before term ended—the Exam Paper Heist. Shortly before the 1959 finals, fifteen-year-old Conrad Black—one year behind me and destined for much world media coverage in coming years—masterminded an act of rebellion to exact revenge on the college he loathed for its smug arrogance and vicious canings. Having discovered master keys, he recruited three fellow students to help him break into the principal's office and other rooms where he could mess up teaching assignments and discover the guarded exam questions. Moving with impressive stealth, they copied the answers and then sold them in a remarkably profitable black market to worried students they had carefully identified by searches of their previous scores in school documents.

This daring sneak attack failed, however, when teachers noted that normally low-scoring students were suddenly acing tests. Confessions came easily. When the aghast school authorities grasped the breath of the plot, they hoped to keep it quiet by not calling in the police. But the press picked up the story, causing much tongue wagging across the city's upper crust. The plotters were expelled, and Conrad left the gates to some jeers and fist shaking from the students.

I picked up not a whiff of this underground operation. I had already struggled through several exams when the school was summoned to assembly and told every single test would be redone. We innocents regarded this decision as collective punishment. And so my heart sank in equal measure at the beginning of my UCC year and at the ignominious end.

I was done with UCC and, I hoped, with upper-crust pretensions. To save for a future trip to Spain I got my first summer job, handling giant boxes in a large and dusty store warehouse. I had hoped physical labour would build me up my strength, but I spent most of the time writing invoices and reports on the astonishingly high number of crates that arrived from the docks with items pilfered. Still, I enjoyed the gab-fests workers had during the frequent slow periods. I was always a good listener, truly curious about people's lives, and found everyone interesting in this milieu, including war vets and immigrants from Europe who talked easily of their life adventures, ethnic customs, and political views. Apart from just relishing their company, I felt I was doing my study of life in the raw while practising a reporter's fact-finding skills.

I had not lost sight of my goal to become a foreign correspondent, and I was fortunate in having enough resources to keep up with events. At home we had an unusually large flow of newspapers and magazines, which Dad needed to keep abreast of advertising and sales trends in Canada's hottest merchandizing struggle: Simpson's v. Eaton's. We had more television news than in England, with access to US channels along with CBC TV and radio. And I was still an avid shortwave radio listener. At the time, the world of the UN and international diplomacy was covered far more than now, and foreign policy specialists like Walter Lipmann got star billing in scores of publications, along with the CBC's "eyes and ears on the world," James M. Minifie and Matthew Halton. There were many sources to keep those interested informed.

Why were some stories so clear, I wondered, while many others were flabby and left little impression? I began to take long, complex stories, such as the ongoing Algerian war of independence, and write down the essential core elements as clearly as I could—and then revise the text for still more compression. I also practised different styles by copying out the first few paragraphs and the conclusions of the articles I liked—much like imitating a pro batter's hitting swing or copying a masterwork in an art museum.

Most urgently, though, after UCC, I needed a cram school (a co-ed one, thank you) to handle my mishmash of UK and Ontario curricula and strengthen my self-confidence. I realized that to cover world affairs, I needed to become more *worldly* by expanding my cultural horizons. Now seventeen, I finally got the break I needed: entry into a small private school, Thornton Hall, located in a large house on a central residential street. It specialized in small classes, intense individual supervision in preparation for Ontario's grade thirteen final exams, and emphasis on the fine arts and humanities. Though the atmosphere was informal, manners and the dress code were firmly enforced: smart jacket and tie for the boys; prim skirts for the girls. No one objected: we liked looking grown-up.

The dominant staff person was an exotic-looking, sharp-featured, and intense Scottish intellectual and polymath, Angela Grieg. She was vice-principal and headed humanities courses ranging from ancient Greek philosophy to Chinese poetry, classical civilizations, drama, and modern European history. She offered seven language courses and a strong literary program. With a small enrolment, she was able to personally appraise each new student and soon pounced on my need to dig much deeper into the arts. Years later she noted, "Brian was strongly under the influence of Hemingway when he came to me, and I was trying to break this grip."

Over the next two years I absorbed a lot of classical novelists, poets, and dramas—and studied Russian language, music, and literature. This immersion led me to appreciate that vast nation's rich culture and humanity despite its history of appallingly awful governance. Later, when covering the collapse of the Soviet Union, I found I could win some credit from harried officials in Moscow or Leningrad by praising Pushkin's poetry.

Overall, Thornton Hall pushed me to expand my interests and shore up my confidence. While Ms. Grieg often joined in the general staff lamentations over my uneven work habits, she also noticed I had an ability to grasp and explain key issues clearly, writing in one report, "He always seems to understand the point of view which is being discussed . . . [and has] excellent insight into the subject." After years of being justly judged underperforming, this was exactly the encouragement the future journalist in me needed.

I also embarked on a more promising social life, making an interesting range of new friends and starting on my delayed dating experience. After I met a lovely girl at Thornton Hall, I was also able to snag a sliver of the late-fifties teen life that would still dominate the first few years of the sixties: dancing at a weekend hop, ordering hamburgers and cokes at quaint mom-and-pop restaurants, meeting dubious looks from her parents and older brothers, and sitting through squishy-romantic movies—some sacrifices, I learned, just had to be made.

As the sixties began, world events also grew more fascinating. John Kennedy became the US president; Cuba joined Berlin on the tension front burner; the space race entered an existential struggle for scientific domination; and the Cold War grew frostier. Britain also started pursuing its "winds of change" retreat from colonization in Africa; and Belgium withdrew from the giant Congo it had so long toxically misruled.

Of all the conflicts, the most dramatic was France's struggle over control of Algeria, where nine million Arabs sought independence and one million European settlers, aided by hard-core factions in the military, insisted that the country remain part of France. It all played out in increasing violence as President Charles de Gaulle inched France, at times duplicitously, toward leaving.

The Algerian War had been my main foreign news fascination ever since our holidays in France, and now it became the spark to an enduring friendship. One afternoon during a school break I noticed a new red-haired, lean student standing off by himself on the sidewalk, smoking. He had the look of a loner. I asked someone who he was: "That's the guy, Conrad Black, who was expelled for stealing those exams at UCC. He's very into this French in Algeria business." I was intrigued not only because of the UCC notoriety but also by the chance to talk Algeria with someone who knew about the war. I introduced myself and inquired if he was following the latest crisis in Algiers.

"Indeed I am, and I am quite confident de Gaulle will prevail within days," he answered. He proceeded to give me a remarkably detailed assessment of de Gaulle's strategy, the overall military versus rebel balance, and the key players, mainly café owners, ex-soldiers, and local business figures in the settler resistance, soon to become the notorious OAS (Secret Army Organization) underground. And so we began six decades of discussions and frequent debates over world events.

Conrad was as much a foreign news junkie as I was and even more of a political one: he was then a "progressive," being pro-liberal, pro-Kennedy, and fanatically pro–Franklin Roosevelt and the New Deal. We were both equally fascinated by history, particularly twentieth-century events and military affairs. Conrad had a strategic grasp of the core issues at stake in complex, fast-moving events. He had been studying on his own the military theories of Napoleon, Carl von Clausewitz, and historian theorists such as Admiral Alfred T. Mahan and B.H. Liddell Hart. We were both members of the History Book Club and the Military Book Club and spent hours looking at military campaigns and searching for keys to the strengths behind political campaigns and mass movements. This early interest in strategy and tactics proved useful in guiding much of my work as a foreign correspondent. Conrad took his adoration of Roosevelt's politics, including battles for welfare and workers' rights, to the point of buying a recording of his major speeches and playing them at full blast in the family mansion until his conservative father, George Black, demanded that FDR's ghost be heard no more.

The small student body at Thornton Hall was filled with interesting characters, several of whom became friends. David Pringle, a brilliant math student, dreamed of driving a powerful speedboat over Niagara Falls as a high-paying stunt, but eventually settled into filmmaking and lighting effects, eventually winning two Oscars for inventing super-high-lighting systems (up to five hundred thousand watts) that had a significant impact on the way movies are made. Carlo Derege, son of the Italian consul in Toronto and a great humourist, eventually ended up as a senior UN Refugee Affairs official.

The dating, partying, and club scene (innocent as it was) continued, but road travels took up more spare energy. We explored Greenwich Village in New York, the epicentre of the sixties counterculture, as well as the city's jazz clubs. We visited Washington and Montreal to check out the pace of political and social change there.

I had to concede major change was happening in Toronto, too, where the modernist new City Hall set the tone for glittering developments, while the Victorian mindset in city politics began to loosen its grip. National politics often seemed uninspiring under the leaderships of Conservative John Diefenbaker and Liberal Lester Pearson, but party ranks were agitating for change as the New Democratic Party was launched. In Quebec, Liberals promised a Quiet Revolution after dumping the long-running power machine of the conservative Union Nationale.

Although life in Canada was becoming more agreeable, I still yearned to cover news overseas. In the fall of 1961, I applied to one of the few journalism programs in Canada, at Ryerson Institute of Technology (now Toronto Metropolitan University).

When I met with program director Ted Schroder, he asked why I wanted to go into the news business and laughed when I said, "to become a foreign correspondent." "They all say that when they get here," he explained, "but no one ever seems to achieve it. They lose interest." I assured him I would not lose mine—and I was in. Over the next three years, Ryerson gave me solid building blocks for my career. The courses and most of the teachers were excellent, schooling us in every discipline we might need in journalism, from basic reporting and news management skills to a wide range of the humanities, including literature, drama, sociology, geopolitics, and economics. I also learned layout design, sound editing, interviewing techniques, and photography. Although I had no interest in ever working in TV, we print students shared a year with the Radio and Television Arts Program to expand our future options. I was sincerely touched when, decades later, Ryerson University conferred on me an honorary doctorate in journalism.

During my first summer break, I worked as a news intern at the *Globe and Mail*: half the time I spent as junior reporter in the sports department, and the rest as a "copy boy" rushing incoming wire items to various parts of the office and fetching coffee. Given my near invisibility, I could drift through various departments—a great chance to watch, eavesdrop, and learn. I had also started a diary on New Year's Day, which I kept for four years as I recorded news items and my reaction to them. On the first day, for instance, I recorded that months earlier, "they threw up a brick wall in Berlin—it's still there and likely will be for some time to come." I never imagined it would stand twenty-eight years and I would be there the night a joyous population started ripping it down. As for South Vietnam, "outlook very glum . . . I don't see how they can keep it out of Communist hands for more than 5 years." Actually, it took thirteen years.

At the time, I saw my future as evolving within a print news environment, with the same pounding typewriters, clanging teletype machines, and smoky hubbub, little changed in a third of a century. But on July 23,1962, standing in the *Globe*'s newsroom, I saw its future rocked by the first live satellite television broadcast from Europe to North America. That night I gushed into my diary: "Today I saw Telstar!!! I saw a direct TV broadcast from England and Rome . . . God knows what it will be like when I read this in 40 years . . . the world is getting smaller and smaller." I could never have guessed that in just twenty years I'd be a creature of satellite TV, reporting from far-off wars and revolutions by spoken words and images rather than typed-out copy.

Through the Cuban Missile Crisis in October 1962, I kept a running diary commentary of the high and low moments. After the opening announcement by President John F. Kennedy on the twenty-third, I wrote: "I was very uneasy . . . all that we care for is threatened to be blown to oblivion . . . I cannot deny though certain excitement over it all; we stand at a crossroads." I drew a skull and crossbones at the top of each diary page during the crisis, light coloured on average days, blacked in on the most alarming. Life went on—during the crisis I was made co-editor of *The Fifth Page*, a Ryerson literary magazine. Only when it was over did I take stock of my feelings at the height of the Cold War: "I'll admit I was scared stiff for a while during it. At one point I probably doubted I would ever get to see 1963."

I was certainly influenced by one outstanding professor, the charismatic David Crombie—later a popular Toronto mayor and federal Cabinet minister—who led a nervous class through a quiet appraisal of the strategic aims of the superpowers in the showdown, illustrating why one side wanted missiles in Cuba and the other insisted they be removed, until wise heads in both the White House and the Kremlin defused the crisis. His calm clarity of reasoning added to my determination to develop similar analytical abilities. Sixty-one years later I was able to thank him when I interviewed him for this book.

Personally, I was obsessed with going to Spain over the next summer. I saved money so I could study the culture there as well as the history of the Spanish Civil War (1936–39)—to many foreign correspondents a classic object lesson in how democracies can fail. On my first visit there with the family in 1956 I had seen a bullfight, and, inspired now by Hemingway's description in *Death in the Afternoon*, I wanted to follow key fiestas across the country for several months. I even practised my passes with a capote (large cape) and a muleta (small cape). I find this ambition difficult to comprehend now because, over the last six decades, ever since Spain refused to follow Portugal in banning the killing of bulls in the ring, I have boycotted bullfighting.

I managed to pull off a dream summer by taking a freighter from Montreal to Lisbon for five dollars a day. I was the first passenger in two years on this small and rather old vessel, so had a stateroom and deck to myself for the ten-day passage as well as the full run of the ship as a sort of honorary member of the crew. I read much of the day and prowled the ship from wheelhouse to engine room, except during a heavy storm that blew off Newfoundland. Once arrived, I mostly stayed at the University of Madrid for $1.50 a day, one meal included, and toured the country extensively by bus and on a Euro Rail pass. I made friends with several medical students who were keen to practise their English as they introduced me to the city's folk and flamenco clubs and told stories of political repression and fear under the dictator General Francisco Franco.

I spent one day testing my capework at a school for aspiring toreros in which the master's assistant charged with a pair of bulls horns in close imitation of the animals' actions. I was pleased with my artistry in the veronica passes and in my muleta right- and left-handed moves. I was thought promising, although rather old at twenty-one to embark on the gruelling apprenticeship such a career entailed. After I attended a couple of bullfights, however, I decided the spectacle could not be morally supported—and that was that. A fantasy died, but my passion for Spain continued.

I graduated from Ryerson in 1964, when the news industry was profitable, entry-level jobs were plentiful, and the burgeoning youth movement brought new energy to newsrooms. There was a feeling of impatience in the air, stirred by the Kennedy assassination the previous November, the start of the Vietnam antiwar crusade, and the nonviolent antisegregation movement, especially in the Deep South. It was clear that American politics at all levels were undergoing fundamental grassroots upheaval and reform. Internationally, a strongly revived Europe was showing its muscle again, while the so-called Third World was demanding urgent attention and influence. Khrushchev was overthrown as Soviet leader, and China tested its first atomic weapon.

Core concepts of government responsibilities were changing. President Lyndon Johnson's liberal Democratic administration put new emphasis on consensus building and expanding programs such as his key war on poverty. Canadian and British governments followed the Big Government with Big Ideas model at both the national and the municipal level—with futuristic park planning, public housing, and freeway construction, for example. All this ferment meant more beats for the media to cover and expanded job potential in journalism.

The swing to bigger, more ambitious government in the United States brought a counter-lurch to the right in the Republican Party, as seen in the dramatic rise of Barry Goldwater's movement in the primaries. In Canada, the age of deference was crumbling, as people protested more and increasingly expected concessions from governments or their employers. Almost overnight we seemed to enter a new period of "affluence and its discontents," as historian Robert Bothwell termed it: "Canadians reacted to prosperity in the 1960s not by coming together but by coming apart. The problem with affluence, it turned out, was there wasn't enough of it—or paradoxically, too much."

My own discontent manifested in my impatience to get overseas to work. With few openings in Canadian media for foreign positions, the only course was to get work overseas, build a reputation, and hope to be picked up by a major newspaper or wire service there. But first I had to work for a year at least to raise enough money to launch a career abroad. I had two job offers, one from a TV station in Sudbury and the other with the vast Thomson newspaper chain, which promised to place me "somewhere" local. I chose newspapers—and was posted, at a salary of seventy dollars a week, to the *Oshawa Times*.

On my first meeting with the management, I was warned of labour unrest that had targeted the *Times* as the first Thomson newspaper to be unionized, but I still joined the union drive a week later. I also booked a room for seven dollars a week in a cheap rooming house and quickly settled into life on a local paper. Given the small staff, I shared responsibility for covering courts, school boards, city hall, civic organizations, and obituaries, and also for doing photo work. I was encouraged, in any spare time, to write features and opinion pieces. The hours were often brutal, but I loved it, especially as I came to understand that all levels of democratic governance have the same basic dynamics. On city hall committees, the characters were colourful and certain types emerged—the power broker, the idealist, the fixer, the problem creator—that I found later in most political environments, from Ottawa to Nairobi to Brasilia.

In August, Conrad Black, now a temporary addition to the Canada–United States Inter-Parliamentary Group, invited me to go with him to the Democratic National Convention in Atlantic City to affirm Lyndon Johnson as a presidential candidate. I begged a few days off work in return for writing several features on my trip, and we drove down together. On one level the convention, held in the gigantic, ocean-front arena, became a requiem for JFK; on another, a coronation for Johnson, whose every appearance was stage-crafted to make him look like a towering monarch of proven power to lead his party's battle against the right-wing threat of Goldwater; and on yet a third, as a civil rights protest for the inclusion of Black representatives from Mississippi as official delegates.

The convention ended with Johnson and his family standing on a floodlit balcony outside the arena basking in the cheers of tens of thousands of followers while fireworks blazed over the waterfront. During the next year and a half, Johnson pulled off astonishing reforms, including the Voting Rights Act, and was credited as, possibly, the greatest legislator in the country's history. Yet less than four years later he was driven from office following failures in Vietnam and continuing racial unrest at home. I never forgot this proof of the transitory nature of leadership and the destabilizing speed of power shifts in politics.

By the time I returned to Oshawa, I had begun to wonder if I should concentrate on reporting on the United States rather than the wider world. I mulled it over for a weekend, but was unable to shake my original determination to work overseas. The following summer I left for Spain.

I arrived in Madrid in 1965 with $1,100 I had saved—sufficient to live frugally for three months while I travelled and looked for work. Life was pleasant, the food exciting, and I was able to reconnect with the medical student friends I had made at the university two summers earlier. Several were involved in serious antiregime movements and were always on alert. We went horseback riding at a location used for Italian western movies and served one afternoon as extras in a hillside scene, where I was told that my horse was a prominent screen veteran of the film *Lawrence of Arabia*.

I went on a side trip to Morocco for eight days to gain experience in travelling in exotic places. I got severe sunstroke and was bedridden with splitting headaches for two days, saw a mirage as I crossed a flat desert area—sailboats on a lake surrounded by mountains—and to my amazement was evacuated from two buses in a row when their wheels caught fire.

Still mesmerized by *The Sun Also Rises* and other Hemingway novels, I went with some friends to Pamplona, determined to take part in the historic running of the bulls. I felt making myself a target of the horns was an allowable indulgence. I was not prepared for the frenzied bedlam that six fighting bulls cause when let loose into a throng of risk-takers to run the four fenced-off blocks through the old town to the bullring. The bulls slash with horns to left and right, sending runners flying and creating dangerous pileups. As I set off I was surprised by the excited screams from spectators, but I soon became aware of the thunder of fast-approaching hooves. As the first bull passed nearby I saw one body, severely gored, pinwheel above the crowd.

I sensed other bulls close behind and tried to climb the next lamppost, only to be kicked off by two other runners who got there first. I dove into a narrow doorway, but the door was locked. Another couple of bulls passed, and more bodies went flying. I decided to run for it, stepped out, and was immediately slammed by a terrified runner going full speed, a collision that sent both of us crashing to the sidewalk. Two of his friends grabbed him and carried him off, leaving me behind, seriously concussed, bleeding profusely from my nose.

I staggered to my feet and saw, only five metres away, a bull charging down the sidewalk right at me. It seemed all in slow motion and I thought quite calmly, "I may be killed now." I hit the ground in a half faint, sensing only a large black force passing over me. After the last bulls passed, someone helped me to my feet, and I wobbled like a drunk toward the bullring. More than two dozen people were injured that morning, so medical staff were busy. Fortunately, friends spotted me and led me to my room, where with ice pads I waited, in darkened gloom, for the worst of the concussion to pass. I vowed never again to take unnecessary adventure-seeking risks and, henceforth, to put myself in danger only for solid professional reasons. It was a promise I kept.

I had a key contact in a fellow Ryerson graduate, George Hawrylyshn, who had landed a job with Associated Press in the capital and also freelanced for a Spanish illustrated news magazine. He asked me to help him on some assignments, and I was glad to do so gratis for the press passes and the experience. When he invited me to help him cover a Beatles concert in Madrid's legendary bullring, I readily agreed. I had first seen the Beatles the year before when, on the evening of February 9, 1964, I was relaxing after a boring day and, along with tens of millions of others, tuned into the Ed Sullivan entertainment hour on television. Later, I wrote in my diary: "I saw an incredible sight—*The Beatles*! This is a rock and roll team from England of four scruffy-looking youths with damn little talent . . . There is something disturbing about them—they seem as if they would attract the lunatic fringe, while in fact they attract millions. Not at all likely to last long." So much for my music judgment.

Despite my initial dislike, I had come to appreciate their genius and had followed their explosive popularity with interest. This concert turned out to be one of their most remarkable performances, not because of its magnificence but because of the surly and paranoid atmosphere Spain's government imposed on it. Even before the event, there was tension because the security services under General Franco feared that Beatlemania might set off anarchic rebellion among the young. They ordered that only half the seats could be sold and that the lights should remain on full beam throughout the concert. George wanted me to cover the behind-the-scenes arrival of the Fab Four while he kept a watch in the arena on both the crowd and the throngs of grey-clad security troops who circled the seating areas.

I was in the bowels of the bullring when the Beatles arrived in a British embassy limo and followed them as they were led to the holding area at one of the gates into the ring. It was odd seeing such famous individuals taking stock of their most unglamorous surroundings. "Is this where the bulls come out?" Ringo Starr asked. "No, it's where the wounded toreros are raced to the operating room when they are gored," came the reply. They seemed relaxed as they milled around smoking. Shortly before they were introduced, I saw them huddled before the grates of the gate whispering with serious looks, which I assumed was their reaction to seeing they would be performing before a half-empty venue surrounded by scores of security police.

After they were introduced and led through the gate, I joined my friend for what was to be in some ways a bummer of a concert. Their performance was standard but seemed smaller under a harsh glare of light. They must have seen acts of astonishing brutality by the police, who used their batons on any youths who acted "wild." Fans who stood to wave handkerchiefs or scarves were ordered to sit immediately or be arrested. The Four made no sign of having noticed the crackdown but left the stage after a mere twenty-four minutes.

As we made our way back to the office by subway, a youth standing near us muttered some low-key comments about a group of security police who were heading home in the same car. One of the "greys," as the state security police were called, came over and grabbed him, twisted his arm behind, and yanked him by his hair toward the door. When the door opened, he belted the lad in the back of the head and hurled him onto the platform. He then casually returned to his laughing mates. No one in the car protested; most looked away. It was one of my first experiences of seeing raw state police power and the paralyzing effect it can have over many citizens. I noticed looks of silent rage among many of the younger passengers, however, some of whom likely became part of the blossoming anti-Franco democratic movements in coming years.

None of these learning experiences were getting me closer to professional work, and by now I had figured out I was not likely to be successful in Spain. So, I launched my Plan B and, in the summer of 1965, headed to Britain, where I had a line on a reporting job in the lively Richmond-Twickenham area of Greater London. All hell was breaking loose there as the Swinging Sixties ushered in the birth of modern Britain.

The sheer volume of change was unprecedented—in music, theatre, fashion, modern art experiments, film and photography, sexual mores, and above all in a surging youth movement that demanded heightened respect and influence. "It was the year when everything changed—and a year that everyone knew it," wrote art historian Christopher Bray.

For the next year and a half, I worked as a reporter and district editor for the *Richmond and Twickenham Times* newspaper. I covered the workings of a complex local government as well as the cultural scene, service clubs, police and courts, the odd conspiracy theory, and a host of colourful personalities (see "Conspiracy Theories" interlude). The novelty of Canadian status gave me a neutrality in disputes between the reformers and the rearguard conservatives. All the while the UK Labour Party government was deeply influenced by the new can-do style of Kennedy and LBJ big initiatives politics, providing enormous leaps in funding for all the social services—a 45 percent gain in three years that helped win the historic landslide election I covered a few months after I arrived. I learned there how citizens work out their differences, plan vital services, debate budgets, and usually make the best of flawed situations.

My life was pleasant, living close by the eighteenth-century Richmond Bridge on one of the most beautiful stretches of the Thames River. My austere one-room apartment with a separate communal kitchen was rented out by a theatrical landlady who brewed her own beer. Rarely seen, she occasionally emerged to characterize noise coming from her strikingly polite tenants as "sheer bloody thunder." The newspaper office was old and scruffy, replete with reporters who made amusing companions, including a future historian, Gavin Weightman, who became a lifelong friend. I devoured foreign news: the first wave of anti–Vietnam War demonstrations was spreading worldwide, the Cold War remained tense, and the antinuclear movement in Britain was strong. My personal news interest focused on two areas: military matters and human rights. In the mid-sixties, Amnesty International was one of the few sizable international agencies, and UN actions in humanitarian issues were cautiously limited.

Although I explored new job opportunities, even getting meetings at the *Times* of London and Associated Press, I soon realized that, as a Canadian, my chances of landing a foreign posting were slim. My best hope was to return to Canada and try to make a success with a large news operation with bureaus abroad. The irony was clear: the only way to seize my prize abroad was to go home first. I also missed some things I thought of as uniquely Canadian—that band of crimson at dusk along the western horizon in late fall, the smell of ice in hockey rinks before a game, and the sharp fall Canadian colours in the clear frigid air.

In 1967, as I was about to turn twenty-five, the next destination seemed obvious: Montreal, host to the World's Fair Expo 67 during Canada's Centennial Year. I couldn't think of a more enjoyable location.

After a round of dinners with friends, I left London in early May. My landlady emerged from her odorous cellar brewery to give me the British version of a hug—a pat on one shoulder—and, with sad eyes, intoned the traditional rooming-house matrons' send-off: "Do take care, lad! Nasty old world out there, isn't it?"

INTERLUDE

Conspiracy Theories

I am nostalgic by nature, but I don't recall life during the sixties with wistful yearning or through rose-coloured glasses. I would take a time-machine trip back, but a weekend stay would be plenty.

The sixties did have a few advantages over today. At the height of the Cold War you could say one thing for the Communists: they were so widely viewed as a singular global threat that they monopolized the market in conspiracy theories. That meant you weren't bored all the time by people offering up ever wilder conspiracy alarms at social gatherings and at work. There was usually just one big conspiracy to deal with, not hordes of fresh ones every month.

We had no idea how lucky we were. It was possible to mingle with people without having to hear someone rant about how vaccines were secretly designed to capture your mind or how a known cure for all cancers was being suppressed by deep-state governments for dark financial profits.

It was a time before politicians might insist there were two realities: a mainstream media one and another, virtual reality where truth reigned. We could even be confident that a political or media figure who was caught in an outright lie would be punished with swift dismissal and not rewarded for repeating the fiction.

A small percentage of the population is always ready to believe anything outlandish, but these individuals were infinitely fewer then and conspiracy notions were easier to pinpoint and address. Cries that Communists were trying to infiltrate all levels of government, while grossly exaggerated, at least had some basis in truth. The old anti-Semitic forgery "The Protocols of Zion" kept appearing every few years as a crazed warning that Jews were really angling for world domination. Then the Kennedy assassination became the most active item in the conspiracy market, but a lot of the cover-up claims grew out of predictable doubts resulting from the many loose ends left by official investigations. Historians and writers inevitably revisited that day in Dallas looking for angles, and now, sixty years later, the speculation continues.

Back then it was also much easier to discuss the latest news because most people read the same few print media and watched the same few TV shows. In Toronto, for example, there were three or four somewhat similar newspapers, radio stations, and the CBC, as well as three American traditional TV networks that arrived via Buffalo. *Time* and *Newsweek* were widely read for the US and some foreign news, while *Maclean's* and the Canadian Press wire stories kept the focus on Canadian events.

Political news coverage was still relatively deferential: reporters addressed Cabinet ministers with respect, and those in the top rank revelled in whatever privileges their status offered. People participated in civic and national affairs far more than now, and campaign rallies were often well-attended events. I saw Maple Leaf Gardens filled to capacity twice for political rallies, once for the newly formed New Democratic Party and again for the Liberals. Voter turnout in the 1963 election hit 79.2 percent, a full 17 points above the 2021 level.

But nostalgia for the "exciting" sixties should be kept in perspective. A lot of public life was narrow, ethnocentric, and self-righteous. Those who think political correctness and "wokeness" are uniquely modern scourges from the left have no idea how many very real imposed restraints dominated public discourse in the more conservative past. School and university teachers alike had to take great care to watch their words lest they be deemed "Red" in politics or "peculiar" in social and sexual tastes. Parents lodged complaints when they heard of teachers who seemed radical, and school boards and many employers kept strict watches on attitude. On university campuses, the RCMP were known to scour student and faculty activities regularly for supposed subversive tendencies. Files were kept, and nobody wanted to end up in one. You could be judged radical simply by your clothes.

Though the sixties had more stability and clarity of focus, people still made predictions that proved comically off-key over time.

- The Cold War would last forever, barring a nuclear war. There was no chance Communism would collapse for a century or more.
- Russia would outpace the West in science and technology and surely reach the moon first.
- China would remain mired in abject poverty, forever cut off from the outside world. India would stay a helpless giant, of no economic consequence in the wider world.
- Africa, however, faced a brilliant future as the "winds of change" roared through the former colonies, bringing progressive reforms that would ensure the solid success of democracy there.
- The monarchy would be gone by 1984 at the latest. Religion would be a dying force of no real account anywhere in the world.

These miscalculations seem bizarre now, and over the years I've come to beware of fashions in geopolitics and of sweeping political views generally, even though journalism and politics remain addicted to them. Whether we are underwhelmed with information as in the sixties or overwhelmed as now, the search for big-picture answers is understandable and deeply human, even though our myopia so often means such bold and broad forecasts seem doomed to irrelevance.

4

Passionate Montreal in Years of Ferment

The early summer of 1967 was the best of times to settle in Montreal, "the city of the future." Expo 67 had just opened, stunning Canadians and visitors from abroad with its instant success. Simultaneously, praise poured in for the city's effervescent lifestyle and culture, and the taste for the urban grandeur that its dynamic mayor Jean Drapeau kept extolling.

Before landing a job, I tried to update myself on the broad political picture in the city. Conrad Black introduced me to the outstanding political facilitator Peter White, fiercely energetic and equally at home in both language communities, who asked me to co-author a six-part series he'd sold to the *Montreal Gazette* on the need for a fundamental overhaul of the two separate language systems in Quebec schools. The articles made a big splash in the *Gazette* and convinced management to offer me a prized job as a reporter.

Ironically, although I covered many crises over my career, the one I was physically closest to occurred just before I began working at the *Gazette*—French president Charles de Gaulle's state visit to celebrate Canada's centennial year. Ominous warnings that de Gaulle's visit would bring trouble began building when he chose to skip Ottawa and land at Quebec City aboard the French naval cruiser *Colbert*. He received a rapturous reception amid enormous crowds waving blue Quebec fleur-de-lys flags and the French tricolour. A committee of Quebec nationalists had arranged this "French second coming." The next morning de Gaulle and Quebec premier Daniel Johnson set off in an open limousine to Montreal along the north shore of the St. Lawrence River in a victory-style procession, passing through triumphal arches in small villages as crowds everywhere sang "La Marseillaise" to honour Quebec–France amity. At several stops de Gaulle urged Quebecers to become "masters of your own destiny."

In Montreal, where hundreds of thousands awaited him, the air was electric with the sense of history being made. Conrad and I were determined to see his arrival at Montreal's City Hall and got a perfect location close to the balcony he would appear on. It soon became obvious that the event and the presence of so much media, including live broadcast coverage, was stirring up the wildest passions of both sovereigntists, who sought a more independent Quebec in association with Canada, and separatists, who demanded a complete break by any means possible.

When de Gaulle emerged in his olive-drab general's uniform with his arms spread regally in a cross between a wave and an embrace, the crowd roared their approval. The officials behind him, including Mayor Drapeau, seemed more nervous than celebratory. De Gaulle began speaking slowly, describing how the emotional receptions on the long drive that day reminded him of "another liberation day"—his entry into freed Paris in August 1944. "Vive le Montréal," he continued, "Vive le Québec," culminating after a dramatic pause in the crescendo, "Vive le Québec libre."

The crowd went wild. In mere seconds the course of Quebec and Canadian twentieth-century history was altered before our eyes. National survival seemed at stake as the crisis of unity that had been brooding beyond the horizon became the dominant political reality for decades to come. Like many across Canada, I was furious at this betrayal of my country. Canada had offered shelter and aid to de

Gaulle's Free France cause during the Second World War and had lost tens of thousands of its sons fighting to defend and liberate France in both world wars. I was disappointed Prime Minister Pearson did not immediately order the French delegation to leave. While separatist crowds rejoiced in the streets, Pearson waited until the next day before calling an emergency Cabinet meeting and only then delivering a mild wrist slap for "unacceptable intrusion" in Canadian affairs. De Gaulle did leave that day, but at a stately pace, after visiting Expo and attending the banquet in his honour hosted by Drapeau.

Broadcast live coast to coast, Drapeau's speech hit the perfect balance, showing respect for de Gaulle while chiding him, and France, for that country's previous two centuries of indifference to francophone Quebec and reminding him that France's role in Quebec affairs was limited by this history. Quebecers had survived on their own, often in harsh conditions, "practising resistance before the word existed." Those who wished to help the province launch a renewal of French Canada must know Quebec, "so that French Canada can better serve the whole of Canada." Any future ties between France and Quebec could only be within the "Canadian context."

Drapeau's speech was hailed as one of the landmark addresses in modern Canadian history: "Drapeau the Magnificent," trumpeted the headline of the Toronto *Telegram*. In the coming months, Drapeau was seen as a national unifier and possible provincial or national leader. Both Liberals and Conservatives tried to woo him. "Why would I move?" he lectured me many times in later years. "Running a city like New York, Chicago, or Montreal is the best job in the world. Here we get things done!"

These extraordinary events made me all the more anxious to start reporting. I already had good contacts in the anglophone community but needed to explore the left-wing activist world, including francophone movements. These separate worlds were plainly heading for collision, a prospect many participants in this hyper-excited city seemed to relish. "Wait for me!" I responded.

The *Montreal Gazette* I joined that September was a historic paper, founded in 1778 and still a bastion of the anglo community. Though outgunned by the bigger and livelier *Montreal Star*, a niche following helped it survive.

I entered through the imposing bronze doors, boarded a creaky elevator with sliding thin steel bars, and rode up to the fourth-floor newsroom. Amid rows of steel-grey desks, phones rang incessantly, teletype machines dinged and roared as they spewed out domestic and foreign stories, and reporters, many smoking cigarettes or pipes, pounded their typewriters or stood in groups trading news tips and gossip. The heart of operations were the two main desks that controlled all local and international stories, where the editors sat, several crusty veterans of print.

Nearby lay a large logbook that carried the current assignments for general reporters like me without a set "beat." There I'd find, for example, next to my name:

- Tues: low-cost housing protest, St. Henri
- Wed: feature on Chinese New Year celebrations
- Thurs: Police union airs grievance against Drapeau
- Fri: Chamber of Commerce lunch, city economic forecast.

Although I welcomed this opportunity to get acquainted with the city, build contacts, and improve my French, I soon realized that the *Gazette* intended to promote me rapidly as a political reporter and future columnist. The paper was intent on reacting to Quebec's tumultuous era of change by bringing on a younger, more hard-driving news team of "hot prospects." We'd be watched over carefully, of course, as we wrote for anglo communities that acknowledged the need for rapid change as well as traditional conservative readers who feared any rocking of political boats. I found it a thrilling, high-stakes atmosphere to work in, so long as I could survive the risk of a CIF (career in flames) moment.

I loved the old place and settled easily into the stimulating but draining social life. The office was only a few blocks from the most thriving bar, restaurant, and dating scene in Canada, and, after our working day ended around 7 p.m., many reporters and editors would drift over to Mother Martin's restaurant to decompress at the sweeping L-shaped bar.

This after-work milieu was an important source of gossip on politics, radical organizations, and the city's five organized crime families. There we also got a sense of our standing in the newsroom. One senior editor tipped me off that I would soon be assigned to big political events and even coverage in the United States. I should, he added, keep an eye on the federal Liberal leadership race early in 1968: he had "inside dope" that the veteran external affairs minister Paul Martin was almost sure to win, but suggested I closely watch the reforming new justice minister, Pierre Elliott Trudeau, as a dark-horse candidate. "He's a not very impressive know-it-all," he said, "but you never know."

My desk sat in a corner that editors labelled Red Square because of the number of radical, New Left reporters working there—a garrulous group that cheerfully poured scorn on their employers' conservative instincts. They cheered on Cuba and Fidel at the same time they denigrated the United States for its racism and the Vietnam War. They made entertaining colleagues, seeing the world as part theatre and lacing their rants with humour. One of them, Nick Auf der Maur, proved to be my best pilot though the political rapids as well as the most congenial cafés and bars. Later he became a legendary *boulevardier*, political activist, investigative newsman, author, columnist, and broadcaster, friend of the powerful and downtrodden alike, and creator of several municipal parties.

Auf der Maur introduced me to the "seven stations of the cross"—his name for the nightspots where every evening he met his astonishing array of friends and offbeat characters, from famous authors such as Mordecai Richler to disbarred judges, shadowy pro-separatist activists, labour organizers, politicians, academics, and foreign journalists. The first stop would usually be the Bistro on Mountain Street, run by former French settlers in Algiers, which thrived on its smoky Left Bank atmosphere of literary and political debates across marble-topped tables and a long zinc bar. Conversation flourished easily in Montreal night spots of that era as music was played at a moderate volume. There I met Mark Starowicz, the firebrand editor of the *McGill Daily* who was destined for a spectacular career creating CBC current affairs shows and directing documentary series.

After the Bistro, several of us might go to the Swiss Hut, where city poets, socialist intellectuals, and hard-core activists would debate and sometimes conspire in dark booths. Tense debates raged over the "viability of violent rebellion" of the kind currently being waged by the Front de Libération du Québec (FLQ), several of whose members were rumoured to be circulating among the customers, as were police spies trying to fathom who was who in this kaleidoscope of agitation.

It was a busy life—a statistic at the time recorded that more was spent in Montreal on "entertaining out" than in any place on earth except Hawaii. But the lifestyle was ruinous over time, for even after the bars closed at 1 a.m. (later 3 a.m.), journalists would often adjourn to the Press Club for nightcaps and smoked-meat sandwiches sent over from Ben's Restaurant next door. I vowed to be self-disciplined, and, although there were several rocky periods, by and large I was.

I was soon caught up in the most extraordinary political whirlwind in Canadian history: Trudeaumania. Apparently I was the first reporter to use the term, although, after all these years, I feel petty even mentioning it. While I was covering the Trudeau campaign in the 1968 election, the editor who monitored Canadian media coverage of the election, an anti-Trudeau grump to the core, pointed an agitated finger at my story of Trudeau's Toronto rally: "Ever since you used this damned word, everyone has picked it up." And this, he noted, was "only adding to unfair excitement over him alone."

There was no doubt, however, that "mania" accurately depicted the reception for Trudeau that I witnessed across Canada. I had used the term not to praise but rather to note how the wildest enthusiasm for Trudeau came from the very young fans mobilized by Liberal Party workers. Reporting on the Toronto rally in the *Gazette* of June 20, I mentioned the frenzy among kids and teens, "some of whom began lining up six hours early and surged in screaming waves around the platform area. The mass rally was not all Trudeaumania," I continued, "and the people of voting age were clearly in the majority."

The phenomenon happened so quickly; even six months earlier I'd seen no sign of it. Trudeau was soaring in prominence as a result of his enlightened reforms to laws covering divorce, abortion, and homosexuality, marked by his terse assertion, "The state has no business in the bedrooms of the nation." As he argued for a Bill of Rights in a reformed constitution, his pugnacious stance against Quebec nationalism brought him extra attention in the wake of outrage over de Gaulle's speech. Seen as an enlightened francophone with a plan to defuse extreme Quebec nationalism and strengthen "one Canada," he was for many Liberals the obvious man of the hour to replace the retiring Lester Pearson. He was definitely a rare politician—an adventure-travelling, yoga-meditating, highly educated intellectual and former union activist who also styled himself a playboy, simultaneously restless and austere.

Still, as 1968 dawned, he seemed the last person who would induce mania of any kind. Before the full glare of TV cameras and flashbulbs highlighted his every move, I was struck by the aura of remoteness behind his thin smile that suggested a strong wish to be elsewhere. Though flawlessly bilingual, his speeches in English could ring rather flat; in French he was more animated. He would soon prove extraordinarily photogenic and camera savvy. Pictures highlighted the high cheekbones and stiletto-sharp eyes and, as biographer John English later noted, "somehow missed his pock-marked cheeks, the faintly yellow tinge to his complexion and his less than normal height."

Trudeau's road to victory was also well paved by his enemies. When Quebec nationalists targeted him for abuse, he slammed them back as "jokers and jerks," to the great delight of many across Canada. In February, when the wily and theatrical Daniel Johnson squared off against Trudeau in a nationally telecast, invective-laced debate over constitutional powers, Trudeau was widely judged to have outfenced the premier. Media were riveted by this "duel of the century" and made much of Johnson's desire to destroy Trudeau's standing. My sources close to the premier's office tipped me off that his real aim was more Machiavellian. In a half-page "insight" report in the *Gazette* on March 2, I laid out that strategy: to use the exchange to promote Trudeau's popularity outside Quebec and promote his takeover of the Liberal Party while weakening Trudeau's standing inside the province. Johnson was sure Trudeau's muscular federalism and "insulting and arrogant manner" would turn Quebecers against the Liberals and toward his own ally, the Conservative Party under Robert Stanfield, which needed to win Quebec. That would leave the new Conservative government indebted to Johnson's Union Nationale and, critically, its cause of solid, irreversible, special status for Quebec.

Had Johnson's strategy worked, the nation would have had a very different future. But clearly, it backfired with a vengeance. Weeks before the convention, Trudeau became the man to beat. The more he held the intensifying spotlight, the more the term "charisma" was applied to him. Also, the *Gazette*'s polling showed him running well in Quebec and everywhere across the country, heading for a fourth-ballot convention victory.

I liked the bracing spring air of Ottawa in the first week of April, when I arrived to cover the convention at the Civic Centre. It fit the mood when everything about the gathering seemed momentous—the unprecedented excitement over the Trudeau phenomenon was mixed with nervous awareness of extraordinary turmoil across the globe. It was a time of wars, rebellions, and mass movements of people in scores of countries demanding, as if by spontaneous combustion, dramatic changes in politics, laws, and, inevitably, social customs.

In the early days of 1968, the Soviet Union was shaken by the Prague Spring in Czechoslovakia and its demands for far less influence in its affairs from the Kremlin. Simultaneously, US confidence in its Vietnam War operations were shaken by the surprise Tet Offensive by Communist forces who poured into Saigon and other major cities in the south. The United States was rocked by campus rebellions, Black power eruptions, and antiwar protests, and a growing air of chaos undercut the once triumphant presidency of Lyndon B. Johnson. Canada felt the chill of Quebec's political hostility to federalism. Then, on the eve of the convention, Martin Luther King Jr. was assassinated, triggering extraordinary riots across our southern neighbour.

Strolling through the convention halls, I felt an intense mix of high spirits and unease. Bands blared, supporters chanted, and horns hooted as rumours flared about "fires spreading only blocks from the White House" and "Windsor watching nearby Detroit burning in rebellion." The struggle during four rounds of voting was brutal: "the most chaotic, confusing, and emotionally draining convention in Canadian political history," the *Globe and Mail* concluded. There were eight candidates in all, but the Trudeau team was remarkable for the atmosphere of out-of-control fan and media worship it orchestrated, inspired to some extent by Robert Kennedy's dynamic primary campaign in the United States. I wrote cynically about the "spontaneous demonstrations" featuring young enthusiasts, especially miniskirted teenage girls: "Most of the demonstrators were recruited from local high schools and served willingly—some out of conviction, many 'just to get out on the floor.' For the most part inducements were simple, the promise of group fun and a steady diet of hamburgers and cokes."

The new mobility of TV cameras helped focus a blazing attention on Trudeau. Wherever he appeared, camera crews with their portable lights, photographers with their flashbulbs popping , and swarms of reporters thronged him and his adoring entourage. He looked generally amused, sometimes bored, occasionally uninterested—a most peculiar convention candidate who refused to appear eager to please. All the candidates ran hospitality suites across the city, but Trudeau's nine were the only ones that served no alcohol. The message: we're not here to party but to shape up! His approach in policy workshops was more hectoring than visionary, to the point of suggesting the party should be ashamed for being sluggish for so long. Even though his message gave few specific reform suggestions, it thrilled the young and increasingly won over older party members, even as it infuriated and mystified those who regarded him as a self-adoring playboy product of media manipulation.

I was fascinated by the painful rejection of Paul Martin Sr., who for decades had been the always reliable warhorse of traditional Liberals, the strong man in dark times. He knew the night before the vote on April 6 that he would lose but put on a brave face even when his first-round defeat brought embarrassing gasps from the arena: "The whole hideous affair continued throughout the day," I wrote. "Martin continued to vote, continued to comfort others, and continued to watch as the prize he has striven all his life for fell into the hands of another."

After the first vote I noticed Martin scribbling on the back of a voting sheet he then cast aside. Later I found it on the floor, the beginning of a concession speech: "I have been caught in a generation gap," he wrote. He never used the lines, realizing it was a cheap excuse, only partially valid. In truth, the traditional party leadership appeared inadequate for new challenges, and they'd been outperformed by a new force they barely understood. After four rounds, Trudeau won with just over 50 percent of the vote.

Even after weeks of covering Trudeau, I was puzzled by both the man and his message. At the historic moment when he vowed a Just Society, I thought it a vague imitation of LBJ's Great Society. But what did he mean by "just"? Still, ambiguity and the excitement of the unknown seemed to work political wonders that summer. Record numbers in every corner of the country had watched the convention on TV, and soon huge crowds were pouring into city streets and exhibition grounds to catch a glimpse of the man that a starstruck media couldn't get enough of.

No sooner had Trudeau become prime minister than he called an election. I was assigned to join the campaign in its final weeks crossing the nation as enthusiasm built to its greatest pitch. Vowing not to be intoxicated by the spectacle, I packed my bag and jumped abroad Trudeau's flying crusade to see for myself.

The first thing that struck me was the sweet smell of an election kill—a winner's mood percolated through his media entourage and dominated his staff, an easygoing crew touched by the arrogance of supremely confident victors. The new prime minister had all the breaks, and we reporters with Trudeau commiserated with the colleagues assigned to his Progressive Conservative opponent, "Gentleman Bob" Stanfield. Terry Haig, a *Gazette* colleague crisscrossing the country with Stanfield, was a baseball nut and future sports broadcaster who likened the PC campaign to "playing out the baseball season with a second division ballclub."

The contrast between the two leaders could scarcely be greater. Stanfield, the dignified Nova Scotian, appeared almost Victorian in his gracious manners and low-key delivery. Intelligent and thoughtful, he was also slow and dull in public speeches. His campaign machine seemed to epitomize sluggishness, travelling in an aged, propeller-engined DC-7; Trudeau, in a sleek new jet DC-9, moved at twice the speed, made more stops, and looked more glamorous.

Travelling with his campaign, I felt in the eye of a hurricane, above an unreal world of frenzy on the ground, in placid calm in the clouds above. Trudeau rarely mingled with media in the plane and was openly contemptuous of camera lenses. He was moody, sometimes seeming pleased and amused by the mania he inspired and at other times bored, even pissed off. He was most emotional when he was given a well-used paddle by a group of campers, and he reminisced about his solo canoe trips through the vast wilderness.

Trudeau's campaign message—that Stanfield would give disastrous concessions to Quebec, while he would stand firm for One Canada united and for constitutional reform—obviously worked across the country, especially in urban areas. As I wrote at the time: "The nation was giving way before him," and "his personality was carrying the day and might yet stamp an age."

Meanwhile, the media struggled to understand just what Trudeau stood for. Followers who hailed him as a bold progressive were puzzled to hear him advocate tough budget discipline and a clamp-down on government subsidies. In the west he praised "rugged individualism" while scorning payouts: "Every region if it had its choice would want subsidies." He made no effort to pretend he respected hecklers, sneering at one, "He can't read anything but the garbage distributed in his backyard." To the young he spoke of the difficulties that lay ahead, as I wrote: "He pleaded with them not to fear the future and its distant challenges . . . the future will be what we make of it and it's up to us to know what to do with this country we love."

In the final week, he seemed weary of the whole business. Once he made a rare visit back to the media section of the plane in shirtsleeves to listen to a song recorded at the previous rally that reporters thought he'd enjoy hearing: "Vote Trudeau and Blow Your Mind." "Good God, isn't it pathetic," he sighed, and made his way back to his solitude.

No other democracy had seen a political figure like Trudeau, and *Time* magazine wrote that US voters should envy Canada's luck: "Along with intellect and political skill, he exhibits a swinger's panache, a lively style . . . a great many US voters yearn for a fresh political experience."

Trudeau's lack of clarity fascinated communication guru Marshall McLuhan, who saw the prime minister as uniquely suited to a new age when cool TV supplanted print and its outdated emphasis on solid issues, programs, and facts. Now politicians had to embrace image, "because image will be more powerful than the message could ever be." Trudeau, McLuhan wrote, was the new political ideal: "The story of Pierre Trudeau is the story of the Man in the Mask" that nobody could penetrate. Rather than spell out details, Trudeau seemed to realize that vagueness only increased his chances of expanding support across a Canada that, in the afterglow of Expo, seemed ready to gamble on the new and experimental. As American Mark Kurlansky wrote in *1968: The Year That Rocked the World*, "The Trudeau approach to leadership (style over substance) has become entrenched."

After the nonstop pace of the campaign, I wanted to duck the St-Jean-Baptiste parade on the night of June 24, the day before the upcoming federal election. Even though I thought trouble a real possibility, I'd had enough excitement to satisfy me for a while. When Auf der Maur confided, "There's going to be major violence, a bloodbath," I knew he had better intel than police authorities, so I listened carefully to his tips: "Several groups are joining forces. I've heard that shortly after nine o'clock, when the third float goes by, that's the prearranged signal to let loose. With Trudeau, the premier, and mayor all together, hundreds will break through police lines to storm the podium—all live on TV."

That was enough. I grabbed a notebook and soon found myself in the middle of one of the most brutal riots in Canadian history. I had no byline that night but would at least get my name in print—as one of five *Gazette* staff injured by flying rocks, bricks, and bottles.

The threat of impending violence was so dense that night I thought

Trudeau was reckless to insist on claiming an honoured place at the one festival guaranteed to bring out Quebec's most pro-separatist elements in force. Around the main reviewing stand at Sherbrooke Street and La Fontaine Park, hundreds of tough-looking Montreal cops faced a surly crowd: they looked keyed up for battle on horseback and on foot as they took their places, along with patrol wagons and ambulances. Deep within the wooded park opposite I could see dark shapes of hundreds of protestors also forming ranks to rhythmic chants of "Tru-deau au pot-eau" (Trudeau to the gallows). They'd had weeks to stockpile empty pop bottles and other weapons to throw and marshal supporters among anarchists and the extreme left.

Sporadic arrests were already underway by 8 p.m. I made my way over to the largest, most aggressive separatist force, the Rassemblement pour l'indépendence nationale (RIN), expecting to hear a speech by their firebrand leader, Pierre Bourgault, a writer and intellectual of remarkable oratorical powers. Instead, I witnessed the precise moment the predicted riot was sparked into premature explosion. I saw a line of police in riot gear confronting several hundred RIN supporters while, within the crowd, Bourgault was being hoisted awkwardly onto the shoulders of a tight group of four men. Strong cheers and chants greeted what seemed a triumphant moment. Bourgault tried to wave but looked puzzled and was clearly fighting to keep his balance. He motioned to be put down, but his carriers kept him aloft, working their way through the mob toward the police line. Suddenly, he looked alarmed, realizing too late that he was in the hands of plainclothes police, who deftly heaved him over the blue line onto the pavement. Next he was roughly pitched into a police van and rushed away. His arrest injected an almost berserk flavour to the night as both rioters and police immediately let fly with all they had. Officers needed little excuse to vent their loathing of young radicals with truncheons, fists, and boots. Quebec's notorious Lundi de la matraque (Monday of the truncheon) would rage on for more than five hours.

A year later, I testified at Bourgault's trial for incitement to riot that he had not gestured for supporters to turn violent but, rather, was fighting hard to balance himself. He was acquitted.

As dusk turned to dark night, the glare of TV lights and smoke from fires made it almost impossible to see the missiles hurled by the crowd, making head injuries the main danger. Twelve police cars were smashed or overturned, and at least one burned to a hulk. Amid the smoke and cacophony of police and ambulance sirens, waves of police on horseback charged into the park to attack the rioters, then returned with the mounts streaming blood down their sides from broken bottles and flying glass. On the viewing stand, the rigid figure of Trudeau sat beside Premier Johnson and Mayor Drapeau, a human bull's-eye. Crowd cheers or boos were drowned out by the sounds of rioting mingled with marching bands, but several people riding on the twenty-six floats in the parade expressed their feeling by pointing thumbs down at the prime minister.

I remember pulling a bleeding *Gazette* reporter with a head wound to an ambulance. When police caught rioters, they often dragged them across the broken glass before pummelling them and throwing them into the overcrowded police wagons. Auf der Maur pled with three cops to "have some humanity," but it fell on deaf ears. One officer on horseback rode over to a few of the bottle-dodging reporters to scream, "They just murdered one of ours on a horse! Pulled him off and slit his throat"—a false rumour that passed like lightning through police lines.

When a portion of the crowd breached the security lines and raced toward the dais, I ran forward to follow the action. In what seemed like slow motion, at least two bottles landed and smashed amid the dignitaries, who started to flee with family members. An RCMP bodyguard tried to pull Trudeau away, causing him to slump to one side, and fearing he'd been shot I instinctively checked my watch to log the time. But he was not injured and he angrily shook himself free and stayed put.

Somewhat later, I was hit in the leg by a bottle, sidelined at the height of the action. I hobbled away toward a pay phone to deliver my notes to the office, but it was occupied. So I went into the lobby of a nearby apartment building where residents had gathered out of curiosity. "I'm a reporter, and could anyone let me phone my office?" I called out. One sweet middle-aged woman volunteered immediately and led me up to her apartment, where an attractive second lady rushed forward with a phone and gushed over me. They produced coffee, cigarettes, and a glass of red wine. "Do stay for a while and relax," the younger one cooed. "Take your jacket off. You look like you could use some fun." Disorientated by the evening's events, only then did I realize I was in a mini-bordello! I politely begged that duty called and bowed out the door with a pathetic "Madame, the news never rests."

I got home around 2 a.m., with, as luck would have it, a root canal scheduled for 9 a.m. Police cells overflowed after 293 arrests, and many were let go after a sound police thumping. Rioters did their worst: forty-three police and eighty-three spectators were also injured.

Next day, the country gave Trudeau a whomping majority victory: 154 seats to 72 for the PCs, and only 22 for the NDP. The Liberals fared well in every part of the country, easily winning Quebec and blowing apart Johnson's hopes that Trudeau's arrogance would contribute to a Conservative victory in the province.

As for Trudeaumania, it quickly faded as the PM got down to the severe and plodding efforts of governing. He had emerged, however, as an international star of the new politics, another surprising hint that Canada could actually be cool, and his pop-star status abroad would linger for some years. But at home the country's mood soon seemed more morose than manic. The sixties had turned nasty.

I graduated to political columnist and a writer of lengthy "insight" pieces on subjects ranging from US elections to human rights. At the time, the expanding climate of violence was much on my radar as Montreal emerged from its post-Expo high shaken by rough dissent in the streets and rising levels of urban terrorism. Often at night the dull thud of yet another FLQ bombing and the distant wail of police sirens broke the silence. Some forty-five explosions ripped through the city in the six months after the St-Jean-Baptiste riot.

The siege seemed mysterious: we forget that the FLQ violence preceded the revolutionary urban terrorism campaigns elsewhere in the West, such as the Red Brigades in Italy, the Red Army Faction in Germany, and the Weather Underground in the United States. Police seemed not to know what to make of the FLQ, clueless as to how many cells were active or how they gathered unlimited supplies of powerful explosives. Mayor Drapeau did not help jitters with a Christmas message bemoaning that his city was sinking into "dangerous and depressing violence and disorder, rancor and conflict." Not to be outdone, the influential newspaper *Le Devoir* described the whole province as ensnared in "intellectual, spiritual, moral and social anarchy."

What concerned me even more was the mental state of the thirty-eight-hundred-member Montreal Police Force. It appeared to be ill-trained, reactionary, and dangerously embittered toward politicians. Even the FLQ picked up on the anger, offering to "lend police a strong hand" in their fight against City Hall. It was a time when police across the United States were rallying to "blue power" movements demanding concessions from governments they despised. But the Montreal Police Brotherhood (their union) took rage to unprecedented levels. After more than a thousand police tried to storm City Hall to protest against pension cuts, Drapeau established an elite and heavily armed riot squad there to act as a paramilitary guard. I suspected the squad but soon had reason to be grateful when I was among a group of reporters they rescued from the notorious riot and fire at Sir George Williams University (now Concordia University) in February 1969.

For months, the downtown university had seethed with student unrest after six Black students complained a white biology professor had discriminated against them by giving them unfair failing marks. After months of negotiations and student sit-ins failed to resolve the dispute, about a hundred students of various races barricaded themselves in the ninth-floor computer centre. On February 11, when the new riot squad was summoned to evict them, I made my way up there to cover the action. Events happened fast: almost immediately as police started dismantling the furniture that made up the barricade, smoke began coming out of the computer centre, followed by yells for help, fire alarms, water pouring from ceiling extinguishers, and a charge of firemen into the chaos. I sought shelter in a classroom, crawling on hands and knees to stay under swirls of darkening smoke. The windows were sealed, so one cop picked up a chair and smashed the glass to give us air to breathe. Gasping, I peered out on a surreal scene: thousands were massed in the street below, pushing and shouting chants, while a blizzard of computer cards fluttered down from the looted centre like giant snowflakes. Thankfully, police remained calmly in charge and led us to a safe stairwell.

Once the fire was suppressed, ninety-seven occupiers were arrested in a surprisingly businesslike manner. When I finally left by the basement garage where police had gathered, a lone, dishevelled figure in a dark coat, the large crowd assumed that I was a police detective, and I received a resounding roar of boos, jeers, and angry whistles until I wearily waved my press pass. In just months I'd narrowly escaped being beaten by police, and, now, being beaten for being a cop.

Nothing, however, disrupted my enjoyable life as a big-city reporter with a broad beat in a hyperactive town awash in fascinating news and an improbable range of characters. I was living a romanticized version of print journalism, in an age when urban newshounds were still expected to mine their sources and prospect for fresh story angles across a range of favourite cafés and bars. Other areas of romance were less fulfilling, as my girlfriend finally concluded my addiction to news was incurable and broke off our relationship. I moved into a nineteenth-century apartment building in Old Montreal, where at night the horse-drawn calèches rattled by with the sounds of a century past. There, listening to Leonard Cohen, so identified with the area, I brooded over the pace of mankind's calamities in the dying slivers of the once shining sixties.

The urgency of police grievances over pay and work conditions kept growing. Drapeau was not at home on September 29 when fifteen sticks of dynamite half-demolished it in the middle of the night, terrorizing his wife and son. A week later events happened that had reporters debating the best headline: Day of Anarchy or Night of Terror?

My phone rang early on October 7 with the alert from the news desk that all thirty-eight hundred police had walked off the job and were about to be joined by the entire fire department—the strikers all heading for a mass protest meeting at a sports arena. For the next sixteen hours I charged around getting a sense of what real anarchy looks like: traffic chaos as citizens desperate to get home ran red lights; burglar alarms ringing through the downtown as robbers had a magic payday hitting a dozen banks and scores of stores; and mass looting on main shopping streets. The so-called elite riot squad, now throwing their weight behind the rest of the striking police force, raced through every station house ensuring the walkout was total, seizing all the city's emergency communications, and threatening provincial police to stay well clear. By evening we had a major riot raging and shootouts downtown—a lawless rampage that FLQ cells, biker gangs, and various radical causes inevitably joined.

Drapeau, who had been out of town in yet another attempt to sell the glories of Montreal, was now in hiding. The troops were called in, and fully armed soldiers of the famed Royal 22nd Regiment (the Van Doos) took up patrols that gave the fun-loving city a toxic public image of martial law. Finally, a shaken province signed back-to-work legislation for the police, and, slowly, the anarchy retreated. Within weeks, the city and the province agreed to award the strikers all they had asked for.

Later, in my talks with Drapeau, I sensed growing paranoia and a clear drift toward authoritarian government. He ditched his two-man police detail as unreliable in favour of a massive guard dog that glared at me whenever I approached His Worship. Drapeau was less patient now when I raised again his reputation for "dictatorial" instincts: "You don't understand, Mr. Stewart . . . that people elect me to the hard work of ruling because they don't want to be bothered with it themselves." Looking increasingly tired and worried, he ended meetings by asking if I knew any new jokes. Sadly, I never did.

The mayor's growing distrust of his own police force was a major reason why troops would return to Montreal a year later to confront an even graver threat that challenged the whole nation. The October Crisis exploded in 1970 when the FLQ kidnapped a British diplomat and murdered Quebec's deputy premier, Pierre Laporte. By then, the FLQ's seven-year-long campaign for total Quebec independence had set off more than two hundred bombs, stolen vast quantities of explosives from building sites and weapons from military armories, robbed scores of banks, and hijacked a plane. Now, the FLQ was studying Latin American guerrilla manuals on the killing and assassination of politicians and diplomats. The terrorist organization was flourishing in the city and had hundreds of active sympathizers offering financial aid and thousands of passive ones among intellectuals and the far left on campuses. Police ineptness was stunning: after the kidnappings and the murder of Pierre Laporte I discovered that they had previously captured the guerrilla manual for attacks on officials but had not alerted foreign officials or politicians that kidnappings were planned.

I was covering City Hall, the ground zero in the crisis, as three powers—Trudeau, Drapeau, and the new Quebec premier, Robert Bourassa—struggled through faulty intelligence and deepening alarm to manage events. The War Measures Act and the infamous mass arrests are mainly attributed to false warnings from within Trudeau's Cabinet that a full insurrection was planned in the city involving thousands of FLQ supporters. I have always believed the overreaction was equally caused by Drapeau's deep fear that the critical police force couldn't be trusted to stand firm and might use the threat of another walkout at the height of danger to blackmail the city into more benefits.

Just hours before the first secret call to mobilize troops went out, I stopped Drapeau as he rushed through a City Hall corridor to ask if there was anything new in the crisis. He said, "You will not believe what will happen in the next few hours. You do not know how serious the crisis is. We are one step away from the whole city exploding in crisis." "Well, please tell me," I urged, but he raced off with a final "You will not believe it." I got the clear sense he thought an actual revolution or some form of military action was imminent.

Within hours, the first troops raced in to rescue Montreal. Under the War Measures Act, nearly five hundred people were swept into detention, and forty-six hundred police raids scoured the city for weapons and manuals before weary officials conceded an armed insurrection was not likely. Many arrests were roundups; others had a very Montreal tinge to them: my friend Auf der Maur was taken in only after officers arranged to meet him in his favourite smoky bistro for rounds of cognac, coffee, and funny stories. He, like most individuals arrested, was later released with no charges.

This siege of Montreal astonished and appalled friendly nations, to the point that, throughout the crisis, the Press Club was host to a growing cadre of foreign correspondents. In talks with them the irony struck me that while I was aiming to cover overseas stories, they were here covering the drama in my backyard. "Seems to me you've got the perfect beat right here, and it's sure a fun place to boot," one Londoner quipped.

After the October Crisis and the grisly murder of Laporte, strangled with the chain of his religious neck medal, Quebec's horrified reaction effectively killed the FLQ. Thereafter, peaceful separatist campaigns became an even greater threat to Canada. I continued a political beat but was encouraged to keep expanding my work into other investigative areas, including a study of organized crime and human rights violations by the justice system. Almost monthly I lobbied management to be sent for a stint, even a short one, covering the war in Vietnam. They said they were thinking about it, although I had doubts about what kind of thoughts they had. Still, I could at least dream that Saigon was in my sights.

Despite the ludicrous male garb of the period—bell-bottom trousers, flowery shirts of shocking colour, lapels half a foot wide, unkempt hair, and, in my case, porkchop sideburns nearly down to my chin—I did serious investigations into Quebec's practice of holding accused people for long periods in jail without bail while awaiting trial. My full-page feature led to an innocent man being released, followed by a public inquiry and the release of twenty-two more. I was awarded the National Newspaper Award for feature writing, an event the *Gazette* played up to the hilt. It was a year of growing public recognition—earlier I'd been chosen, along with hockey superstar Bobby Orr, to be one of twenty-five "representative young Canadians" to dine with visiting Prince Charles at Government House in Ottawa. I was dancing with Miss Canada until a tap on the back informed me someone was cutting in. I knew instinctively it was bound to be one person—Trudeau—and there he was. "And how's Mayor Drapeau?" the smiling PM asked as they danced off.

Basically, my life was busy with work I mostly enjoyed, including a regular political column. I felt in a good place. And then, unbidden and utterly unexpected, TV came calling.

5

TV Times

Like many print reporters of the era, I stumbled into TV work without having ever sought an on-camera career. In college I had endured the mandatory semester in Radio and TV Arts required for those studying print journalism. Nothing about it appealed to me: going before a TV lens was still a rare experience, and, to me, a distasteful one. I no more considered working in front of the pitiless black eye of a TV camera than joining the Foreign Legion.

I loved the still romanticized world of print, with its daily swirl of multiple stories. I was at ease with its eccentricities and oddball characters: the bookish, the political junkies, the jaunty sports department rogues, the crime reporting connoisseurs of city gang hierarchies, and the fired-up chroniclers of radical causes.

Almost overnight in the sixties, however, TV swept past our vaunted news hegemony when it came to covering big events: from the Kennedy assassination to Vietnam, from the "new politics" ignited by Pierre Trudeau to the October Crisis in Quebec. Print reporters stuck up their noses at this competition—unless offered a network job, of course.

In the spring of 1971 I accepted an invitation for coffee at an outdoor bistro table from Nick Auf der Maur, now working at the CBC's current affairs program *Hourglass*, and one of its producers, Margaret

Davidson. I assumed Nick had another scoop he wanted to share. Instead, they brought up the recent departure of host Peter Desbarats. "Brian, do you know you're being considered for a host role?" Margaret asked. Thinking they were having me on, I shot back, "Well, I certainly would have thought so!" "Stewart, ya bastard, this isn't a joke," Nick snapped. The program, it seemed, was impressed enough by my work and background to view me as a lead candidate. I instantly plummeted into a pit of confusion: in a flash I imagined a new world of cameras, lights, and micro-level celebrity, balanced by a counter-vision of disaster, ridicule, rejection, and tittering over my inevitable stumbles.

As I wrestled with the offer in the following weeks, the *Gazette*'s managing editor, Mike Daigneault, tried to persuade me to stay. Knowing how susceptible I seemed to flattery, he offered me my own "grand ideas" column that would also appear in associated papers across Canada. Finally, pulling the sentimental lever, he swept an arm toward the newsroom, sighing, "You love this place. How could you leave it all now?" (He himself would jump to a CBC management job within a year.)

In the end, I couldn't resist giving TV a shot. In future years I sometimes wondered if I had made the right move, but I remind myself I was also attracted to the national broadcaster because it had promising overseas news operations. The CBC was likely the best route for my foreign correspondent ambitions.

However, I was plagued by my nerves. I had learned to keep my social anxiety veiled behind a laid-back demeanour, but a live slot in a glaring TV studio might push inner jitters into panic. I was haunted not so much by regular performance butterflies as by fear of an uncontrollable twitching of facial muscles and hands that had occasionally afflicted me since my teens when under stress. This curse was diminishing with age and eventually disappeared, but at the time it added enormously to my stress on TV. This half-hour interview show was the most watched of the dinnertime current affairs shows across Canada. As host, I was thrown in the deep end with no real training. I stealthily relied on help of my own devising: a Valium-and-vodka mix prepared by a friendly bartender that allowed me to relax enough to avoid flipping out on camera. I had one shot on regular days, and an extra quarter-shot for special shows such as a panel interview with the premier.

Fortunately, a good portion of the show remained pretaped interviews and documentaries, which I recorded without my vodka-valium mix. These were enjoyable, and once I even spent time with my boyhood hockey hero, the Montreal Canadiens' Maurice "the Rocket" Richard. I had lobbied my youthful teammates to call me Rocket, and they had obliged, but as I now told Richard, I was so slow at skating the coach stuck me in nets. Richard roared with delight: "Ah, we finally meet. I was the fastest rocket ever, and you were the slowest! I bet you were teased."

After my first TV season, all seemed to be going well. I was more comfortable in the role, and that summer the *Gazette* put me on a generous contract to write part-time as well. Still, at thirty, I was adrift, with no steady relationship, no religious faith, and no deep inner conviction. My mother, too, had died suddenly of a heart attack, adding profound grief to my life.

Shortly after the funeral, I took off to Europe on a two-part pilgrimage: first to Ireland, where my mother had spent her first fourteen years in severe poverty, and then, though not a Catholic, to Italy on an inept mission to see if I could reignite some form of lost religious faith. In fact, neither walks along Irish beaches contemplating the grey sea and immersing myself in the works of John Synge and James Joyce nor touring great Christian art and churches of Florence and Rome provided the spark I needed to escape from gloom. It was the first of the periodic "wannabe religious" quests I undertook at various points in my life, which provided insights but not always the comfort I was seeking. I thought the trip a failure, but it affected me in surprising and positive ways.

The first positive development was a heightened sense of empathy in the wake of our family tragedy, that, frankly, surprised me. As I wrote in a note, I found "a sincere sense of feeling for others that swept aside so much of my self-pity." That led to a growing interest in humanitarian aid projects that helped bring order and assistance amid chaos to the areas I later so often reported on, including Ethiopia.

The second jolt came when, on a dreary flight from Rome to London, I read the Nobel Prize acceptance speech of Alexsander Solzhenitsyn, the acclaimed Russian writer, dissident, and survivor of Stalin's terror. His words, read in absentia, were a searing condemnation of societies that cared only for local outrages and not the vastly more terrible ones in distant tyrannies. He reminded the world that entire cultures could die in darkness as a nation's literature was "cast into oblivion not only without a grave, but without even underclothes, naked, with a number tag on its toes." Who would bear witness? One of my favourite poets, Anna Akhmatova, put it succinctly in her "Requiem" poems after her husband was executed and her son long imprisoned. As she lined up by the prison walls of Leningrad in the bitterest winter of the purges, someone in the crowd recognized her: "Behind me was a woman, with lips blue from the cold, who had never heard me called by name before . . . she started out of the torpor common to us all and asked me in a whisper: 'Can you describe even this?' And I said: 'I can.' Then something like a smile passed fleetingly over what had once been her face."

I realized that ability to bear witness is not only for artists and poets but journalists as well. They too are in a position to shine light on global misery and to report the truth. At the time, there was nothing like the vast number of NGOs we see across the globe today, and there was far less official concern for misery in the developing world. Within a few years, however, recognition of both human rights and other humanitarian causes surged, which coincided with the revolution in television's ability, thanks to satellites and video, to broadcast searing reports on conflicts and disasters with a speed that profoundly elevated public awareness.

Back in town, I resumed my host duties on *Hourglass*, but I was now impatient to return to news with a new sense of mission. Walking along Sherbrooke Street on a bracing spring day in 1973, I ran into a news manager I much admired, Denis Harvey, my old boss at the *Gazette* and now chief news editor at CBC TV.

"I've been looking for you," he called out. "I want you to come to News and head to Ottawa as our first investigative reporter—help shake up the place!"

It was the time of Watergate exposés by *Washington Post* reporters, and Canadian media suffered from severe scoop envy. "Sounds tempting, Denis, but I really want a foreign posting," I answered.

"Perfect move then: do well, and you'll nail a posting. Ottawa's a perfect place to build your credentials and make contacts in foreign affairs and military circles."

I was sold and made the jump in September. It was an easy departure, as I'd recently had another romantic bust-up and retreated from my usual social rounds after ditching Valium cold turkey. The struggle to stabilize my stampeding nervous system had me bouncing off walls. The CBC put me on political reporting for a year, adding me to a new "youth wave" of first-rate reporters including good friends Peter Mansbridge and the always colourful Mike Duffy. We became a remarkably productive bureau and a regular target of aggressive poaching attempts by powerful American networks, or Amnets as we called them.

My early months in the capital, which some predicted would be dire after the intoxicating charms of Montreal, instead turned out to be uplifting. Now free of Valium dependency, I appreciated the clean stone splendour of the Parliament Buildings and the reassuring air of serious business being done by, mostly, sincere people.

I had to learn the business of fast-paced TV reporting—a condensed style of writing built around pictures and sound bites (clips)—and editing techniques. I also worked on my reading style and memorized the on-camera stand-up we were expected to end reports with. My progress was uneven: one Toronto editor said I came off "like a stentorian pulpit-pounding Presbyterian minister, and the old-fashioned sort at that." I needed to be less ponderous. I had started in Montreal when CBC still broadcast in black and white and arrived in News when the bureau still used film rather than video. Film was costly, so we were limited in how much we could shoot, and the time needed to develop film before editing added to deadline pressures. On busy news days there could be heart-stopping backlogs in the edit suite. One night, four of us with major reports all missed the *National News* deadline, causing chaos and fury on the news desk in Toronto. Before long, the far less restrictive videotape replaced film—one of the great revolutions in the television industry.

Overall, it was a time of bracing and enjoyable new challenges, crisscrossing the country on election campaigns and covering the House of Commons across the street from our office. Even my often lamentable romantic life took a turn for the better. I met Leigh Beauchamp, a market researcher in advanced computer technology, and we soon moved in together in an apartment with a stirring Canadiana view of the majestic Ottawa River and the Quebec shore beyond. After so restless a life, I discovered the relaxing pleasures of domesticity, including staying in at nights, shopping forays for books and antiques, and luxuriating in one another's company. I overplayed the domesticated gent role by taking up pipe smoking, but the look was too pompous, and I could never keep the damn thing lit.

When I eventually did get to dive into investigative reporting, I found the city notorious for the way its civil service, true to its prim Scots ancestry, tightly guarded access to information. Ottawa was, compared to Washington, a closed tomb. Powerful bodies, including the military and the RCMP, regarded probing questions as impolite, unpatriotic, and possibly posed at the secret bidding of the Kremlin. In the end, however, I was able to break a series of scoops even bigger than the CBC had counted on, and likely more than it wanted.

In the United States, the approach to scandal in the wake of Watergate was "follow the money." In Ottawa, I felt it should be "follow the Mounties." Although revered in Canada, there were dark signs that the force was misusing its power, sinking deeper into unlawful acts, and posing an increasing threat to civil liberties. My work on civil rights issues in Quebec made me aware there were too many serious complaints of RCMP black ops to be dismissed as fantasy. In British Columbia, investigative reporter John Sawatsky had exposed four hundred illegal Mountie break-ins in that province alone.

Something in the setup of the RCMP felt wrong. It was divided into two parts: the Criminal Division and the deeply secretive Security Service, which chased spies, ran security checks on senior politicians and civil servants, and worked to counter domestic threats to national security (which it defined vaguely). The lack of sophistication in this branch was astonishing. The McDonald Commission of Inquiry later concluded that officers were inadequately educated in political matters and in differentiating between legal dissent and insurrection. They rejected any civilian oversight, especially by Parliament. Anyone who inquired too insistently into the Mounties' ways ended up in their secret files, often with a chilling sense that continued curiosity would trigger serious unwanted attention.

In 1976, while working on a two-part documentary examining the October Crisis, I looked into the role that police intelligence had played in overhyping the danger of a popular insurrection. I got a clear sense that even in a widely admired democracy like Canada, some police-state tactics such as harassment, break-ins, and intrusive surveillance were being used. During this project I linked up with an extraordinary character who oozed investigative smarts from every pore—Joe MacAnthony—who had been Ireland's most famous reporter-sleuth before joining the CBC. With a naturally curious mind, sharp intelligence, and a seemingly irresistible charm that made everyone want to tell him secrets, he was the best investigative journalist I ever worked with.

Comparing our notes over drinks in smoky taverns, we found we shared the conviction that the Mounties, rattled by their belief in foreign intervention (Soviet, Cuban, or French) in Quebec's nationalist and separatist movements, were throwing their considerable weight around in dangerous ways: black ops run not just to gain intel on imagined enemies but to sabotage them as well. We each had ex-Mountie sources who confirmed that the force was going off the rails.

"But Jeesus, Brian, I know you're not as thick as you look and must realize this is far, far more than coppers going bad," Joe said. "The government has to be deeply involved. Right at the top."

"More likely," I suggested, "it's a case of the politicians saying get results, but don't tell us how."

"That's even worse. It encourages the worst cowboys to stop at nothing, for there are no limits."

In both Ottawa and Montreal we worked on our own quiet investigation, convinced it would be politically explosive. We had meetings in secret locations with possible whistleblowers and spent hours trying to tap into former officers' sense of conscience or depth of grudges. Meanwhile, the country remained unaware that the RCMP was unlawfully disrupting the lives of thousands of Canadians, spying on anyone it chose to with no civilian oversight.

All that changed in November 1977 when I was able, with Joe's help, to break two major scandals within days. On the ninth I revealed the existence of Operation Cathedral, the RCMP's secret and illegal opening of Canadians' mail across the country, without court order or Parliament's approval. The operation was carried out with the secret connivance of the Post Office, so a great many people had to know basic laws involving privacy were being flouted. Although I had double-sourced all the details in the exposé, I still spent a nervous night waiting for the reaction—every scoop is a potential career-in-flames moment. The government seemed stunned, with Trudeau saying that if opening mail was illegal, maybe they should simply make it legal. Cabinet ministers insisted that if the story was true, the Mounties must have lied to them. Then the RCMP jumped in, admitting they'd actually been opening mail since the 1950s!

The uproar in Canada was enough to attract rare interest from the *New York Times* under the bold headline: "Canada Says the Mounted Police Opened and Copied Mail Illegally." The article pointed out that when similar mail tampering by the FBI and the CIA had been exposed, it led to a US Freedom of Information Act, which Trudeau insisted was not needed in Canada because "police irregularities of that nature had not occurred."

A few nights later I produced another exposé on Operation 300, a program of illegal break-ins over twenty years. I reported that the Mountie burglars had become so brazen they went on joint heists with Quebec police to steal documents and plant bugs on radical targets.

Parliament had just opened Question Period to live TV coverage, so the storm there attracted huge audiences as opposition MPs demanded to know how the government could not have known. Was it lying or grossly incompetent? As the Cabinet struggled with two scandals, both the CBC and I were the targets of furious criticism. Veteran broadcaster Knowlton Nash later wrote: "Night after night CBC News uncovered more RCMP security service misdeeds, mortifying the government and leading to further attacks on CBC. Solicitor General Francis Fox said the CBC was wasting public money on 'irresponsible' reporting, and he suggested funds should be taken away from the CBC and given to the RCMP." Opposition MPs accused the government of attacking freedom of the press. The tension only increased as the Canadian public overwhelmingly supported the Mounties over the CBC, and letters to the editor poured in to newspapers blasting muckraking reporters.

The storm went on for weeks. Two Tory MPs claimed their offices had been bugged and documents taken, and stolen dynamite was connected to an alleged police kidnapping. The CBC office and my own apartment were visited by burly men with bags of equipment to sweep for bugs. It was a lonely time and, not being radical in politics or by nature, I felt uncomfortable. To me, these were straightforward human rights issues: the government had a sacred mission to ensure everyone's rights were protected, even those of objectionable minorities, and when it failed, it was media's job to ring alarms.

As nerve-racking as it was for CBC top brass, my news editors were supportive throughout. In time, both a Quebec inquiry and the federal McDonald Commission proved an extraordinary range of police illegal acts, and my stories were shown to be accurate. No direct government complicity in the wrongdoing was proved, but plenty of testimony emerged showing serious political negligence. My illegal letter-opening exposé led to strict laws in force today to permit openings only with judicial warrants and overseen by a civilian review committee. With so many scandals established, the RCMP was stripped of its Security Service, which was formed into the civilian Canadian Security Intelligence Service we have today.

The RCMP affair, as it was called, was the highlight of my investigative reporting role. Office mates bestowed the title "Scoop" on me, and it stuck throughout my career. But I was hungry for new challenges. Although I would do some major investigative reports occasionally in future, I lacked the long-term patience to thrive on such challenges. Fortunately, CBC management, having gotten more scandal from my stories than they bargained for, soon appointed me as external affairs reporter—one giant step, I gushed to myself, up the ladder to a foreign posting.

While still based in Ottawa for a few more years, I made forays abroad, covering prime ministers' overseas trips, international conferences, and diplomatic controversies. I was also called on to do lengthy feature stories on conflict zones and quick analysis "think pieces" on sudden international developments or seemingly intractable wars. I enjoyed the beat and dived into the research as the world entered another phase of great upheavals. There's nothing more exciting in journalism than surfing atop a rolling sea-change in societies and nations. I'd been lucky, catching the sixties in London and Montreal as well as the new political age ushered in by Trudeau's early media magic. Now, in the late seventies, everything was in flux: first the Helsinki Accords (1975) altered the shape of the Cold War by formalizing relations between the West and the Soviet Union, and this was followed by the arrival of serious interest in human rights advocacy.

Earlier in the seventies, human rights had been a side issue, with Amnesty International the only prominent non-government organization. By the time it won the Nobel Prize in 1977, however, scores of new ones such as Human Rights Watch were forerunners of thousands of NGOs that sprang up to campaign for liberties and confront state repression, particularly in areas of Latin America and Africa where the United States and the Soviet Union competed for influence. The swiftness of global change meant that media faced a scramble just to keep up with all the new sites of turmoil and crisis.

Canadians had a problem: they saw themselves as a middle power, yet needed far more information on the world than they were getting. A wealthy country, Canada, with a population of twenty-six million, had just been accepted as one of the leading industrial nations, turning the Group of Six into the Group of Seven. Canada was involved in developing foreign aid projects and peacekeeping and had to differentiate its stances from those of its mighty US ally. But its national broadcaster, the CBC, had little ability or funding to report on the world. Although the CBC was a hefty domestic network with scores of stations and thousands of employees, its grand total of TV correspondents working overseas was five.

The closer I came to a posting abroad, the more I saw the CBC was weaker than I had imagined and how much of a shell game editors had to play to make it look semi-respectable. We had offices in London, Paris, Washington, Hong Kong, and, temporarily, Johannesburg. Bizarrely, there was just a radio reporter in Moscow. Only the London and Paris reporters had the means for serious travel, so they essentially covered the world outside North America. The high quality of senior correspondents like David Halton and Joe Schlesinger made the CBC look far stronger than we were. Ominously, we were dependent on a one-sided partnership with a major US network (first CBS, later NBC) to help us file reports and plug gaps in our nightly newscasts. The foreign editor at the time, John Owen, in a memorandum to CBC brass later looked back on years of news penury: "Our foreign news coverage was sporadic and erratic, our travel budget was paltry. We routinely aired one or two American network reports each night on the *National*."

Fortunately, during this bleak period a spirit of change swept the newsroom. Younger reporters and editors, who tended to be internationally attuned and aware of the need to differentiate our reporting from US media, also wanted to make the CBC a serious player abroad. Executive editor Trina McQueen, a commanding and charismatic leader with an outstanding background in print and private TV, was quick to seize on the need to expand foreign coverage. That challenge fell to John Owen and Tony Burman, the news desk editor. They prioritized the new global human rights revolution, distinguishing us from the Amnets, as Canada became a vocal advocate against horrific acts of state terror in Latin America—the mass torture, murder, and "disappearance" of tens of thousands of people in Chile, Argentina, Brazil, Guatemala, and El Salvador. My first major foreign assignments sent me south to look into the struggle for political and economic rights and the counter-reaction of terror.

In late January 1979, I was awakened on my first night in Mexico City by an earthquake. It shattered my sleep but was also symbolic:

I was there to cover the first trip abroad of Pope John Paul II. His recent election had sent tremors across Eastern Europe, where his strong anti-communism had encouraged dissent but also roused fear across Latin America, where many feared he would discourage resistance to the state. There, the Catholic Church was torn between liberation theology activists fighting for reforms and conservative elements who viewed any real dissent as Marxist, to be opposed with force.

I followed the charismatic John Paul as he rode through enormous crowds, with bands playing and sombreros and balloons flying, to festivities and prayer meetings where still more people packed into squares. But I also noticed growing nervousness among some clergy contacts as the main purpose of the visit approached: the landmark Conference of Latin American Bishops in Puebla. This human rights summit was set to discuss the role of church activism on behalf of the poor, and the whole continent was watching to see where the new pope stood on this explosive subject.

The church had been in ferment since the loosening of doctrine in Vatican II and, later, Pope Paul VI's appearance at the landmark Medellin Conference in Colombia (1968), where he called on Catholics to actively seek social justice. Catholic progressives picked up this loosely defined challenge with great enthusiasm, helping to mobilize citizen reform groups, support union demands, and push for major economic reforms. Other clerics were appalled by any talk of radical change and often stood silent as right-wing military-backed governments took over the majority of Latin American states. Many of these new leaders launched reigns of terror against social activism, using mass arrests, torture, and murder against large sections of the public, including religious progressives. More than eight hundred priests had been arrested, tortured, deported, or exiled. Among them were thirty-five bishops, four of whom were murdered.

The impact of repression was significantly heightened by US support for the new military-dominated regimes. Although criticizing major abuses, Washington, still smarting over the Cuban and Vietnamese disasters, was determined not to "lose" more states to what it viewed as Moscow-directed Communist movements.

The pope opened his address in Puebla by offering some hope to moderates and progressives, mentioning the right of the poor to better lives and criticizing abductions and torture. But he went on to denounce the worldly involvement of Christians in politics and commanded churches to avoid "ideological systems" and the portrayal of Christ as a "revolutionary." Although he did not name liberation theology, he clearly condemned it. His speech certainly encouraged military juntas and far-right dictatorships to clamp down even harder.

After I flew back to Toronto, the CBC expanded the size and the scope of our coverage. In early 1979 I was sent, with Tony Burman as producer, to do a series of stories and features on two of the most important countries under military dictatorship: Brazil, where a junta coup in 1964 had inspired imitators across the continent; and Chile, notorious for the military overthrow of the democratically elected socialist government of Salvador Allende, with much suspected backing from the CIA. In both countries the repression targeted unions, civic groups, media, church reform advocates, legal and political figures, and even families of the detained, and involved mass torture, secret executions, and "disappearances." We went in years before the full tally of the terror was known, so we had many questions: How widespread and deadly was the repression? What was the effect on society? How was it possible that individuals of great courage still risked everything to try to organize resistance? What could Canada and other nations usefully do to protest such abuse?

I was particularly intrigued by the similarity in the tactics of military rule across most Latin American states. I kept coming across a phenomenon called the "national security state doctrine" that was emerging from Latin American military academies heavily influenced by US counterinsurgency trainers as well as French veterans of brutal campaigns in Indochina and Algeria. The core belief pounded home was that Communism was nothing short of an attempt to undermine Western culture and to abolish the sacred nation; it would come in myriad forms and "subversive elements," which must be crushed by active state violence and military action. This pseudo-philosophical indoctrination was used to convince a surprising number of officers and men to commit the most grotesque acts of cruelty. Chile, a nation of only eleven million with a widely admired democracy, became synonymous with fear after the coup: forty thousand people were arrested and tortured, over three thousand secretly killed, and two hundred thousand forced into exile.

In both Brazil and Chile, the generals had justified their power grab by pointing to periods of considerable political unrest, but the threats in no way justified such extreme measures. The question I kept coming back to was whether national security states could ever return to democracy or whether human rights would continue to be crushed under permanent oppression.

Brazil was a fascinating study. The military regime had enjoyed considerable popularity as it boasted of a "miracle boom," but now that severe inflation and human rights protests had returned, the confidence of the regime in its own power plummeted. An unexpected wave of labour unrest caused major shock waves as unions discovered that the generals had lied about soaring inflation figures to keep wages down. To add to the drama, the military leadership was increasingly divided between hard-liners and more moderate officers who felt the military had to return to the barracks to save its professionalism. Younger officers in particular felt the grungy and brutal job of enforcing state control besmirched their own honour, especially as rumours spread of corruption in the high command.

Talk of re-democratization came with a major catch: there could be no investigations, no trials of officers. In short, you'll get democracy back in a few years, but only if you forgive and forget all that's been done (estimated to include hundreds of murders, more than fifty thousand people detained, and six thousand tortured). Cultural amnesia was the price of freedom.

Tension was high. A new president, General João Figueiredo, was sworn in at a new danger point as 140,000 metalworkers walked out in open defiance of the regime and paralyzed São Paulo's industrial zone, including the crucial auto industry. Workers demanded major wage increases to make up for runaway inflation. Our crew set off to cover the showdown, unsure whether we'd be able even to function. We particularly wanted to cover the firebrand new union leader, already jailed once, a man of extraordinary courage called Lula: Luiz Inácio da Silva, later one of the most famous political figures in the world as the highly popular president of Brazil. He had called for an unprecedented rally of a hundred thousand–plus followers at a fairground.

We made it to the rally site just in time, and we found a vast field covered by acres of workers and supporters who were aware of the state security spies in their midst. There was worried talk of army units on standby ready to move. I was surprised to find we were the only TV crew to show up, and as we approached the stand, our interpreter warned us that, despite our proud Canada logo, many in the crowd were muttering, "They must be security spies."

When Lula strode to the microphone, he found it was dead. Organizers frantically tried to make it work, without success. The crowd grew restless—it looked like sabotage. There were no other mics anywhere, except the one held by me. The chief organizer raced to our side with something between a plea and a command: "Can you loan us your mic, like, *now?*"

As Lula gave a thunderous speech demanding justice, lighting the crowd with an electricity I'd never seen before, Burman nudged me and pointed. The mic still had the CBC logo attached. Our jaws dropped—we feared the regime's hidden cameras were sure to highlight the fact that Canada's CBC was endorsing this act of open rebellion!

After the speech, I was led into Lula's presence for a brief interview. Any expectation that he'd show gratitude for our mic was quickly dashed. Magnetic in public, he was cold and in a grouchy mood in private. All we got was a short, offhand interview. When we left Brazil on the way to Chile, clashes between the strikers and the regime were continuing, but it was obvious the power of the generals was starting to wobble. The failure of the regime to intimidate the strikers inspired growing popular resistance to oppression across Latin America. There was some easing of repression across the region as regimes sought accommodation with more opposition factions. The Brazilian labour movement, with its most poignant moment in that speech, marked the beginning of the end of the dictatorships in Latin America and was listed by the *Christian Science Monitor* as one of the twentieth century's "ten economic protests that changed history." If so, perhaps that CBC mic deserves a niche in a Brazilian museum.

By chance, over three decades later Burman was introduced to President da Silva at a conference in the Middle East. He asked Lula if he remembered the mic incident. "Hell yes, I do." He laughed: "For a few minutes there facing out on this stupendous crowd, I really worried what would happen if I couldn't speak. Then, suddenly, there was your mic in my hand." Still no thanks, though.

I left Brazil feeling some optimism the pro-democracy movement was gaining momentum, but Chile afforded no such hope. Six years after the military coup, the self-reinforcing grip of a national security state mindset showed no signs of easing up, and it would last for another thirteen years. Though things looked calm on the surface, everyone seemed wary. I thought of the capital, Santiago, as an artificial stage where a horror show was conducted behind curtains by agents of repression. They vied with each other to invent ever more ghastly brutalities. Rumours reached us of deaths by torture, firing squads, mutilations, drownings, burnings, and electrocutions, as well as a concentration camp deep in the south where people were held and tortured in secret. I had a hard time fathoming the bravery of "civil witnesses"—a handful of human rights and clandestine labour activists—in these circumstances.

Over many years, I would learn another lesson: when full records are exposed by judicial inquiries many years later, the reality is usually worse than even dire initial reports. It's a safe rule of thumb to take very seriously the earliest reports of abuse: Nazi atrocities were incomparably more lethal than first rumoured, as were the purges of Stalin and Mao and the Cambodian genocide.

We expected that in a Chile run by General Augusto Pinochet, we, like all foreign media, would be watched closely. We planned to edit our material back in Toronto. We had to watch our step as our visas could be revoked in an instant, and we were instructed not to tape anything until we had a special pass. On the first morning, we heard the sprightly sound of a military band playing cheerful numbers for civilians in the park opposite. Surely, we thought, a few pleasing images like these would not disturb our state minders. So we went over, spent a few minutes taping this inoffensive footage, and thought nothing further of it.

The next day when Burman went to the ministry, an official glared wordlessly from behind his desk and held up the front page of a major paper. There, over a large picture of our camera crew in the park, was the headline, "Canadians Record Chilean Life." For hours afterwards, I worried how our management would react if our expensive Chilean trip was reduced to six minutes of a band concert in a park before expulsion.

A major part of our stories dealt with repression, but we also interviewed strong-free-market economists who claimed Chile was booming thanks to Pinochet's takeover. In fact, as in other national security states, the claims of economic miracles were greatly exaggerated by state economists: the economy had nosedived for five years after the overthrow of Allende. The Pinochet era saw inequality increase and corruption run rampant, all for a puny overall increase of 1.7 percent in gross domestic product over the first half decade.

The most powerful moment came when I interviewed a mother in a rural town whose husband and five sons had been murdered and buried in a local mine by a regime death squad. At the end of a heartbreaking session, I asked her if she knew who had done the killings. "Oh yes," she replied, "the local police chief led it. I often pass him on the sidewalk when I go in shopping." I could not imagine how one could live in an oppressive state with no hope of ever seeing justice. This lack of accountability has been one of the great challenges of re-democratization in our time, from South Africa to the Soviet Union. The promise of freedom is dangerously weakened when the poison of past oppression remains hidden by the state.

Ahead lay many subjects to pursue: Apartheid in South Africa; the stirrings of peaceful resistance in Poland, Czechoslovakia, and other satellites within the Soviet Empire; and ever graver conflicts in Latin America. Next time, I felt sure, I would be going into my first war.

6

Horror in Latin America

By early 1981, long-predicted armed uprisings had begun against military-dominated, far-right governments in Central America. The tiny impoverished nations of El Salvador and Nicaragua became the hottest flashpoints in US-Soviet Cold War rivalry, and those conflicts threatened to spread to Guatemala and Honduras.

In El Salvador, where a junta held power, a Marxist-led insurgency was fighting to overthrow the generals. In neighbouring Nicaragua, the iron-fisted Somoza family, notorious for brutality, had recently been overthrown by a Marxist-led revolutionary uprising, the Sandinista National Liberation Front, after forty-three years of corrupt rule. This short but bloody conflict led to a second war launched by CIA-backed counterrevolutionaries (the contras) in the countryside. Outside pressures made both these conflicts proxy wars. Vowing "no more Vietnams," the new Reagan administration in the United States backed the anti-Marxist sides. The Marxists, in turn, were supported by Moscow and Cuba.

We heard horrifying stories of atrocities and kill zones that ravaged urban slums and remote rural villages in El Salvador. Guerrillas occasionally launched ambitious attacks from their bases in thickly forested mountain ranges. Both sides committed offences that resulted in the deaths of tens of thousands of civilians ranging from

Marxists to moderate "soft" conservatives, liberal priests and nuns, teachers, university students, land reformers, and alleged do-gooders of any nationality, including the hated foreign journalists. Multiple inquiries since have confirmed that the government committed the vast majority of civilian killings. An American TV reporter for ABC News during the Nicaraguan fighting, Bill Stewart, who was about my age, was stopped by the dreaded National Guard at a roadblock one day, made to kneel, and then shot in the head. Still, I was anxious to cover these wars.

The plan was for us to spend about three weeks in total, mostly in El Salvador where I would send out a series of news reports and collect material for two news documentaries, and then finish up in Nicaragua. There was growing opposition in the United States and across the West to the Reagan policy of backing authoritarian regimes, however appalling their records. A new term, "death squads," entered the language to describe roving bands of vigilantes doing government dirty work and financed by oligarchs who ordered killings with complete impunity. El Salvador had become an important story in Canada too: a broad coalition of lobby groups in universities, churches, and labour unions criticized the government of Pierre Trudeau for doing little to demand justice for El Salvador's terrorized people or to protest US complicity in the war through its supply of arms. Mark MacGuigan, the External Affairs minister, was criticized sharply in the House of Commons after telling a group of reporters in New York in February, " I would certainly not condemn any decision the United States takes to send offensive arms there. The United States can at least count on our quiet acquiescence."

The rebellion had broad support abroad. Within El Salvador, a coalition of five separate Marxist groups called the Farabundo Martí National Liberation Front (FMLN) partnered with a growing hive of independent groups ranging from landless peasants to middle-class academics. What differentiated this rebellion most was the influence wielded by liberation theology supporters, both Catholic and

Protestant. They strengthened the non-Marxist progressive factions and boosted FMLN credibility abroad. To me, though, the rebellion seemed mostly homegrown and nationalistic. Above all, it appeared inevitable, given the brutal unfairness of society in these countries.

El Salvador had been essentially feudal since the Spanish conquest, when Indigenous peoples had been forced off all the decent lands, creating a system perpetuating the cheapest labour possible for the landed oligarchs—the infamous "fourteen families" (about two hundred interconnected clans by 1981). Peasant protests were met by assassinations and massacres. To protest was to die, and your family died with you. During the previous fifty years, all governments had been subservient to oligarchic and military dictates and had avoided real reforms, blocked free elections, banned opposition parties, and even made it illegal to advocate land reform. Even as wealth poured in from coffee and cotton exports, only a minute elite received the benefits. Only 10 percent of the peasant population was literate, and three-quarters of the children suffered malnutrition. Most of the countryside had no safe water or sewage systems.

El Salvador's wafer-thin urban middle class were terrorized by security forces that viewed even moderate opposition as pro-Marxist. Moderates risked being *desaparecido* (disappeared). If found at all, their mutilated bodies would often show signs of torture. The National Guard and Treasury Police were notorious for such semi-official action, but charges were never laid. By 1979, decomposing corpses were becoming commonplace even in the capital because the terror network did not seek to hide its work but to advertise it as a warning to all.

The final straw came in late 1980 with the murder of Archbishop Oscar Romero while he celebrated Mass in the cathedral. He had dared to speak out against atrocities and call upon the United States to end its support of the regime. His assassins belonged to the feared death squad led by the ex-army intelligence major and neofascist Roberto D'Aubuisson, known as "blowtorch Bob" after his favourite instrument of torture. I wanted to get an interview with him but doubted my chances; a year earlier, a visiting CBC radio reporter, Robin Benger, had confronted him with the question "Why did you kill Archbishop Romero?" and was lucky to escape with his life.

A few months after Romero's murder, four US Catholic women missionaries, three of them nuns, were abducted, raped, and murdered by the National Guard's secret death squad as they drove from the airport to San Salvador. Soon after, two US agricultural experts and a journalist were also killed. Death seemed both vicious and casual. Writer Joan Didion remarked after one visit on the country's "mechanism of terror which leaves one demoralized, undone, humiliated by fear. Terror is a Given of the Place."

We received a lot of personal security advice before leaving, and two warnings stood out: try to avoid contact with the notorious Treasury Police, and don't be out anywhere after dark. Concerned about safety, the CBC bought bulletproof vests for our crew, but they soon proved to be far more trouble than they were worth.

Within minutes of our arrival, we were interrogated by the Treasury Police and still faced a long drive after nightfall to our hotel next to a highway notorious for the number of corpses dumped along its way. As I waited at customs with our TV News foreign editor, John Owen, and a two-man crew, we tried to look relaxed, but my mouth was already dry. An interpreter and a driver were waiting for us, but the police, now going through our luggage, stopped at those four bulletproof vests. Were we planning to give them to rebels? Owen explained several times that they were simply company policy, and, after another hour, the police dismissed us, with instructions to pick up the vests next morning at their headquarters—the last place in El Salvador I wanted to go.

We piled into the van and set off through the wooded hills to the capital. Within a few minutes, the driver complained the engine was misbehaving and said we needed to pull off into a small gravel patch beside the highway. I feared it was a setup, something out of an old film noir. As we stood around the van watching the driver fiddle with the engine, Owen muttered, "You know, I think this is the very spot the American nuns were killed." As dire thoughts flashed through my mind, the engine started up, and we hurled ourselves back into the van.

Before long, I noticed a solitary figure on a low hilltop standing stock-still and holding a machete. Then another, then more. "I think they are guerrillas," the driver said calmly, as he switched on the van's interior lighting to advertise we were visitors, not security forces. When we finally reached San Salvador, its dark and empty streets gave no hint of safety. Finally, we turned a corner and pulled up to the entrance of the Camino Real Hotel, where cheerful Latin music and the sounds of a large wedding party poured forth. I wanted time to compose myself, but as I opened the window in my room to get some air, shots rang out below, somewhere in an unlit maze of alleyways. An exchange of fire or an assassination? Or just the regular harassment of journalists?

On our mandatory ride next morning to the police headquarters, there was little talking among the crew. Our press passes and Canadian passports offered minimal protection in a war where media were so often targets. A future CBC documentary team would be stood against a wall by a security squad and subjected to a nerve-shattering mock execution. We didn't know what to expect, but what we got was farce. As we pulled into the parking lot, a group of officers were standing around hooting with laughter as an overweight and sweat-drenched colleague tried to draw a runaway bull back to the cattle truck from which it had escaped. They were so amused they motioned us to film the scene. Just what we needed: we show up and right away one of their own is gored to death, on camera, at their own station. Explain that! Once the bull was subdued, Owen began haggling over the vests, which took significant amounts of grovelling and signed guarantees. We were warned we'd better have them when we left or else it would be assumed they had ended up in guerrilla hands and consequences would be severe. Given the stakes involved, we left the vests locked in a chest the whole time we were there.

As we drove around getting our bearings, we encountered truckloads of army and National Guard troops. The "Prensa Internacional" sign on our windshield attracted mostly contemptuous glares from security squads, who waved us away from any districts they'd just sealed off. There was a sense of siege everywhere. The US embassy had recently been attacked by rebels, and helmeted marines in sandbagged machine-gun posts watched our van carefully as we rode by. The US staff were well aware of the daily atrocities but downplayed their frequency in cables to Washington. The supporting weapons and money continued to arrive.

In the residential areas of the rich elite, posh tropical homes nestled amid a luxurious mix of flower beds, leafy bushes, and palm trees, barely glimpsed behind towering stone walls and bold iron gates manned by private armed guards. Across the city, the deep scars of extreme poverty appeared as if physically poured into the overcrowded slum *barrancas* (ravines), where running water and sanitation were absent and jumbled shacks made of cast-off materials and old newspapers lined narrow lanes. Here, during the nighttime curfew, death squads would sweep in murder and mutilate while residents huddled in terror.

We watched out in particular for the dreaded Jeep Cherokee Chiefs with tinted bulletproof windows that the death squads favoured. On spotting one, our driver would tense up and say "los desconocidas"—the unknown men—deeming it was safer to proclaim his ignorance of who they were. Every day, city newspapers recorded the gory details of corpses they left behind.

Other unmarked vans with no windows were often used to abduct targeted civilians in broad daylight. The vehicle screeched to a halt, men jumped out to grab a pedestrian or a group, and, as doors slammed, the kidnappers raced off. Everyone knew that mobile torture sessions began as soon as the prisoner was gagged, so seeing these vans left a sick feeling.

In one suburb, we passed a suspected torture centre from which few victims emerged alive. People were targeted not just for being opponents but because a family member might be or for some other vague association. Our driver spoke with the casualness of a tour guide highlighting ancient wonders: "That one is where most are tortured around here," as we slid past a two-storey office block. "What would happen," I asked, "if you told them everything right off?" "They would torture you anyway as a warning, and because it's their job, for something to do."

Around this time, the security squads seemed divided over what to do with the corpses: hide them or display them as public warnings? For a while, murder became more methodical as a meat-packing plant was used to dispose of human remains, but in August 1981, dozens of decapitated corpses showed up on the streets as a death squad experimented with a guillotine to better advertise the terror. This urge to show off struck all newcomers. When American poet Carolyn Forché visited, she was pressed into dining with the family of a notorious militia colonel. After dinner he ended pleasantries by pouring a shopping bag of human ears on the table, declaring, "As for the rights of anyone, tell your people they can go fuck themselves." Things were no less lurid in the countryside, where soldiers would proudly display severed heads after some massacres, even for media.

Part of our work involved showing exquisite politeness while chasing interviews with some of the most odious officials imaginable in San Salvador—men in sharp suits who ruled by the gun and gave new meaning to the term "process of elimination." The junta sought to eradicate whole sectors of society through threats, lethal violence, and forced emigration. The CBC did not represent a major power's media, so we had to lobby harder than US or UK networks for access. Any aid cut off by Canada would be modest and quickly made up by the Reagan administration. My main task was to gather as much information as I could about the course of the war and the reality of repression, so I spent long days shooting material in the countryside and, at night, researching, writing, editing, and building contacts while also planning the next day's outing.

In these pre-internet days, I always collected the latest international human rights reports before I left Canada, deleting any material too unsafe to bring and leave in our hotel rooms. We could phone Canada but had to be cautious because security services were presumably listening in on our calls. I read Salvadoran media with the help of a translator for sparse information on government positions and listened to the nightly news from the FMLN's Radio Venceremos, which at least in the early years tried to build credibility by being more accurate than government communications.

The Camino Real was a hive of rumour and tip-sharing for the foreign media. In so mixed a crowd you have to be very careful to sift good sources from bogus ones, but I've always found that the best journalists are highly experienced, insightful, and often better plugged in than diplomats. The CBC was in partnership with CBS at the time, so we took advantage of their visuals and latest information. Correspondents from Mexico, Britain, France, and the Netherlands were in touch with their embassies' military attachés and human rights observers, and news photographers had tips to share on routes to take, towns to avoid or enter, and acute gut feelings for key parts of the story. As expected, I in turn shared my intelligence.

John Owen, on his way to becoming an outstanding international producer, university lecturer, and foreign coverage guru, was a master at developing contacts. Some advice was chilling. When he approached the acclaimed *Newsweek* combat photographer John Hoagland for tips on reaching the rebel zone near Suchitoto, north of the capital, he got a blast: "You stupid bastards, coming in here ignorant, risking your idiot lives and those with you for bloody 'bang-bang' footage. Go to hell!" Ironically, a few years later, Hoagland, shooting action along the same Suchitoto highway, was shot and killed by a government soldier. In such wars, vast experience helps but is no guarantee of safety: famed British correspondent David Blundy, also killed in El Salvador, had survived twenty-three previous wars before falling to a sniper's bullet. Nor is nationality much protection: a Dutch TV crew, just like ours, was stopped on a country road and murdered by National Guard soldiers.

Our media passes allowed us to travel into the countryside "at our own risk." We stiffened when a pickup truck crammed with apparent farm workers, many with sombreros, machetes, and old rifles, passed by and slowed down to give us a look—"Vigilantes," the interpreter warned. I suspected our movement plans were known because media drivers were almost certainly pressured into reporting schedules to security. Simply put, how could they refuse and remain alive?

On one of our first shoots on foot in the country, an army platoon appeared out of the bushes. They seemed very young and, to break the tenson, we explained we were from friendly Canada (more blank looks) and offered our cigarettes, which were snapped up in seconds. Then our cameraman pulled out a Polaroid camera and offered to take portraits—an instant hit as they jostled to line up for a Rambo-like pose. The lieutenant even offered to let us follow a small portion of a patrol in the dry bush looking for traces of rebel movements. Glad for such cover shots, we packed up, smiling in gratitude.

Worry about our own safety was only part of the tension. We needed to talk to rural Salvadorans about the war, their poverty, and the abuses they had seen, but we realized our conversations might put them in grave danger, whether they were farm-rights activists, religious workers, or random civilians desperate to survive. One day we ran into a landless, dispossessed farmer, a single father with four children, all sheltering in a small hut of tin, carboard, and rags close to a bridge. He was willing to talk, and when I asked him what he most hoped for his family, he replied: "I have never known any money, and no security in my life. I know only this and can hope for no more." Just then, several green-helmeted National Guard soldiers appeared on the bridge and looked down intently on us. As we drove away, I worried we had inadvertently put the man and his family in harm's way. We asked a local church welfare worker if he'd check up on them, but his influence was limited, and we didn't hear back. Human rights activists commonly face that same dilemma.

What happens, though, if your absence from a situation increases the danger to the helpless? A few days later, when we pulled into a temporary refugee camp, about two hundred people were sleeping in the open, cared for by two or three volunteers, including a foreigner. We were told they'd been chased off a nearby estate by vigilantes accusing them of squatting and were afraid they might be violently attacked or even wiped out. They had nowhere to go, no place to hide. Although it was late afternoon and we were anxious to get back to the hotel, Owen and the crew went to one part of the camp to take wrap-up shots while I stayed making notes. Suddenly we heard rumours that the vigilantes were in the area, possibly to attack that night. The volunteer I was talking to asked, "They wonder if you could stay here overnight as [the vigilantes] likely won't do anything if news people are here." "All night?" I gulped. We had no communications through which to consult our embassy or the CBC. Our driver and interpreter, already jittery over the hour, would likely refuse to stay, and everyone in the crew had individual veto power when it came to safety. What's more, as journalists, we were there to observe, not play a role. Still, how could we in conscience leave these people now? All these thoughts raced through my mind.

Within minutes, a tattered station wagon that helped supply the camp arrived. It had church markings as well as a Red Cross sign. Three youths leapt out and went into an urgent conference with the organizers. They were edgy, but insistent. They would stay overnight to protect the camp, but the foreign news folk were more useful getting information of the danger back to the capital, to embassies, rights groups, and more media. I nodded agreement, far too quickly, but I was stunned, humbled, and personally shamed by the courage before me. We packed up and left, and we spread the story to useful sources across the media and to some business leaders with close ties to the government and militias. We kept inquiring and, a day or so later, heard that the camp had peacefully moved on. I've run through that drama in my mind many times, but I will never know how I would have acted had the station wagon not pulled up at that moment.

In the war, the army was weak, corrupt, and brainlessly officered. Momentum was with the rebels. The Reagan administration, however, kept sending in arms and counterinsurgency trainers, as did the notoriously brutal military juntas of Argentina and Chile. The FMLN-FDR (this hyphenated branch was a less ideological, non-Marxist alliance of many groups) certainly got advice from Cuba, Nicaragua, and Moscow, but maintained its independence as it prepared for a new phase of "long war" insurgency, based on tactics made famous by Mao and the Vietnamese general Vo Nguyen Giap. The next phase, after the failed 1982 spring offensive, favoured small hit-and-run actions directed at infrastructure, banks, and the assassination of regime collaborators and spies. The rebels were not well armed, and their volunteers were young, often inspired by liberation theology, and included many women and girls. Surrender was not an option for them. An army chief of staff, General Adolfo Blandon, later stated, "Before 1983, we never took prisoners of war."

One night I was relaxing with colleagues over a beer when a passing car sent three or four shots into the bar. I dropped to the floor, drink in hand, and observed another reporter balancing his martini as if by gyro-compass. Many around me seemed amused: one idiot raced to the window to shout "Piss off!" at the gunmen. The bar was not fired on again, but for the next few evenings, groups of scowling "local businessmen," handguns clearly discernable on their hips, came in. Everyone knew they were the "unknown men," here to intimidate the media and scout out faces for future reference.

The day after the bar shooting, another media van just like ours was shot up when driving through a district we often visited. The interpreter was killed, and a US freelance journalist shot in the arm. A cameraman rolling from another vehicle caught the moment one of the crew rushed toward the body and a voice yelled, "Leave the guy for God's sake, he's dead, clearly dead." I'd read a lot about fear, and what I dreaded most was the possibility of being kidnapped and disappeared.

Our El Salvador section of the trip was winding down, with Nicaragua still to come. We had a lot of material showing the oppressive nature of the government, but had not yet come across a vivid example of the murders for which it was notorious. That changed early one morning when the interpreter raced up to us saying we had to come immediately: "Something horrible to see—killing of a whole family." We were the only crew to arrive at the scene in a poor section of the city. No police or ambulance had shown up, and people milled about talking in whispers. Owen raced in to take stock, appearing moments later looking white and shaken. "This is the worst—two sons killed in front of their mother, and her head blown apart." The walls behind them were so spattered with blood and bone chips it looked like an abattoir. "We can't use this on air, so do we even have to be in here?" the soundman, John Axelson, asked angrily. "Yes, editors can use most of what we have and mask the head somehow," Owen replied. "We have to show what they are doing here." I was shaken by the scene but also felt deep rage. There was no sign the victims had resisted, and they were grouped in a way that suggested the sons had been executed first so their mother would witness it—a sadistic impulse common among liquidation squads the world over.

This period was the worst of the twelve-year war. In 1981 alone, the government killed eighteen thousand civilians. When the war was over, an official amnesty protected all perpetrators, and thirty years passed before any serious investigations began. Few have been prosecuted. Despite everything I've seen in other conflicts, El Salvador remains the scariest place I've ever been, a tough first test.

When our flight landed in Nicaragua, the contrast was striking. In El Salvador, the rebels fought the government; here, the leftist rebels had fought their way to power and were expected by their many international admirers to conform to the best socialist probity. "This is not socialist!" one lanky foreigner admonished the aggressive beggars, an appeal met with snickers and even more aggressive begging. After less than two years in power, the Sandinistas were still struggling, in the face of internal fissures and a growing US-supported armed resistance, to make clear what they stood for.

Managua, the capital, looked half destroyed, with cracked walls and vacant lots filled with rubble from a massive earthquake a decade earlier. Under the former Somoza regime, international aid to rebuild had been siphoned off by friends of the dictator. The ongoing celebration of rebel victory gave some of Managua a jaunty air, but the heavily armed Sandinista militia presence was also apparent. The countryside was not safe because right-wing guerrillas, including many former Somoza National Guard members, were staging attacks on bridges and power lines and assassinating people who had opposed them. The Sandinistas protected the media, but this attention soon felt cloying. We were watched with an intensity that gave us the jitters, making us prime targets of rebel assassins or kidnappers. Our small hotel was surrounded by guards with full combat weapons—both to protect us and stop us from straying off on our own.

In El Salvador, our cameraman had relied increasingly on alcohol to cope with the stress, and he deteriorated even further in Nicaragua. He began to act like a stand-up comic, spewing out wobbly one-liners that left some of the locals thinking he was mocking them. As our camera operator could neither walk straight nor shut up, some regime officials pressed us to show we were serious journalists.

We had no choice but to stage an intervention. Owen, Axelson, and I sat him down and demanded full sobriety, offering to give up all drink ourselves if it helped. It was a sad event because we liked this skilled professional who was, in good times, a witty companion. "Man, you might have got us killed in El Salvador with your babble," one of us argued, "and we can't let you risk the same here as well." The session worked, and he abstained for the rest of the trip. This was the era when foreign coverage lifestyle stirred as much high living as possible in with stress, risks, and discomforts, and, incredibly, it would be years before management confronted the problem of sending staff with notorious drinking problems into danger zones.

Although I realized we wouldn't be covering Nicaragua if not for the allegedly high stakes in the Cold War, I felt it was at this stage overhyped. The new Sandinista government did not meet the dark billing Washington gave it of being an "extreme Marxist state" on the Cuban model. For starters, Fidel Castro had launched his first government with mass executions of hundreds of former regime stalwarts, while Nicaraguan leader Daniel Ortega began by banning the death sentence. The Marxists were only one part of a broad rebellion supported by youth and middle-class city dwellers after the Somoza kleptocracy had become unendurable. The short war saw fifty thousand killed in an impoverished country of only three million, and it further devastated the economy. The Sandinistas sought support from moderates and pledged a mixed economy, pluralism in politics, and a nonaligned foreign policy. The alliance was not yet firm and already fraying as some followers joined the opposition, accusing the Sandinistas of power grabs and being too chummy with Cuba. Meanwhile, the regime became ever more militant as the Reagan administration sought to throttle the revolution at birth by imposing a full trade embargo, setting off underwater mines in the country's ports, and unleashing the CIA to arm the underground force known as contras. It was a return to war.

Some elements of the regime did manage to win international praise. Socially, it sharply reduced the illiteracy rate through a massive reading campaign in the countryside, initiated local drives to improve rural work and general living conditions, boosted health services, and allowed the first free-trade unions. Still, I knew revolutions were usually deceiving at first. Unrestrained power corrupts former heroic rebels just as it does others, and early threats to the new shining citadel of power almost inevitably led to increased internal snooping, iron-fisted reaction, and some form of autocracy. I was suspicious of the new neighbourhood "defence of the revolution committees," common in many popular dictatorships, that were modelled on Cuban and East German citizens forces. Though portrayed as a local network for good works and protection, they had already become internal surveillance systems to spot suspected traitors and the ideologically unreliable.

In Nicaragua, in contrast to El Salvador, I was surprised to find that the government held Canada in high regard. Ottawa had recognized the new regime, but it was also critical and had offered scarcely any aid. The Trudeau government's program was clearly to say little, do less, and, above all, not upset President Reagan. There was, however, a remarkable outpouring of support from Canada's labour unions, churches, NGOs, and university campuses.

I was keen to see how human rights were being addressed. After looking into nightmarish abuse in Brazil, Chile, and El Salvador, I was particularly interested in several questions in Nicaragua: how nations emerging from great oppression could avoid slipping into new dictatorships during regime change; and how change, when it came, could conscientiously confront the mass crimes of the past. I would run into these same issues in a score of countries in coming decades, from Latin America, South Africa, and Northern Ireland to Poland and the collapsing Soviet bloc, including Russia itself. If you ignore past mass crimes by protecting perpetrators at all levels with amnesties, surely that too becomes a form of atrocity whose spectre will haunt the future.

Fortunately, I got access to the most intriguing figure in the Sandinista government, the often jailed, tortured, or exiled Tomás Borge, interior minister and secret police chief, an iron-man figure much feared by opponents but revered by followers. The official leader, Ortega, was suffocatingly bland, while Borge's whole life was drama. A skilled guerrilla, he had been a revolutionary since the age of thirteen, and his wife had died during torture by the National Guard. He was also an acclaimed poet, dramatist, songwriter, and author of children's books. Because he was a chief target of assassination, we could interview him only inside the security headquarters. Short, squat, balding, and with thick glasses, he stared hard at me as I asked questions—a wise-looking professorial type who was at the same time predatory and unbreakably tough.

I asked him about internal policing and how he could avoid the government's slipping into dictatorship. He insisted the new Nicaragua was intent on winning outside respect for its justice system. Police would no longer be corrupt; torture was forbidden; local committees would not harass people for their views; security forces were being trained to avoid abusing civilians. I interjected, "Is that possible in the face of far-right counter-revolutionary war?" "Yes, that's how we win the people's trust," he insisted. He was impressive; I was dubious. "Your followers have suffered so much and are now in charge of handing out justice," I began, and he interrupted: "And we who knew such suffering are most keen to end such practices. We will show that in the trials we are arranging for seven thousand of the National Guard accused to unspeakable crimes." I leapt in, "I'm interested in the issue of justice for war crimes, so can I visit some of these prisoners to observe their treatment?" He seemed surprised but quickly agreed.

A day or two later, a well-armed Sandinista convoy accompanied me and my crew to the main prison. We were led to a hot cell block overcrowded with military and police members from the former regime. The railings were bedecked with drying laundry washed in small sinks. It was astonishing to view so many men with appalling records in one spot. A few close to our guard post came forward with surprising boldness to beg cigarettes, but most of their attention was glued on our attractive female Sandinista captain, who was firmly in charge. I felt the same uneasy feeling I got whenever I had a closely conducted tour of a state prison: How much was staged? Were the prisoners coached, and were more fearful conditions kept out of sight?

I had asked to talk to people charged with torture, rape, and multiple killings. Before long, two "very notorious killers and torturers" were led before our camera in a small interrogation room. They looked like simple gardeners or building commissioners, unremarkable and, in these circumstances, craven. They would tell all, they assured me, because their peaceful lives had been ruined while senior commanders fled into exile—in Miami!—leaving them to face all the consequences. They hoped true justice would see they were merely following orders, and might they have a cigarette or two?

Within a few years, most of the prisoners won appeals in court and were let go. Some joined the contra rebels. Nothing that I saw allowed me to conclude one way or another how Nicaragua's need to confront its past would work out. We didn't know, of course, that the Cold War that stoked fires in El Salvador and Nicaragua would end in the late 1980s, causing their wars to soon fade out as well once outside powers had no interest in continuing them, regardless of what locals had to say. El Salvador would stay one of the world's most violent nations for decades after the war; Nicaragua would see the Sandinista regime ultimately corrupted and thrown from office, while immense poverty continued. So began the mass exodus of migrants from these countries north to the United States—a movement that continues to this day.

Arriving home, despite the vivid fall colours, I found that sleep was fitful. My partner, Leigh, said I was restless, jumpy, and sometimes deeply distracted. While shaken by some scenes on my trip, I was still completely hooked on foreign news. I was already investigating human rights, especially in Poland and Eastern Europe, where I believed oppression was being overlooked in the growing media focus on Latin America. Such absorption in world events did not help domestic life. The world events that fascinated me were far less intriguing to Leigh, who was achieving her own career success in the demanding new technology of computer programing. Neither of us understood or had much interest in the other's work, and mine also entailed long periods on the road, followed by moody decompression when home. After a half-decade together, we agreed to split amicably, and have remained friends ever since.

I soon received thrilling word that the CBC was sending me to London for a likely four-year posting—an enormous honour. But before I made the move, my first big assignment was another conflict, the Falklands War. This dramatic air, sea, and land battle over small British islands in the South Atlantic, between invading Argentina and counterattacking Britain, seemed a return to the imperial age. Along with many of my colleagues, I was soon covering events over massive fine steaks and thick burgers in what we came to call "the room service war."

7

Thatcher Years and the London Bureau

In the process of preparing for my London posting early in 1982, I became one of several CBC reporters, part of the international horde of media, covering the ten-week-long Falklands War, which meant filing analysis pieces from three capitals over three months: Ottawa, London, and Buenos Aires. I delivered my possessions, including the library I'd accumulated since early youth, into long-term storage and reduced the belongings I would take abroad to three large suitcases. I had no pressing family, relationship, or financial obligations: my widowed father, now remarried, and my siblings were all doing well, I'd never owned a car, and I had no hobby apart from the "high" of chasing news. During my final weeks in Ottawa, I was packed, restless, and ready to go anywhere within hours.

I felt right about moving on. The world was buzzing with technical revolutions in computers, satellites, and digital communications, while the long Cold War seemed lurching toward some form of dénouement, either diplomatic or military. The dawn of the human rights era meant minority groups and aggrieved nations were demanding to be heard in power centres as never before. In April I watched Queen Elizabeth 2 sign the Charter of Rights and Freedoms on a blustery day on Parliament Hill, making Canada one of the first nations to enshrine not just individual rights but group ones as well, covering race, language, and religion. The eighties were gearing up for profound change.

Leadership itself was different: the oddest people were rising unexpectedly and mastering commanding roles with a mix of suave theatricality, media savvy, and steely determination. Ronald Reagan, America's first ex-actor president, came with a masterful voice and boundless self-confidence; Pope John Paul II, trained as an actor in his Polish youth, almost overnight stood as a towering statesman; and in the United Kingdom, Prime Minister Margaret Thatcher used her Iron Lady image to help mesmerize allies and unnerve opponents (see "One-on-One with Thatcher" interlude). Surprising power figures arose, including Chairman Deng Xiaoping, a diminutive party operative who emerged in China after Mao Zedong's death to turn Communism on its head by preaching "capitalist virtues"; and in Poland, the shipyard electrician Lech Wałęsa shook up the Soviet Empire when his Solidarity movement succeeded in launching the first free union inside the Marxist behemoth—a genie Moscow could never rebottle (see "Glitches and Greatness" interlude). Meanwhile, waiting in the Kremlin wings stood Mikhail Gorbachev, adroitly fashioning a totally new persona for a Soviet leader. Perhaps Pierre Trudeau, as Marshall McLuhan predicted, had started the trend toward image mastery.

To much of the world, the Falklands War between the United Kingdom and Argentina over a pair of small islands in the South Atlantic seemed more comic opera than real. Actually, it was an extraordinary mix of high-stakes combat and blatant theatricality by both Thatcher's government and the senior officers of the junta, seated in the Casa Rosada (Pink Palace) in Buenos Aires.

I had long researched the British military out of historical interest and for my reporting on North Atlantic Treaty Organization (NATO) affairs. I'd also followed the bloody record of this junta as it ran one of the most murderous governments in modern South American history. Since 1974, in targeting both urban guerrillas and political dissidents, it had waged a notorious "dirty war," using death squads to hunt down people for torture and liquidation—killing and "disappearing" more than twenty thousand. Many victims were tortured, drugged, stripped, and dropped from aircraft into the ocean.

In 1982, faced with a growing economic crisis, the military rulers saw a way to pacify discontent by seizing the Falklands, long claimed by Argentina, which knew them as the Malvinas. Wild rejoicing swept Buenos Aires. Led by the often tipsy General Leopoldo Galtieri, the hyper-macho junta felt sure the lady Thatcher would let the islands go without much fuss. She had recently ignored objections from human rights groups when she courted Buenos Aires for lucrative military contracts while also slicing spending on Britain's naval strength. Her government had completely misjudged the junta, ignoring clear warnings that an invasion was possible.

Now, though, Thatcher reacted swiftly by diving decisively and theatricality into an unwavering defence of British honour and prestige. Bolstered by a hawkish Admiralty and a pliant War Cabinet, she ordered a task force thrown together from a much-reduced navy to set sail like a glorious fleet of old to boot the Argentinians off the islands. Tens of thousands of thrilled civilians raced to Portsmouth harbour, waving Union Jacks to "see the boys off." It was an astonishing act of daring: the Falklands were only 483 kilometres from Argentina but more than 11,000 from Britain, and elite units of ground troops with logistical support had to sail for three weeks just to reach possible landing sites. The world as well as the junta was startled by Thatcher's actions: Europeans grumbled that Britain had gone mad; Reagan urged her to reconsider and negotiate. Even in hindsight it seems a preposterous risk for a nation whose previous amphibious operation ended in the Suez shambles twenty-six years earlier.

Having arrived in London, I raced around seeking meetings with military experts and turning out analysis pieces that included news updates. I had hoped the CBC could persuade the British fleet to include me in its small pool of journalists sailing off to war, but

Thatcher waved off international "freeloaders" and imposed a strict British-only press policy on what became tightly controlled and fervently patriotic news coverage. The Argentinians were even more selective: foreign media were not only excluded from its captured islands but watched closely as possible spies. The more TV networks were excluded, the more frenzied became the competition for pool tapes and military experts. Former generals and admirals were more sought after than ex-diplomats, as neither London nor Buenos Aires looked ready to talk concessions.

I was assigned to report on the "Britain goes to war" scene from London, then fly to Buenos Aires as the fleet and its troopships approached the islands. After several weeks in Argentina, I would race back to London to handle the conclusion of the war along with a visit by the pope.

In London I was struck by a revival of the famed British bulldog spirit. The capital had an almost euphoric summer-of-1940 air reminiscent of the Blitz, minus the Luftwaffe bombs. Newspaper stands posted tallies of Argie Air Losses and RAF Victories, while the pro-Thatcher Rupert Murdoch tabloids took jingoism to excess. The *Sun* hailed an early Royal Navy victory with the headline "Stick It Up Your Junta" and later trumpeted the sinking of the Argentinian cruiser *General Belgrano* with the banner "Gotcha!"—withdrawn after it became apparent that hundreds of sailors had drowned. The conservative media were in full war cry and, following public pressure, even the lefty *Guardian* fell in line. One senior BBC broadcaster was labelled a traitor for suggesting a British victory was not guaranteed. "A British citizen is either on his country's side . . . or he is the enemy," the *Sun* intoned, a statement said to mirror Thatcher's intolerance of any antiwar views.

Only years later in her memoirs did Thatcher acknowledge the ferocious strain she felt. The basic need to transport supplies to the war zone stretched sea power to the limit; air cover was inadequate as the Brits had only thirty-four Harrier jets against 230 jets flown by

Argentinian pilots; and landing sites were few and exposed to air attack. While British troops were first rate, the expedition was light on helicopters, artillery, and even communications equipment. On top of everything, weather was deteriorating rapidly with the onrush of stormy winter seas in the Southern Hemisphere. The admiral leading the fleet and the generals commanding troops seemed to detest one another, rarely talked, and complained of weak communications with Britain.

When I landed in Argentina, the theatrics proclaimed wild optimism. Forests of blue-and-white banners and flags made it feel like a World Cup tournament in which Argentina was scoring early victories. Hotel waiters and barmen eagerly greeted me, asking if I'd heard how primed their glorious soldiers on "our Malvinas" were to defeat the odious British sissies. However, while there were pro-war demonstrations near the Pink Palace whenever a British ship was sunk or a Harrier downed, the public mood quickly turned sour when Argentinian loses were revealed.

Most Argentinians were pleasant, but the country was potentially dangerous for English-speaking Commonwealth journalists such as the British and the Canadians. Not far from the hotel were heroic demonstrations of mothers and grandmothers demanding word of their "disappeared" family members, often just teenagers, and these protests drew increasingly threatening counterdemonstrations from pro-military mobs. Tension was always high. Some reporters received death threats; others were followed by ominous men in unmarked cars. An air of menace hung over the splendid city, with its vast array of architectural styles, wide boulevards, lush parks, and famous neighbourhoods that resembled Paris in the 1890s. Occasionally, tango dance music wafted wistfully and seductively in the air, reminding me of the labyrinthine mystery stories of Jorge Luis Borges. The air of instability and nostalgia was heightened by the collapse of the currency, while annual inflation of 300 percent was one more reason for citizens to be on edge and for visitors to remain cautious.

I had special reason to feel at risk. Two weeks before I arrived, a producer working for CBC's new current affairs show *The Journal*, Tony Hillman, had been seized, along with his two-man crew, by security police near a southern airbase. They were charged with espionage—no minor matter in a national security state. I knew Hillman well as a friend of our family in Toronto in the early sixties who had dated my sister, Heather (and, before I met her, my future wife, Tina). A talented producer, he was not given to reckless acts. His crew had not shot anything sensitive, but they were facing years in prison for being near an airbase. I could only assume that the CBC was on the junta's blacklist. If our team were hauled in on trumped-up charges, I could imagine some of the international headlines: "Canadian Spy Ring Busted in Buenos!"

Staying in the capital was no guarantee of safety. I covered the story of a celebrated British TV reporter, Julian Manyon, and his crew, who were grabbed off the streets by secret police, wrestled into a van, and driven deep into the countryside. They were stripped naked, blindfolded, and subjected to a mock execution. When told to turn their backs to the gunmen and start walking, they were so sure of imminent death they clasped hands as they awaited the volley of shots. Instead, their captors roared off, leaving them alive but without clothes or any sense of where they were. They stumbled across fields looking for help and, fortunately, found a farmer who led them to safety. Asked by a reporter later if he'd been scared, Manyon replied: "Very—but probably not so much as the local farmer when he saw three naked Englishmen running towards him out of his corn field."

Even local shoots could veer instantly out of control. When we went to the mothers' protest in the park by the Pink Palace, intending to interview some of them about their missing family members, we were suddenly engulfed by a marching mob of counterprotestors entering the square. Our unnerved driver started howling in English, "These are idiot people, sir, dangerous people! I cannot move!" "Stop talking," I gasped. "Stop using English, only Spanish," but he got even more incensed. "Idiots! Stupid people!" he bellowed. As I was debating whether we'd best stick with the van and risk being inside as it was turned over or take our chances by exiting, the crowd swept slowly beyond us. We were able to move on, even grabbing some quick video of the women who refused to be quieted.

Because I'd recently been in El Salvador, I felt accustomed to risk, knowing we had to be careful in planning every move. It's one thing to read about fear, and another to feel dread the moment you step outside. One very professional, normally unflappable Canadian reporter came up to me twice during dinner in the hotel restaurant to say he couldn't stand the tension. I tried to calm him, but the next morning he bailed and flew home. I respected his decision because his nerves left him with no alternative. Once again I was surprised at how reckless it was of news organizations to send staff who had no interest in becoming foreign correspondents into war zones with zero training and no appreciation of the mental stresses they would encounter.

Most reporters were deeply frustrated by the refusal of the local government to give us more freedom of movement. We started calling it the "room service war" because trips out to restaurants rarely seemed worth the extra risk. The heavy workload also kept us occupied far into the night. Bulletins from both warring militaries came in at all hours: one moment I might be rushing down the corridor to deliver the breaking story of the first British air raid on the island, and the next handling moments of high-sea drama such as the sinking of HMS *Sheffield* by an Argentinian air anti-ship missile. As pictures of the bombing raid arrived from London and Buenos Aires, the news desk in Toronto took a risk and asked me to do a live running commentary on the footage feeding directly into the national newscast. The pictures were blurry at times, but as the Harrier fighter-bombers screamed in low amid ground fire, they were certainly dramatic. I was familiar with the RAF planes and types of Argentinian anti-aircraft guns, but I was increasingly frustrated by having to report from Buenos Aires when London had vastly superior open-source intelligence and quality analysis available. I'd also reached my limit of giant hamburgers and plates overflowing with thick steaks, which hotel and restaurant staff proudly served up as symbols of their country's meat-proud heritage.

Fortunately, I was rotated back to London in the dramatic closing weeks of the war. After the British landed at San Carlos Water and started to fight their way on foot across the island toward the main Argentinian forces, the outcome was constantly in doubt. All could be won or lost in days. I believed the British would win; their military was one of the best trained for real war in the world, while Argentina's army was more attuned to domestic security duties. But still, the highly skilled Argentinian air force had the potential to take out one of the two British carriers or fat targets such as the massive civilian ocean liners, including the *Queen Elizabeth II*, that transported the bulk of its troops. As it was, the British lost six ships, with several more damaged, because the fleet lacked up-to-date air defence missiles. It was widely rumoured that US military estimates considered a British victory unlikely.

The stakes could hardly be exaggerated: a loss would have fatally weakened Thatcher and stunned the confidence of the Western alliance at a critical time in the Cold War. What concerned me most, though, was the certainty that an Argentinian victory would greatly strengthen not just the military dictatorship there but those in other national security states across Latin America. The human rights of tens of millions would suffer. Argentina's defeat, however, might undercut the junta's chances of survival. When I left for London, with several weeks of war remaining, I noticed that the pro-Malvinas war sentiment in Buenos Aires had suddenly faded. And so it was: a year after the British victory, the junta collapsed and democracy returned to Argentina, an event that speeded the crumbling of Latin America's modern age of military despots.

In London, there was no doubting that Thatcher's extraordinary display of nerves paid enormous dividends for her Conservative Party. She had, many Brits took to saying, "put the 'Great' back in Britain." Thatcher would go on to rule party and Parliament through the eighties, her total of eleven years in power making her the longest-serving prime minister of the twentieth century. Although inclined to be a self-righteous bully in domestic matters, she proved herself a first-rate war leader as she left her military commanders to get on with the job. She was decisive, courageous, and amazingly wobble-free, and the notoriously fractious Tories allowed her to dominate as a domestic and global leader until they drove her from Number 10 in 1990.

Even as I was covering the final stages of the war, I was detailed for six days to follow Pope John Paul II on his tour of Britain—the first serving pontiff to visit in the half millennium since the country broke with Roman Catholicism as the state religion. Across nine cities, I was able to study his manner of engaging strong emotions in vast crowds with what the *Guardian* called the "eloquence of an actor and poet." He looked strong and rugged in those days, and, after covering so many dark stories, I was relieved simply to see the enthusiasm and joy on so many faces at mass services in soccer stadiums. John Paul did not meet Thatcher, and he spoke in general terms about the awfulness of war in the Falklands and Northern Ireland, but he often seemed to say far more than he really did. War was decried, yet no regime was singled out for blame. His convoluted sentences, a papal specialty, frequently left secular reporters struggling to make sense of the full meaning of his words. The Queen invited him for tea at Buckingham Palace, and then he held a special mass of comfort for four thousand of the very old and dying at St. George's Cathedral, South London—a service that left many observers, including me, deeply moved.

I had a satisfyingly busy summer as CBC London correspondent, keeping an eye on footage coming in on foreign stories that needed explaining for newscasts and prepping for potential new crises that seemed about to break. Footloose, I leased a furnished apartment in one of the stately Georgian-style houses in the leafy Hampstead district in northwest London, an area favoured by academics, media figures, and actors—Jeremy Irons was a neighbour. Not far away, my producer, Tony Burman, leased a house for his family that H.G. Wells had once owned. The area was restful, but I also found it isolating and somewhat sedate for my tastes.

In stark contrast, the CBC's TV and radio bureaus (English and French) were located in the chronically traffic-jammed and chaotic Great Titchfield Street in West London. The area had undeniable character, a faded bohemian spirit from the time arts and literary types knew it as Fitzrovia. In the forties, it had boasted the smoky pub-land hangouts of writers and poets such as George Orwell and Dylan Thomas, part of the art and academic crowd lured there by the closeness of BBC Broadcasting House and the shadier drinking havens of Soho.

In the eighties, scores of small clothing outlets churned out fashions for nearby Oxford and Regent Street shops. Dotted around were the news offices of British and foreign networks including, prominently, Canada's CBC. I loved the whole slightly shabby but legitimately creative atmosphere: the friendly pubs where reporters and crews could debrief each other over pints or meet up with contacts before flying off to distant stories; and the Turkish, Italian, and Indian restaurants within a block or two where you might meet up with academics, diplomats, and NGO field workers for those "backgrounders" you wanted to keep from competitors. We could fly out of war-torn Beirut in the morning, drop our bags off at the CBC in the afternoon, and stroll over to a gathering of friends in a pub or restaurant.

The Titchfield area was a world centre of foreign journalism, up there with New York, Washington, or Paris. Our bureau was a hive of change, as new technology kept bringing in ever greater reams of video to be quickly edited into items. The CBC's flagship news hour, *The National*, was moved from 11 p.m. to 10 p.m. and split in two parts, with the new current affairs show, *The Journal*, adding documentaries and studio interviews to the news for increased depth and reach. The brainchild of Peter Herrndorf, one of Canada's leading cultural forces, *The Journal* was forged by producer Mark Starowicz, a rare visionary who was fearless, demanding, and very humorous. The show brought a refreshing style and pace to late-night information programming, and British, American, and Australian networks immediately tried to copy it. In mere months, the Canadian media profile abroad was elevated as major new funding flowed into *The Journal* to finance more teams abroad for longer periods.

Despite this euphoria, I learned to control my enthusiasm. My excited early suggestion that my opposite number in Paris, Don Murray, and I should divide coverage of the vast reaches of the Western Hemisphere between us—from Cape Town to the tip of Finland, and the Russian Urals to Northern Ireland—was met with the amused ridicule it deserved. We simply had to be ready for whatever came up, at home or abroad, from the serious to the engagingly silly—from think tank reports to the juiciest tabloid scoops on royals, political scandals, spy dramas, and what we called "British loonie" fare. My predecessor, Mark Phillips, once marvelled that his most lauded CBC story concerned Tiddles, a monumentally fat cat who squatted for years in the ladies' toilets in Paddington railway station feeding on food handouts. I in turn spent hours walking around the sets of *Coronation Street* accompanied by cast members who described the buildings individually as if they really lived there.

Most stories were serious, however: the Falklands War was soon followed by Israel's invasion of southern Lebanon and the siege of Beirut, along with repeated threats of a Soviet military invasion of Poland to crack down on Solidarity's spreading open dissent. The longest-running story of all, the Cold War, was reaching the point where jousting between President Reagan and the Kremlin buried the détente of the seventies and substituted a sense of showdown that heightened fears of an actual Third World War.

A major challenge was to cover the phenomenon of Thatcher, whose gift for holding power surpassed all the legendary British leaders in well over a century—Palmerston, Gladstone, Asquith, Churchill, Macmillan, the lot—and the only one to have a political philosophy named after her: Thatcherism. Though she accepted the term, she made no claims to be a philosopher. She was a scientist at heart, a brilliant opportunist, and a sharp-minded workaholic of astonishing resilience who liked to be portrayed as a thrifty housewife. She was contemptuous of intellectuals, lofty academics, and cerebral civil service gurus, appearing to welcome their hatred as a reliable sign of progress. British politicians are usually quite witty, but she had no discernible sense of humour.

By 1982 she had led her party for seven years, and as prime minister for three. While many portrayed her as rigidly Victorian in outlook, she was really the creation of a miserable age of upheaval in British politics from the late sixties through the seventies. Visiting the United Kingdom in the seventies, I had been struck by the dispirited public mood. Economists termed the debilitating effects of stagflation the "British disease": high inflation, soaring unemployment as bad as in the depressed thirties, low productivity, and a malaise that included race riots, bombings by the Irish Republican Army (IRA), and chaotic labour unrest. Much of the West, including Canada, also faced poor economic times for reasons such as surging oil prices, but Britain reeled with special bitterness surrounding strikes and walkouts by increasingly militant unions. The discontent helped drive the strife-ridden Labour government from office and had Thatcher fighting for survival—until the Falklands War saved her. The speed of her recovery was unprecedented: when I was packing for London in the spring, she appeared doomed, and when I had a chance to unpack some weeks later, she was riding a tide of postwar euphoria that set her on course for landslide victories in the next two elections.

A few months later I was in the thick of what was likely the emotional highlight of Thatcher's decade: the extraordinary Falklands victory parade through the City of London, with thousands of marching troops, flawless bands, the roaring flypast, and hundreds of thousands of cheering spectators. To the horror of media royal watchers, the Queen was not invited to take the review, and Thatcher presided instead, which she did while aping Her Majesty's style of hat, purse, and wave—a regal posture she began adopting on all foreign trips. Whether the Queen was amused or not, it was a triumphalist moment for Thatcher.

Guided by a coterie of neoconservative thinkers, Thatcher set out to upend the progressive consensus of centralized state planning of society and industry that had dominated Labour and Tory governments since the late fifties on—an arrangement heavily dependent on giving in to union demands while also bowing to strong resistance to reform by government departments. She derided the obsession with consensus seeking and set her course on lower taxes, privatization of nationalized industries, free markets, and small government, fighting inflation by higher interest rates, and encouraging a tougher line on union demands. Those in Tory ranks who opposed her views she labelled wrong-headed "wets." Many who respected her abilities in power and high intelligence still found her manner too hectoring, her legendary rudeness either appalling or darkly amusing, like watching a villain in a pantomime. She was known to answer a minister's admission in Cabinet of making a mistake with "Not a mistake, gentlemen, utter incompetence!" Thatcher fired more Cabinet members than any modern predecessor, usually after first using media leaks by staffers to denigrate the victim.

I marvelled at her ability to rise above her unpopularity to score such victories. "She is that extraordinary paradox," historian David Cannadine wrote, "a populist who is not popular." But many factors played into her hands: she was lucky in her opponents, from Argentina's wobbly General Galtieri to the bumbling heads of the fractious Labour Party she defeated three times, to the dismal state of the UK economy which made any improvement seem almost magical. I could go weeks without running into someone with a sympathetic opinion of her, whether traditional Tories, liberals, religious workers, academics, or students. The snobbery of elites was part of it; and being a woman (though avowedly no feminist) surely provoked some extra resentment, although a male leader as humourless and bullying would almost certainly have met open resistance even sooner. On the world stage she presented herself as a major leader in the Churchillian mould. Even here her sharp, undiplomatic tongue, which astonished Brian Mulroney when he first encountered it, rattled powerful equals. Historian David Cannadine noted that Helmut Schmidt compared her to "a female rhinoceros, charging." François Mitterrand muttered to aides that she had the "eyes of Caligula."

Still, she did introduce significant reforms, even if not as many as her reliably grandiose rhetoric suggested. Like much of the media, I often underestimated her; she was more complex than we thought. I covered her for years and met her personally twice in odd circumstances—once face-to-face for an interview in the garden of Number 10. I found her pleasant enough, although I suspect she thought I was someone else (see "One-on-One with Thatcher" interlude).

London always had enough stories to keep us busy in between forays abroad, including the constant risk of terror attacks, especially IRA bombings. That June a guerrilla unit from Ireland created mayhem with two bombs in Hyde Park and Regent's Park in central London targeting military ceremonies: eleven soldiers were killed, along with seven army horses. It shocked the nation and increased the air of watchful tension in public places, including pubs, restaurants, and outdoor gatherings.

A few weeks earlier in London, a team of assassins from a Palestinian militia unit attempted to murder the Israeli ambassador, the event that Jerusalem cited to justify its invasion of south Lebanon. The stated goal was to drive Palestine Liberation Organization (PLO) and Syrian units away from Israel's northern border, but soon the campaign became a destructive drive up the coast and into the suburbs of the capital, Beirut—a disaster that escalated Lebanon's long civil war into one of its bloodiest phases.

I was fortunate to miss the worst incident of this period: the Sabra and Shatila massacre in a Beirut suburb in September. There Israeli allies, the Lebanese Christian Forces Militia, were allowed passage by Israeli occupation troops into the camps, where they murdered between five hundred and a thousand civilians, mainly Palestinian refugees and Lebanese Shias. The world was doubly shocked, as was Israel, when it became apparent the Israeli invasion force could see the massacre underway from watch posts and appeared complicit. So soon after El Salvador, I was relieved not to be there to witness the clearing up of the corpses, mostly mothers and children.

I would spend much time covering the war in Lebanon, on and off over the next two years, but in 1982 I did reports in Israel and on the occupied West Bank, where the controversial new settler apartment buildings blazed boldly in the sun—a warning of coming conflict that even four decades ago seemed inevitable. I went with Israeli troops on a patrol into south Lebanon which wound up mountain roads notorious for mines and ambushes, past an ancient Crusader castle recently fought over by Israel and PLO units, and on to the stone encampment of a mysterious private force. The few-hundred-strong South Lebanon Army, predominantly Christian, was financed by Israel as a proxy occupation force to keep various Palestinian militia from returning. Gloomy young soldiers stood around looking impatient for something to do while the chain-smoking warlord, Major Saad Haddad, offered few words and even fewer details. It was later alleged that some of these cross-wearing warriors had participated in the Sabra and Shatila bloodbath. In a way, my lacklustre encounter with them resembled much of the Lebanese story at the time, always complex and never settling long in place, as new units kept arising and disappearing or merging with others. The warlord died soon after of natural causes and was succeeded by another, while the South Lebanon Army failed to guard itself and disappeared in the years after Israel pulled out of the country.

Back in the bureau, I spent a lot of time studying all I could find on the shifting political and military blocs in play in Lebanon. An increasing amount of attention, however, had to be paid to history's greatest military standoff, the Cold War in Europe. More than six million armed personnel regarded each other across the Iron Curtain, millions from nations in the North Atlantic Treaty Organization, versus somewhat larger forces under the Warsaw Pact, which comprised Soviet-allied nations under the command of the USSR itself. After a decade of East-West détente, the early eighties were memorably tense, for new threats of conflict, possibly a nuclear one, were unnerving governments and inspiring massive antinuke protests. Détente had been popular for years but contained the seeds of its own destruction: it froze superpower competition in place in Europe and left the Soviet Empire intact, and, it appeared, unchallenged. That standoff was intolerable to conservatives in the West like Reagan and Thatcher as well as to dissidents behind the Iron Curtain, who felt betrayed by the recognition of Soviet permanence.

Moscow had signed the Helsinki Accords in 1975 because it gave the USSR the right to clamp down on any satellite that attempted to move out of its orbit. The various Communist governments, meanwhile, simply ignored the human rights provisions of the accords. Dissidents anywhere in the Soviet bloc faced prison and forced labour, and, in Russia, entombment in mental asylums. Despite such threats, agitation was spreading, adding to increasing tension and distrust of détente.

On the military front, technological advances in tactical nuclear weapons, smaller than the intercontinental ballistic missiles, now saw them deployed to special arsenals on both sides of the Iron Curtain. In the West that sparked massive protests in capital cities and military bases. A renewed fear of nuclear war led to many TV shows on that theme and a bestselling novel, *The Third World War*, by a retired UK officer depicting how vast megatons of nuclear destruction could be tactically and strategically best used—all the "if they wipe out Liverpool, take out Minsk" type of calculations. I began to wonder how it would be to cover such a war, assuming networks remained on air, and London was not vaporized at the start.

The more I researched military thinking, the more it seemed likely any vast conventional war would precede, but the risks likely negate nuclear exchanges. Despite easy doomsday dramatizations, I doubted leaders would prove suicidal maniacs ready to toss away cities and whole civilizations at a whim. The United States, soon after Vietnam, started working on an all-arms concept of deep penetration war called AirLand Battle. Soviet planners still imagined mighty drives to the Rhine in Germany, if not beyond. In coming years I'd cover a lot of military exercises, risking frostbite with Canadian units in northern Norway.

Also on my beat was Poland and the dissident movement Solidarity. This drama swung between grey auras of fear during the introduction of martial law and ecstatic jubilation covering the homecoming of the pope in 1983.

I didn't have to cover many royal events, which were the tedious side duty of reporters in London. I was not anti-monarchist, just not much interested. I marvelled at the stamina of the royals, particularly as the security around them grew tighter with the rising fear of terrorist attacks. It seemed only a matter of time before something happened, especially after a drunken intruder broke into Buckingham Palace and entered the Queen's bedroom.

By fall I'd had a chance to catch my breath, settle into London, and get caught up with old friends. Most Fridays when free, I went to dinner parties given by an old mate from my previous reporting days in England, Gavin Weightman. He was now a TV producer of documentaries on social issues and the making of modern London, and he became an invaluable guide to the best bookshops and literary events when I needed escape from news. A woman I dated for a while introduced me to poetry readings, which I enjoyed. I also found the right shops to buy the safari suits common among foreign correspondents, feeling only vaguely like a poseur.

To find quiet time to reflect on events and life, I sometimes sought out the quiet escape of nearby churches. One was the amazing All Saints on Margaret Street, a High Victorian Gothic masterpiece of staunch Anglo-Catholic allegiance. Inside were dazzling stonework, gilded panelling, and nineteenth-century panels making it, according to writer Simon Jenkins, "England's most celebrated Victorian church." There, in the stillness broken only by a distant choir practice, I also caught a faint air of incense that made me wish for personal discoveries even deeper within.

INTERLUDE

One-on-One with Thatcher

While working in Britain during the tumultuous Thatcher years, I took solace in the fact I would not have to interview the Iron Lady herself. That opportunity was carefully doled out by Number 10 only to very senior media celebs. I had watched enough of these solo sessions to know the chance of humiliation was ever present. She could be coldly pleasant one moment, then, if mildly irritated, would give a thrust of the notorious verbal stiletto she was so proud of. Stab one might be "That is a very silly question," with a look of contempt. The second jab might dig even deeper: "It's quite clear you've never even read my speech." And it wasn't just the media. She could be equally roasting when she met with foreign leaders.

My peace was shattered one afternoon in May 1984 when a manager in our office informed me and producer Tony Burman that we were to show up next morning at Number 10 for our requested interview with the prime minister. "Huh?" we gasped. "What interview? It must be a mistake. We didn't request one."

The only detail we had from her office was that Thatcher was going to do four sit-downs with three US and one Canadian network before her upcoming trip to North America. But no CBC show knew anything about a request for an interview. "How bloody embarrassing," I raged. "We'll get there and be turned away, in front of everybody, as Canadian gatecrashers." Burman shrugged. "Well, we can hardly phone back to say CBC flatly refuses to come over, so we'll go."

I dropped everything to prep, and at the appointed time we entered the historic door of Number 10 Downing Street. After rigorous security checks, we were led to the back garden, rarely seen by the public, where interviewers and producers were gathering by a shared-camera setup. It was immediately clear from the chatter that the others were all from morning shows, and Number 10 staffers were coordinating live roll times.

"You're going fourth. What's your show's roll time?" a staffer asked us. "CBC has no live morning show, and therefore no roll time to worry about," Burman said, calmly. Shocked looks followed as staffers huddled. We were about to be exposed, I thought, and the fact it was their screwup was little comfort. Burman whispered the likely explanation: "They must have sent us CTV's invite by mistake, meant for their *Canada AM* morning show."

"Let's just roll with it. Do it as if live, with cues and all," I suggested, just as the craggy-faced, glowering figure of Thatcher's press officer, Bernard Ingham, bore down on us. Thatcher called him "tough, blunt, humourless," high praise from her, while media characterizations favoured "an obnoxious rent-a-spleen" and the "Yorkshire Rasputin."

"This will run when?" he growled, likely imagining how his unforgiving boss would take such a foul-up.

"We'll be showing it through the day on many shows, and likely over several days," Burman replied, somehow keeping a straight face. Ingham gave us a sour grimace and stomped away. I took my place in line with the other interviewers as the prime minister emerged, smiling pleasantly, to take her garden chair beside a wide-branched tree.

The first two interviews, quite short, went well, with no unpleasantness. The start of the third, however, was delayed when falling buds from the tree caused Thatcher to cough. As they continued, the interviewer leaned over with a concerned expression and suggested, "Try a sip of water." Irritation flared over Thatcher's face at such impertinence. Still, she sipped, recovered, and plunged on.

Now my turn. I breathed deeply and slipped into my chair pretending cool confidence, hoping like hell she wouldn't ask after consulting her hand notes, "So, CTV, is it?" Instead, she smiled briefly and flashed a "let's get it over with" look. I quickly glanced at Burman, nodded as if getting a signal to roll, and began the interview, pausing for five seconds in the middle to get another "cue" from Burman. Our chat ran about seven minutes, and I survived without a verbal stiletto as we discussed economic summits and Canada-UK relations. Later we had to lobby puzzled CBC shows to take the interview. Years later when I looked at it, I found it frankly dull.

If it was a mix-up with CTV, we never knew. We weren't about to call their London office to suggest they stop waiting for the Thatcher interview: "We got her instead. Not sure why."

My friend and CBC anchor Peter Mansbridge was not so lucky, as he describes in his book *Off the Record*. In his interview with Thatcher during her 1993 book tour, after she left office, he endured "a parade of verbal slaps in the face." Although he had read her book from beginning to end, the jabs still came.

I wonder what she would have said to me if I'd simply begun with the words, "Prime Minister, I don't think I am who you think I am, and I'm not sure why I'm sitting here."

8

Beirut Furies and Fascination

Lebanon is a country you could fall in love with even at a time of war, and I was easily seduced in September 1983. Driving north to Beirut on the coastal highway from Israel, you travelled along the rock-ribbed shore of ancient Phoenicia and through the narrow lowland of fruit farms, orchards, and small settlements that rose sharply into legendary Mount Lebanon, the collective name for the row of peaks ranged parallel to the sea along the length of Lebanon. Contested for over five millennia, the land was drenched in history and in the glittering blue-green light of the Mediterranean.

In the Old Testament, Lebanon was held in awe for its trees and mountainous beauty. Its position midway up the eastern edge of the sea—the Levant—made it a major east-west trading hub, the best link between the Mediterranean world and India and Asia, even before the empires of Egypt, Greece, Persia, Carthage, and Rome. I passed by the five-thousand-year-old port of Tyre, which Homer would have known, and the equally fabled harbour of Sidon. Not far on, when I caught my first distant sight of Beirut, I gasped to my crew, "My God, there it is," the way you might exclaim on seeing your first view of Rio, the Nile, or Mount Kilimanjaro. This awe eased the tension I felt entering a dangerous land. Set on a headland jutting out into the sea, yet three-quarters ringed by mountains, Beirut seemed highlighted, mirage-like in a whitish-grey glow. This was the city the world had swooned over only a decade before, when it was still a tourist magnet as well as the economic, diplomatic, and intellectual centre of the Arab world. Its Western facade led to the label "Paris of the East," while mountainous Lebanon was hailed as "Switzerland on the Med."

Of course, the vision was a trick of sea-light and my own anticipation, for the closer we came, the more reality set in. Now, in the seventh year of war, the city was frayed and battered to hell. It was still striking, the image of resilience, but the southern suburbs were filled with rubble and rotting refuse, while the artistically cherished inner quarters and old souks were reduced to stone ruins and weeds. The once glittering business and luxury hotel towers near the seafront had been heavily scarred or fully gutted by waves of shelling and militia firefights. As we passed the international airport, I caught my first glimpse of the sandbag dugouts and armoured vehicles of the US Marine base, quiet at that moment but increasingly exchanging shell fire with rebel militias commanding the overlooking foothills and mountains beyond. The fact that busy life still continued within the jumble of remaining buildings was a proud but grim reminder that cities take a lot of killing.

On the way up the coast, I'd seen many signs of accumulated war damage, especially from the year before when Israel pushed its invasion of southern Lebanon right into the heavily populated suburbs of Beirut's western, Muslim section. The assault was aimed at driving the Palestine Liberation Organization (PLO) out of Lebanon and at strengthening an alliance with the Christian forces in East Beirut, but the main outcome was to further destabilize the long-fractured country. The Beirut siege lasted over two months, with air assaults plus shelling from land, sea, and mountains. The death toll was so shocking that President Ronald Reagan phoned Israeli prime minister Menachem Begin to demand that the potential "holocaust" be stopped.

The 1982 invasion, which encouraged, first, Syria to expand its own invasion lines within Lebanon and, second, the Christian militia to massacre hundreds of Palestinians in the city's Sabra and Shatila refugee districts, was the worst single catastrophe of the war, but not the only one in a country that seemed bent on national suicide. The term "Lebanonization" came to mean a country's disintegration—political, ethnic, religious, and class—to the point where social cohesion crumbled and the state was left ungovernable. Nowadays, we say "failed states." Reporters struggled with how to get stories out safely and with the challenge of figuring out who was fighting whom, and why.

In the barest outline, Lebanon was part of the Ottoman (Turkish) Empire until that realm collapsed after the First World War. It was then occupied by France. While the population's basic divide was between Christian and Muslim, the sharp differences among mountains, valleys, and shoreline encouraged strong, separate communities. Christians dominated in northern mountain strongholds, and Beirut was home to Maronite Christian, Greek Orthodox, and smaller Protestant groups. Muslims included the Sunnis in Beirut and Shiites in the south. The Druze, an offshoot of Islam but long a separate faith, held traditional mountain strongholds southeast of Beirut. When France left in 1945, it regarded Lebanon as a Christian redoubt in the Middle East and used the census of 1932 to establish lines of power in Parliament: Christians would pick the president; Sunnis, the prime minister; and Shiites, the speaker.

Theoretically, that plan might change under a new census, but, given the explosive stakes, no new census was permitted. Even as Muslim numbers soared, Christians clung to power. Numbers became even more unbalanced after more than three hundred thousand Palestinian refugees poured in following Israeli independence in 1948 and a failed uprising in Jordan in 1970–71. Unrest increased as the PLO and other Palestinian factions used Lebanon as a base for attacks on Israel, which brought inevitable retaliation and undermined

Lebanon's weak central authority. Soon other factions—Christian, Muslim, Druze—spawned their own competitive militia and sought informal alliances with other nations ready to assist with supplies of arms. Private armies became a Lebanese speciality, even as the tiny, ill-trained military was viewed as a "cabaret army," good for the odd parade but little else.

The fatal danger grew through the economically promising sixties and early seventies, when oil money inflows and soaring tourism encouraged visions of a tolerant and democratic Lebanon. The role of Beirut as an exile nest for various rebel causes and foreign spies added a spicy air of intrigue. Then, after war erupted in 1975, an estimated fifteen different militias took up arms, struggling for domination within their own communities, and cut the country into pieces. Beirut was divided into east and west by a Green Line that saw periods of ferocious fighting and almost daily sniping attacks.

The Christian community, believing it was fighting for its very existence, struggled to keep control of the government, while the dominant private Christian militia—the "Lebanese Forces"—was controlled by the right-wing Phalangist Party (Kataeb), inspired in 1936 by Italian and Spanish fascist movements.

Among Muslim groups, militias were diverse and frequently clashed. The wide class divide between rich and poor in Lebanon spawned extreme leftist militias as well. In the era of the Cold War, the struggle to reshape so strategic a nation turned many warring factions into proxies for outside powers: Arab nations and the Soviet bloc poured support into Muslim and leftist causes; Western nations sought to shore up the central government; and Israel sent arms and expertise to Christian Lebanon and the Lebanese Forces in hope of establishing a regional ally against its enemies.

Within Lebanon, militias constantly forged and broke alliances. In writer Jean Said Makdisi's words: "Yesterday's allies are today's enemies; yesterday's enemies are in close conference today. Yesterday's hero has become today's villain, and yesterday's villain, today's martyr." A sickening characteristic of the conflict was the propensity for massacres. Sabra and Shatila were the worst areas in terms of numbers, but not unique in fury. As correspondent Jonathan Randal wrote in *The Tragedy of Lebanon*, his history of the fighting: "In Lebanon it is not who you want to massacre, it's who you can."

I was heading to cover a whole new round of horror breaking out in the Chouf Mountains east and south of Beirut. The Mountain War had erupted as Israel began withdrawing from its invasion lines to regroup closer to its border, and the abrupt vacuum pitted Christian Lebanese Forces against a Druze-led coalition army, supported by Syria, along with some Shiite and Palestinian units. This Christian-Druze conflict was ultimately for the domination of the mountains overshadowing Beirut, and thus for the city itself and control of government. The militias were well armed, with machine guns, mortars, rockets, heavy artillery, and even some armoured units. The struggle entailed ethnic cleansing that would see more than two hundred thousand villagers fleeing for their lives. Even during our drive into Lebanon, the road was frequently blocked by swarms of refugees. One man rapped on our window and warned us of a total "lack of social conscience." Wagging a finger like some Old Testament scholar, he cautioned, "There will be massacres!"

To further complicate matters and make it a major news story, Beirut was aflame again, and a multinational peacekeeping force composed of US, French, Italian, and British soldiers was dragged into the violence. That thirteen-hundred-strong US Marine mission dug in around the airport came under daily attack by Druze and Shiite militias, who saw them as favouring the Christians. Fearing the nation was approaching total anarchy, the United States and allies were preparing a mass evacuation of foreigners by sea. The US Sixth Fleet sailed much of its massive force to patrol the coast off Beirut, with naval guns and carrier fighter bombers standing by to attack

Druze positions if needed. Harried diplomats and the media speculated that evacuation might begin within days—in which case, our crew suggested, I would check into the city just in time to wade out to sea in a mini-Dunkirk exit.

I did not know at the time, but, as I was approaching Beirut, two Canadian journalists I had looked forward to seeing were caught between the lines in the mountains, under fire and with their transport destroyed. Only one would survive. The US ABC network had sent two camera teams up to the Druze town of Kfar Matta in the Chouf. They included Brian Kelly, a Canadian-born cameraman with ABC's London bureau and one of the best professionals I knew. On earlier assignments, I'd met Clark Todd, CTV's London bureau chief, a lively companion and raconteur.

Other organizations regarded Kfar Matta as far too explosive to enter because the Israelis were pulling out and Christian forces were forming to attack. The CBC's *Journal* reporter in Beirut, Ann Medina, was known for her daring coverage, but she flatly refused to take a crew there for fear of a massacre. Indeed, when the poorly defended town was attacked by Christian Lebanese Forces, the ABC crew was pinned down under heavy mortar and rocket fire. After hours of shelling, they took their chance to flee, but a round exploded nearby, and as they dove for the ground almost simultaneously Clark was hit by a sniper round near his heart. Kelly helped drag him into a nearby dwelling, where, as hours passed, Todd slid toward death as shelling intensified. He insisted the others leave and try to break out before they were killed. They resisted, but he handed Kelly his wedding ring and passport, saying, "Tell Anne [his wife] and the children I love them." Kelly heard him gasp, "The crazy thing is no one's ever heard of Kfar Matta. It's not the death that scares me. It's the embarrassment."

The team felt helpless. As was standard at the time, they had been given no training in war zone survival or medicine, and no helmets or armoured vests (which might have saved Todd)—an indication of how poorly prepared news teams were for war coverage. "My only thought was to survive," Kelly wrote later in an unpublished manuscript, "and I didn't have a clue how to do that." What followed was a terrifying flight down wooded areas, avoiding militia patrols.

When my crew arrived at Beirut's Commodore Hotel, the foreign media's main quarters, the first person I saw at the entrance was Ann Medina, awaiting transport. She was part of a combined news effort to push the Red Cross to search for the missing news team. I checked in and raced to the CBC's makeshift office to alert the London and Toronto offices that I was in place to start reporting. My producer, Tony Burman, and I began making plans to cover both the drama in the city and the war in the mountains, including the constant fear of massacres. This would have been a challenge on our own, but the networks formed alliances in the field, and we shared visual resources with CBS and an Australian broadcaster.

Next day while I was in the lobby, cheers broke out when Brian Kelly walked in. Badly shaken, he told me about the still missing Todd and raced back into the mountains to join the search. It was a week before the Red Cross was able to enter the town and find Todd's body. The incomplete details released over months by management cast an unfair shadow on Kelly by implying he was alone with Todd, rather than part of a team. Fellow journalists believed him blameless, as did Todd's family. Still, twenty years later, Kelly's flashbacks triggered a mental collapse linked to post-traumatic stress disorder, although with therapy he recovered to continue as one of the most admired cameramen in the business.

There was no time to acclimatize to a city at war. The first night the windows of my room rattled as the Marines' heavy 155 mm howitzers blasted out replies to Druze rocket fire. I planned to head for the base in the morning: the fate of Beirut and the US base under fire were the top crisis news story. I wasn't complaining: I had always yearned to be in a ringside seat to history, and here I was.

The US Marine base beside the airport lay in the war-battered southern outskirts of the city. To get there, along with Burman and a two-man crew, was a nerve-racking race in our marked van along the coastal road, passing the Marines' Green Beach landing zone for troops and supplies, which would become evacuation central if needed. Vehicles making this run were watched closely by militia spotters, snipers, and Marines in guard posts, so our driver put his foot to the floor just in case.

My impression entering the base was that it looked like the film set for a Vietnam War epic bizarrely located near the luscious Mediterranean Sea. Overhead, helicopter gunships thudded to and fro as Marines in camouflage combat gear, including Vietnam-era pot helmets, went about their duties. The troops looked calmly businesslike, but the air seemed thick with the anticipation that action could happen any moment. Our military escort stressed that if he dove for cover, we should instantly do the same: "No questions, just do as I do!"

I've generally found Marines to be well trained, proud of the Corps, and hospitable to foreign media—far more so than the French and British units. It was well known, however, that they hated playing peacekeepers where there was no peace to be had, required to respond with minimal fire to attacks from enemies they knew nothing about. Their commander, Colonel Tim Geraghty, looked hardwired for action but stressed the need for restraint to the higher command, knowing the danger of being drawn into the Lebanese vortex. That was the key point in stories now: the base had little chance of a positive outcome, but an enormous potential to be a monster failure. The Marines were hunkered down in part because Washington did not know how to finesse a way out without reviving memories of the fall of Saigon. When I asked the soldiers their view, they always replied, using the epithet with pride, "I'm just a grunt, sir—that other stuff is for higher-ups."

A well-meaning peace effort initially, the mission was now tasked with shoring up the much-hated government by training the official Lebanese Army. To Muslim and Druze factions, that support amounted to taking the Christian side in the civil war, so the base faced threats on three sides: to the south, Sunni militia were potential foes; directly east, along a front of suburban hills and nearby mountains, were the approaching Druze and Syrian positions; and due north, amid a maze of poor suburban housing, were the powerful Shiite militia Amal, highly influenced by Iran's anti-American passion. Already there were artillery duels with the Druze and frequent firefights with Amal, and it was only going to get worse.

When we toured the perimeter, the danger of Shiite ambushes seemed as real as Druze shelling. Our Marine lieutenant guide drove us in a Jeep to visit the perimeter bunkers, but before setting out he slapped rounds into his M16 and pistol, casually instructing us, "If we come under fire, jump out on the side opposite the fire and do whatever I say." At one of the bunkers the canvas roof was shredded with shrapnel from an artillery round that had killed two Marines the day before. One of the survivors came up to chat and handed me a small piece of metal: "A souvenir, sir, from the attack."

We were at the base for some heavy shelling, watching from atop one of the five-storey unoccupied concrete buildings. We witnessed how the main fire-control teams operated with ground radar that picked up where incoming rounds had been fired from. An alarm would send Marines across the base rushing for cover before the Druze rockets and mortar rounds slammed in. I worried our position on the roof was highly exposed, but it was the best chance to see all the action. Marine sniper teams kept watch on neighbourhood suburban buildings for opposing shooters, commenting on what distant men with guns were doing. "Guy here is aiming at the highway, no targets I can see," one said; another noted, "This one is following a moving target . . . Bastard! He just shot a cat—all for fun." Then a sniper team spotted a uniformed figure hiding in deep bushes outside the base, spying on the troops through binoculars. "How about we just put a new crease in his butt?" one asked. Permission denied.

Was he Druze, a Shiite, or from some other faction? One shot could escalate yet another miniwar.

The war was never distant. At night, with the city largely darkened by power cuts, I could watch from the Commodore Hotel's roof the flicker of tracer bullets zipping between building blocks and the slow arc of rockets fired into the dark mountains or between East and West Beirut. Occasionally a powerful car bomb would shake the downtown district. The Commodore had recently been hit by a rocket that shattered several rooms. Longtimers covering the war advised us to sleep with our US dollars in one sock, passport in the other, in case the hotel was demolished in the night and we survived. Although I knew the hotel paid handsomely in protection money to local factions, I instinctively looked for cubbyholes to hide in throughout the building in case we were overrun.

The growing naval buildup offshore now included a French carrier fleet. Many civilians continued to depart along the northern road to Syria and Damascus or on the ferry to Cyprus. One morning, halfway along our shoreline drive to the Marine base, tall columns of water suddenly leapt high in the air as a barrage of shells landed. Our convoy of three vehicles pulled in beside a vacant building where there were ditches. A mortar round screamed in, exploding with a prolonged *blaaammm*. More shells followed and, with my face in a ditch, I marvelled at the way each blast sent up minute puffs of earth. The metallic sound of shrapnel and shell parts clanging against concrete pavement jarred me with thoughts of what they'd do to one's inside. As we ran for cover toward a Marine guard post, I was reminded, absurdly, of scenes in the war comics of my youth, Johnny Canuck and G.I. Joe. We were all rattled, but we shook off the dust and continued about our day, anticipating a few extra drinks at the bar that night.

Journalists who ventured into suburbs or up into the contested mountain roads routinely returned with accounts of close misses or hostile gunmen, reminding us of what civilians, most of whom wanted no part of war, faced continually as they struggled to survive. We planned our trips as carefully as possible in this turbulent environment, carrying different media passes in Arabic from various militia and making sure on approaching a checkpoint to pull out only the right one. We were also wary of criminal elements that looked to steal or kidnap for profit.

Probably no city of the modern era had faced more predictions of doom than Beirut, yet we grew increasingly sentimental about its lacerated charms. Despite years of destruction, it remained well populated. Many shops, restaurants, and small businesses strained valiantly to stay open, university classes remained lively, the newspaper presses rolled, radios blared news and catchy Mideast music, nightclubs faced down the dangers of the dark hours, and people remained remarkably well dressed. Good manners prevailed, but under the surface, nerves were stretched taut and a black market in tranquilizers flourished.

In the nearby Mountain War, Christian attacks on towns were matched by Druze offensives. Thousands of Christians fearing mass killings fled the major town of Bhamdoun, strategically close to the road to Damascus and the famed resort town of Aley. Fighting was heavy, but as it waned, we approached the smoking ruins, where the smell of death lingered. While we collected footage, I came across a badly disfigured corpse bound by rope. Our Druze guide caught my attempt to alert our cameraman and ordered us away.

As we left the town, we pulled over onto a roadside stop to get a shot of the beautiful view toward the coast. When I went to the rear of the van to help with equipment, my heart stopped—an unexploded mortar shell stuck out of the sand, maybe eight centimetres from our right tire track. Hitting it would have blown us to shreds. A day later, we stopped at another point for my stand-up, overlooking some of the contested mountain sites across a wide valley. I was just stepping before the lens when a car screeched to a halt and the driver yelled, "Get out of there! Armoured cars across the way have been firing at anyone stopping here!"

Later that day in Beirut's southern suburbs, as we were led to firing points by a local militia, our guide warned that we would have to run past a five-metre gap in a collapsed wall to beat an enemy sniper. "Short run, no problem," he assured us. As we sprinted, we realized how long a few seconds can seem when you're a potential target. Though often subject to fear, I found such action a bit exhilarating as well, preferable to the gnawing dread I experienced whenever I drove along streets, once full of life, where emptiness reigned. One such stretch between two hostile factions in Beirut's southern suburbs usually took, by my nervous count, twenty-seven seconds at regular speed. Decades later, memories of that road are still unpleasantly vivid.

The Commodore lobby and bar provided a brisk market for exchanging news tips and safety cautions. Early on, Burman and I were bemoaning that we couldn't get to the ancient Chouf town of Deir al-Qamar, once a Crusader mountain stronghold and now a crisis hotspot as some twenty thousand Christians crowded its relief camps. Diplomats, fearing an unprecedented massacre would evaporate the last fragile efforts at peace talks, desperately sought a mass evacuation. It seemed cut off from the world, only forty kilometres from Beirut yet near impossible for journalists to reach. Overhearing us, a young French photographer sauntered over and whispered, "I just got back hours ago and can show you the route I took. Seems passable, for now." He gave us a briefing with maps, local Druze posts to check in with, and side roads to avoid.

Setting out early next morning with Burman, our crew, and driver, I was too sleepy to talk much when suddenly there was a sharp *crack* just above our car. The driver hit maximum speed and threw us into a zigzag motion. "What the hell," Burman gasped. "Are we under fire?" "No problem," the driver predictably muttered, but clearly the shot had been aimed our way, either a sniper's near miss or his morning warm-up shot for practice.

Driving into the Chouf, I felt the relief of fresher air among the forested heights as we broke free of Beirut's thick humidity. Before the war, the area had been a tourist retreat, with lush valleys, thick pines, and distant views of the shimmering sea. But, as we rounded a curve, we encountered another checkpoint, manned by glaring young militiamen demanding passes and passports as they inspected our TV gear. Canadian nationality often helped us but not always. "Canadians—we know you're just Americans in disguise, yeah?" was thrown at us once. "No, we are here to cover your brave efforts. That's why your leaders gave us these passes." This time we were waved on and finally reached the last Druze military post about five hundred metres from Deir al-Qamar and its thousands of Christian refugees. A captain gave us a warning: "Advance slowly along the road, but do not look back or to the sides." Tapping his binoculars, he added, "We'll be watching you the whole way and, if you look around, God help you!" Heading forward across the short no-man's-land, our heads were firmly set forward, but out of the corner of my eye I made out the grotesque figure of a decaying corpse wrapped in transparent plastic.

Entering the square, which some claim is the most beautiful in the Middle East, ringed by stone palaces and the religious sites revered by both Christians and Druze, we met refugees beseeching us for cigarettes and news. As we toured refugee sites, I found the mood nervous but steady—food rationing and health services were disciplined, and aid agencies and local officials had worked hard to keep hopes high. As always when visiting endangered refugee sites, I was dogged by a feeling of helplessness at being just a witness. We conducted interviews, filmed relevant scenes, and set off back to Beirut. I had a feeling, given the stakes involved, that an evacuation was still possible, but my report emphasized the dangers to so many people and the consequences if talks failed. It would be months before a truce permitted evacuation, straining relief efforts to near breaking point.

By late September the Druze were pushing hard to take all the foothills and mountains overlooking Beirut. The Christian (Phalange) militia fought to hang on to their positions and had new support as the government, fearing collapse, ordered the official, nonsectarian Lebanese Armed Forces to fire on Druze positions. At the same time, the Druze duel with the Marines was so threatening that two US warships joined in with their 5-inch guns. Day and night, mortars and artillery shells blasted back and forth along the landward rim of the city. Even seemingly quiet areas could hold nasty surprises: once, doing a stand-up in a cemetery, I was sent diving for cover when a shot cracked close overhead.

We set out daily to shoot footage that might make sense of the many separate battles. Cameraman Philippe Billard, who later captured amazing footage in Ethiopia's famine, was calm, urbane, and elegant in every situation. Soundman Matti Lansoo, a free spirit from British Columbia, had just signed on and was still learning the basics of field recording. That might have been a serious drawback, but his remarkable wacky sense of humour and unflappable good spirits made him a godsend in times of stress.

Like other TV crews, we would visit, when possible, the people firing those mortar and howitzer shells. "Bang-bang" combat footage is an inevitable part of war coverage. It may seem repetitious, but crews do their best to portray the reality of war. What bothered me most was that some of the firing done at gun emplacements visited by TV crews or photojournalists was for media show—a sort of brand advertising for militias hungry for an international audience. One morning we pulled over on a hillside outside Beirut where one of the Lebanese Armed Forces mortar crews were taking a break between lobbing shells toward Druze villages in the Chouf. Their leader gave us a cheery smile, motioned us to set up our camera, and, grabbing a new shell, checked the mortar's aim for firing. I was horrified to think that, somewhere, a mortar might soon be crashing into a town square or schoolhouse for the sake of a five-second shot on CBC national news. I motioned him to stop and, through our interpreter, told him we wanted to see only the preparation part but no firing. He looked dumbfounded and disappointed, but complied with a trace of a sneer. It shook me to see again how easy it is to step over a moral line in war, when the deadly becomes routine.

The work was hard and the hours long. I wrote the stories, and Burman oversaw editing and logistics. Without satellite communication, we had to get everything ready for a late afternoon taxi run to Damascus, or a feed point to the south in Israel, which we referred to in code as "Dixie" to avoid trouble from militias. I enjoyed the comradeship of others living life on the edge, and I was still smitten by that urban marvel of Beirut set between mountains and sea. Most residents loathed the war, but here it was, intruding on every aspect of society, feeding on divisions so deep no power appeared able to contain the fury. Journalist Robert Fisk, writing after three decades based there, concluded: "Warm and gentle Beirut may be. But tough and cruel."

Even with an armada offshore, Beirut had a rugged seaside flair, with its salt-tinged air, beaches, bluffs, and limestone Pigeon Rocks islands just offshore. The inhabitants had an extraordinary work ethic, keeping repair and rebuilding efforts going throughout most of the fighting. As truce talks spluttered on, there was great friendliness when people had a chance to show their better side amid short lulls in the fighting. Then life would gush back to seeming normal, and families emerged to enjoy the famed waterfront.

I enjoyed life at the Commodore, and, in retrospect, many who worked there regarded it as the greatest media war-zone hotel ever. Whatever the turmoil outside, management was tireless in serving media needs, paying off potential attackers, offering excellent restaurant and bar service, and somehow ensuring vital communications to the world. In the lobby, a glass cage held the phone for long-distance calls. That booth was our lifeline, and reporters had priority. I once saw the lobby manager sternly inform two Foreign Legionnaires from the French mission that they'd have to wait behind "Miss Ann Medina of Canada" to use the phone.

In the famous horseshoe-shaped bar, you could meet foreign correspondents who had covered conflicts from Algeria to Vietnam and all Mideast wars since Suez. Embassy attachés and academics also came to hear the latest rumours. War historians passed through and, helped by my long interest in military history, I had several useful chats with John Keegan, a leading historian on the psychology of battle.

The city had an infinite supply of characters. I featured "the man with the worst job in the world," Beirut's bomb disposal chief, who daily risked all to defuse unexploded shells and car bombs. He showed up with his young teenage son, who he boasted was keen to follow in his profession. Along with a story I got an enthusiastic course in bombs, booby traps, and the tricks of defusing.

Another time I did a feature on the lead architect working on the master plan for postwar Beirut. In his picturesque hillside studio overlooking the city, he kept me fascinated showing off his sketches and designs even as pillars of smoke from urban battles rose to join the haze over the city. The work seemed the epitome of futility, but I later treasured the moment for spurring my growing interest in the way societies can recover from the worst of war and catastrophe. This would become a major focus in my foreign reporting.

However much I threw myself into my Beirut work, I was still the CBC London correspondent, responsible for a vast beat, so I was rotated back every three weeks or so. I wanted to spend more time in Lebanon, where I felt history was being made that would affect the whole Middle East as well as the course of the Cold War. I also felt that the deep complexity of the conflict foreshadowed a new form of highly fragmented yet well-armed internal warfare swirling within a failed state, nourished by outside supporters and historic grievances, which becomes self-perpetuating. “Bellum omnium contra omnes,” the nightmare image of Thomas Hobbes's *Leviathan*, “the war of all against all.”

Compared with our US counterparts, we had remarkable autonomy on story choice. Burman and I had mutual veto over the degree of risk we'd face, which balanced out well: he had more grit and determination, while I provided the essential ballast of a nervous nature. Nowhere in Lebanon was really safe. A few days after my first rotation to London, producer John Owen, reporter Don Murray (in from his Paris bureau), and the crew were held up at gunpoint by a bandit who snatched their expensive camera and fired a warning shot near Owen. Later, a Druze patrol returned the camera, indicating the bandit had been summarily executed.

Even during my time back in London, it was impossible to shake the effect of Beirut. I had switched apartments to be closer to town, and on my first night back I was awakened by a powerful blast nearby. I shook my head, believing it a mere nightmare. In the morning, I learned it was a real terrorist bomb, planted in a newsagent's shop just blocks away. A few days later, I was awakened again, this time by a call from the office directing me to head back to Beirut immediately. The US Marine barracks had been blown apart by an immensely powerful truck bomb that killed 220 Marines of the 241 military personnel there. Some of those Marines had been so helpful and welcoming to me. When I arrived back, the frantic digging for victims was still in progress under floodlights, and the concrete building I'd known well was obliterated. I did stand-ups amid the glare of the rescue efforts, then raced to the Commodore to file. The bombing was a major international shock that no one had anticipated. Only much later was the Shiites' Hezbollah blamed. The era of terrorist mega-attacks, leading to 9/11 and beyond, was at hand.

In Beirut, there was much talk of how to improve one's survival chances. Was the Commodore, packed with Western media, an obvious prime target? Some reporters left, but most bet on the hotel management's proven survival skills. We could feel the escalation of war in our bones as the cacophony rose. As the Druze and Syrian shelling continued, the counterfire roared and US warships added hundreds more shells to the combined weight of US Marine and Lebanese Army bombardments. Under Reagan's orders, the United States fought more vigorously to shore up the Christian-dominated government, despite warnings from its allies that it could drag the West into a disastrous quagmire.

As always, the city adapted to the war's wheel of misfortune. Radio bulletins flashed like echoes through the city—Lebanese stations, BBC, Voice of America, Radio Monte Carlo, Radio Moscow. Once, when I developed an inflamed gum, the dentist crammed my mouth with padding and started digging and drilling. He stopped whenever a shell exploded near the neighbourhood. As I gagged in frustration, he reassured me: "Just a mortar, some ways off. No problem."

After the barracks bombing, the Marines were less welcoming to visitors, media included, so we focused more on local fighting campaigns and human rights abuses. The big story also involved, of course, the suffering of civilians. Once we arrived at the car bombing of a nine-storey apartment building that killed fifteen and injured over a hundred, where we taped a crying relative emerging on a ladder holding the limp body of a toddler, clearly dead as her head lolled backwards. The large crowd gathered below screamed with pure rage, demanding revenge and "jihad." As we withdrew it was difficult not to step on body parts. Our footage was widely circulated, but we were depressed by the thought that our role as witnesses could not bring peace or justice one minute closer. As usual, the perpetrators were never found.

I did not lose my urge to stay longer. Every day there were developments, and the drive to make sense of the madness increased. One morning the fleet offshore was joined by the biggest naval artillery puncher of all, the fifty-nine-thousand-ton USS *New Jersey*, the last serving battleship from the Second World War, whose nine 16-inch guns could fire twenty-seven-hundred-pound shells with a range of forty-two kilometres. It was supposed to be a major deterrent to Druze and Syrian artillery and was held in considerable awe. But that winter, when the *New Jersey* finally started firing the super guns in salvoes, they caused mostly civilian collateral damage and only further enflamed anti-American anger.

The longer we operated in Lebanon, the more the CBC won the respect of other international news organizations. When *The National* and *The Journal* combined resources to set up a temporary Beirut bureau for four months, I leapt at the chance to join. It was headed by the redoubtable Ann Medina, a star correspondent with a highly personalized broadcast style. She ran a complex bureau in the media hub of wartime Beirut, producing insightful documentaries for *The Journal*, while I handled the news side. Early on, she stunned CBS, our US partner in the field, by dropping it in favour of a new alliance with NBC—a far warmer and more cooperative team player. She also negotiated a suite of offices in the Commodore Annex, next to the hotel. She brought with her a parrot that sat on her desk next to her favourite teapot and never grew fazed or rattled, no matter the tense drama around us (see "Dangerous Doodles" interlude).

Serious battles beyond Beirut and the mountains also needed coverage. Just before Christmas, I went north to Lebanon's large city of Tripoli, where hundreds were dying in a war between competing Palestinian movements. The PLO, under its chairman Yasser Arafat, bombed out of Beirut by Israel the year before, had returned to other areas of the country and was now desperately trying to hang on in Tripoli with barely forty-five hundred war-weary soldiers against a combined assault by more numerous rebel Palestinian groups strongly backed by Syrian guns. For weeks the fighting had torn the city apart, and I arrived to cover Arafat's last stand before the PLO sailed again into exile. I managed to squeeze into Arafat's final meeting in Lebanon with journalists, huddled in a narrow street by his small headquarters. As always, Arafat smiled, looked triumphant in defeat, and seemed madly unrealistic about world support. I looked up to see three Israeli fighters flying reconnaissance, glinting silver at perhaps twelve thousand feet. What a chance, I thought, for a pilot to take out the hated Arafat, even if the horde around him became collateral damage. I later went to a hospital where several PLO fighters lay wounded. One fifty-year-old with a leg wound fought to hold back tears as he explained that his whole life had been a struggle, and now he had nothing left.

Next day, just before Arafat arrived to board one of the five Greek passenger cruise ships hired to take his army away, bedlam reigned. Several men fired automatic rifles skyward in defiance. A shoulder-fired rocket joined the cacophony, sending our driver diving under a truck for protection. More grenades were tossed in the harbour, seemingly to catch fish and for fun. Overhead, the expected Israeli fighters circled and watched, causing the PLO crew of an anti-aircraft gun to rip off a spray of tracers skyward, almost inviting an Israeli attack and causing us to dive for cover. Order was eventually enforced by the PLO's disciplined security squad, and an hour later we taped the departure of the PLO for foreign exile in various nations, protected by French warships and carrier air cover against a possible attack from Israel. One saga in the war had ended with the PLO vanquished, but Israel had no reason to celebrate as other, more dangerous, militia threats would soon rise to take its place—in particular, Iran-backed Hezbollah.

Lebanon is a small country, so racing back on the coastal highway from Tripoli to Beirut took less than two hours. We needed to hurry, not just to get our story out but because a new one was exploding only minutes from our office. Several militias in Muslim suburbs, especially the battle-hardened Shiite Amal force, were fighting furiously to throw back a government army drive to impose full control over the city—a reckless action by deluded Christian political leadership that was bound to fail, and did, after some of the heaviest urban fighting of the war. The crew and I spent some of Christmas Eve covering the latest fighting, sharing footage with our new NBC mates.

It was a tense Christmas Day: passions were so inflamed in West Beirut that an extreme Islamic faction threated to shoot at any visible signs of Christmas celebration. We felt a bit adrift, but as usual Medina rose to the occasion. After ensuring that the windows were well curtained, she provided a small Christmas tree and a sack of silly gifts for us to share—toy Jeeps, colouring books, and such. It was all great fun as we were crazy kids again. Someone joked we were like early Christians hiding in the Roman catacombs as they prayed. But I remember thinking that, throughout history, there have always been believers in a religion or a cause who could express their faith only in deep hiding.

I worked on through the winter, growing more pessimistic about Lebanon, where everything seemed to be getting worse despite the wonderful humanity of so many citizens. I needed a break, a return to the simple pleasures of normal life and some optimism about the future. I knew that covering traumatic events risked psychic scar tissue, but friends said they noticed little change except that I seemed distracted and a bit jittery at times. I was still enjoying the job and its often bizarre mix of experiences—that feeling of covering history-making events.

I left Beirut in late spring to return to my London base and new assignments. That June I took the chance to cover Pope John Paul II's flights to and from his first visit ever to Canada. I used the fourteen days in between for vacation in Montreal. Even there I couldn't quite escape Lebanon: I passed a brick wall with the painted message, "Blood of Beirut I flow with you." I soon lost myself, however, in reunions with friends and in efforts to revive a romance with a wonderful woman who was ready to consider long-distance dating.

I returned to London to start planning a major swing into Africa, particularly the anti-apartheid struggle in South Africa as the Free Mandela campaign gathered growing global support. However, doing the rounds of international aid agencies in London, I was also picking up early warnings of a possibly catastrophic drought and famine in remote Northern Ethiopia, where civil war also raged. We started a steady campaign to gain a visa for that area, a weak long shot because foreign TV crews had been firmly excluded.

Then, one morning in September, Burman raced into the office exclaiming he had got them—visas!—and we were going to Ethiopia. From that moment my life changed in ways I could not have imagined.

Covering that famine in 1984, so monstrous a mass killer it shocked the world, and meeting with Birhan Woldu and her family left me shaken to the core even as the experience became a pinnacle of my career as a foreign correspondent. But I have already told that story in the opening chapter, so chapter 9 recounts how both growing success and the inner damage clung to me as I moved still deeper into the great swirl of world news in the 1980s.

INTERLUDE

Dangerous Doodles

When veteran correspondents gather for dinner, the chatter often turns from personal highlights to their memorably stupid mistakes. Some are funny; many not.

Everyone knows of a war correspondent who took a road he was warned to avoid and was never seen again. Or crews that arranged a stand-up without first checking it was not in a line of fire. Or a reporter, convinced he had trustworthy sources in a dangerous militia, who ended up kidnapped.

Some blunders can be expected when working in unfamiliar hostile territory while sleep-deprived and distracted, but they can get you and those around you beaten up, abducted, or killed. I thought I was too cautious to act stupidly in the field, but then I let my guard down and a doodle I'd made on a map almost did me in.

While covering the war in Beirut, I'd spent time at the US Marine base that was under daily rocket fire from rebels in the overlooking mountains. I also followed speculation that a far larger US landing force would deploy to protect the evacuation by sea of foreign nationals. What defence lines, with artillery, would be needed? How long a stretch of beach must be held? That kind of war-gaming had long interested me.

Back in my hotel room, too restless to read, I'd sometimes pull out my map of Beirut and surroundings and start doodling in my best estimate of the major evacuation operation. I sketched likely defensive lines and firing posts in the foothills, showed where armour units could expand the defended beachfront, sketched in likely helicopter landing sites for Marine commandos, and added symbols for the US fleet's offshore covering fire. It wasn't everyone's idea of relaxing artwork, but to understand, you had to be there.

Once finished, I put the refolded map in with some research papers I intended to take back to my London bureau. I forgot about it as I continued to cover the war.

Weeks later the fighting had become even worse in the mountains beyond Beirut as Druze, Syrian, and Palestinian forces fought artillery duels with the Marines and bloody hillside combat with Christian militia, who their opponents believed were supported by the Americans. Inevitably, rebel fury over US fire from land, sea, and air was intense, so suspected US spies could expect no mercy. Many US crews wisely avoided the rebel areas, and even our CBC presence drew increased suspicion and closer searches at roadblocks and a few taunts that we were just Americans in disguise.

One afternoon when our van was stopped at a checkpoint manned by gunmen from a hard-line faction allied with the Druze and Syrians, we knew we were in for a tough search. We piled out displaying our best "jolly Canuck" smiles, which were met by glowering pat-downs and barked orders to open everything up for inspection.

I was impressed by their expertise: every book had pages flipped, tape cassettes were inspected one by one, and all electronic gear was probed for suspicious parts. The contents of our overnight bags were dumped out on the ground.

Nearing the end of the search, I was standing by the front passenger door and, glancing down at the map-holder, I was stunned to see my doodled-on map prominently resting there. The earth swayed, and shock waves rattled my entire being. They had already opened the driver's maps, and surely they would do the same to mine.

There was no way I'd be able to convince them my sketched battlefield positions were not the work of a US agent. I could argue they were mere doodles—"Hey, all for fun, guys!"—but almost certainly I'd be taken away and subjected to torture, long imprisonment, or a quick death. My poor innocent crew might be dragged off as well.

Suddenly, the officer in charge noticed several other vehicles that had drawn up and were waiting to be searched. After a quick consultation, the roadblock gunmen told us to go on and turned their attention elsewhere. It was that close.

I've always wondered how the map got into the van. Perhaps a crew member saw it and innocently took it along. Or perhaps I was distracted enough one day to grab it by mistake on the way out. Regardless, it was an act of inexcusable stupidity on my part.

9

Greed, Grievance, and Generosity

Back at my London base in the mid-1980s, as the CBC poured unprecedented amounts of money into foreign news and documentaries, there were plenty of big stories and historic moments to chase and feed by satellite back to Canada. "Feed the bird; feed the bird!" harried news teams mockingly chirped as they raced to shoot, write, edit, and uplink reports to the bird in outer space. To keep my perspective in balance, I found my love of history a lifeline to reality.

The study of decades has always fascinated me—news viewed in hindsight and corralled as the Roaring Twenties or the Dirty Thirties. But how to label the often glitzy, fragmented, schizophrenic 1980s? The age of greed, or grievance—or even generosity?

Some observers focused on the mania for consumerism and financial investment spurred on by the dominance of Reagan and Thatcher free-market economics and epitomized by the phrase "Greed is good," taken from the film *Wall Street*. Most tellingly, the sixties Yippie activist Jerry Rubin had morphed by then into a multimillionaire capitalist. "Politics and rebellion distinguished the '60s," he wrote in a *New York Times* article as the new decade began. "Money and financial interests will capture the passions of the '80s."

From my vantage point, however, generosity on an unprecedented scale became the defining characteristic of the times. Bob Geldof's Live

Aid concert in June 1985 helped to mobilize a whole new generation of youth in humanitarian efforts, from fighting famine to the campaign for human rights. Though seen as the pinnacle, the concert was only the most spectacular event of a longer-term phenomenon that saw the rise of thousands of NGOs across the globe and made humanitarianism, according to the World Bank, "one of the world's largest growth areas." Never before in peacetime had so many people given so much to so many.

However, grievance came in many forms. I remember the eighties as a decade filled with political and social animosities that often turned violent. In Britain, the largest industrial dispute of the postwar era pitted the striking National Union of Mineworkers in a brutal battle of wills against the Thatcher government; the astonishing escalation of soccer riots made British fans the scourge of Europe; and major urban race riots, along with the continuing IRA bombing campaign, resulted in a seemingly irradicable state of conflict and stress. Across Europe, similar grief led to the fragmentation of furious movements of the far left and far right as they increasingly clashed violently with other factions and the police. Then, before the decade ended, came the ultimate drama, the thunderous collapse of the Soviet Union's hold over Eastern Europe. The shock waves are still enraging the Kremlin and shaking confidence in the stability of Europe.

The impact of Britain's miners' strike of 1984–85 is hard to overestimate. The turmoil threatened the traditional way of life in communities around the coalfields and, for almost a year, left the country's economic direction unclear and challenged the survival of Thatcherism itself. Margaret Thatcher and union president Arthur Scargill fought with an intensity that gave no quarter, seeking the crushing and total defeat of the other. The struggle mesmerized the nation, as Thatcher's steely political will battled big union muscle. Surging phalanxes of angry miners clashed with truncheon-wielding police ranks, leading to thousands of arrests.

British political fortunes had long been dominated by the ability of giant unions, especially in the nationalized power and transport sector, to fatally weaken both Conservative and Labour governments—and Thatcher was determined to destroy this power. With their walkouts in 1972 and 1974, the miners had helped to topple Edward Heath's Conservatives from power. Five years later, another wave of strikes caused a "winter of discontent" that led to the defeat of the Labour government. Although, ironically, this election brought the hard-line Thatcher to power, union kingpins were confident she too would have to bend to their demands. Thatcher, however, more confident than ever after the Falklands victory, moved to break the union's power first. Coal might still dominate UK energy sources, but offshore oil and nuclear plants were coming online, enabling Thatcher to insist that long-profitable pits be closed. She knew the first tranche of twenty pit shutdowns, at a cost of twenty thousand jobs, would cause a strike, and she prepared carefully for an industrial war, stockpiling six months of coal supplies, passing laws to reduce union rights to picket and intimidate nonstrikers, and ordering the police to draw up mobilization plans for all-out confrontation.

I was always struck by how lucky Thatcher was in her opponents. War with the brutal but profoundly inept Argentine junta was followed by a showdown with Scargill, a Marxist firebrand, folksy in demeanour, rousing in oratory, hungry for combat but devoid of strategic sense. His authoritarian leadership was resented by many, but he did nothing to dispel that impression. When he called the strike, he refused to allow union membership a vote, which caused lasting strife within miners' ranks: 120,000 men walked out, but 40,000 refused to stop work. The continuing output of coal was an early symbolic win for Thatcher. The British courts ruled that the refusal of a vote was unlawful, and it cost miners the critical support of other major unions and even the Labour Party, whose leader, Neil Kinnock, felt Scargill's "suicidal vanity" was walking miners straight into Thatcher's trap. There was widespread speculation that the radical

Scargill saw the strike less as an offensive to save the pits than as an attempt to destroy Thatcher's government.

The showdown led to divided loyalties among the public, though widespread "up the miners" sentiment flowed from the long history of suffering and courage in coalfields in Yorkshire, Scotland, and Wales. I found people vacillated between misty-eyed support for the miners' willingness to stand up to "our dreadful PM" and scorn for Scargill. They were tired of disruptive strikes and power-hungry union bosses.

I drove north to cover clashes between strikers and the large police mobile units. TV images made them look ferocious, as they sometimes were, but often they seemed choregraphed on both sides. Two lines would face each other about forty metres apart, waiting for the next round to begin. In the way that humour infiltrates every aspect of British life, miners would sing, chant, and laugh as they threw insults at the police, who looked rather bored as they chatted and exchanged jokes among themselves. Everything would seem fairly casual until, suddenly, the miners' chants would switch to "Here we go, here we go!"—a familiar call to action among soccer fans—and a police captain would shout "Form up!" Blue-clad arms linked, plastic shields swung into place, and both masses collided in a shoving, swaying mass that, for a few minutes, looked like a massive rugger scrum. As arrests were made and the walking wounded on both sides staggered away, the miners backed off and the waiting game resumed.

Given my experiences in conflicts, I felt encouraged that such a determined challenge to the state could be carried out without massacres, torture cells, and the mass disappearances of strikers. But injustices were still done on a disturbing scale: nonstrikers could face terrifying threats from union goons, and the police often overreacted. Some eleven thousand miners were arrested and eight thousand were prosecuted, often losing their jobs as a result. Many of the communities that lost pits never revived, and unemployment in former coal areas remains high today.

In March 1985, with morale collapsing and their war chest

exhausted—despite Scargill's characteristically reckless appeal to Moscow for funds—the union had to give in. The strike ended without winning a single concession from the much-strengthened Thatcher. The prime minister liked nothing better than what journalists covering her came to call "the smack of firm government," and she went on to close still more pits in coming years—the beginning of the end of Britain's legendary coal-mining culture.

Even more momentous, the miners' defeat marked the beginning of privatization for many nationalized industries and utilities—a transformation that fundamentally changed the face of modern Britain. Having passed firm laws to limit strikes, Thatcher now destroyed the enormous influence of unions to resist economic reforms. She sold off most of what she could to private interests: railways, steel plants, shipbuilding, telecommunications, gas and electricity companies, and water supply. Foreign governments and financial markets were impressed, adding glitter to City of London bankers and global traders. Yet, even as many people made money and property values skyrocketed around London, a boom-and-bust uncertainty remained—among the 3.2 million unemployed were thousands cast out of jobs by privatization. I found an intense new bitterness in this still class-ridden society and filed reports such as "Crumbling Britain," detailing how whole regions experienced intractable joblessness as plants and underfunded public services closed down, creating a country that, while growing richer, simultaneously fell into a prolonged decline.

"As an *economy,* then, Thatcherized Britain was a more efficient place," historian Tony Judt wrote of the period. "But as a *society* it suffered meltdown, with catastrophic, long-term consequences . . . private affluence was accompanied by public squalor."

I remember it as a scuzzy, dispiriting time. London looked more tattered, more homeless people were sleeping in the streets, and there was rising racial tension, more fear of crime. A surge in urban violence was seen most bizarrely in the fury of British soccer riots. In stadium after stadium, rampages by gangs of hooligans broke out during or after games, terrorizing local districts. The viciousness wrecked area cafés and pubs, destroyed vehicles, and intimidated neighbourhoods in spasms of fighting that left scores of fans, bystanders, and police injured. When the rioting crossed the Channel for games away from home, European host cities were horrified. As I reported, some rowdiness has always been a part of UK soccer rivalries, but it now metastasized into a major national problem. Thatcher listed her three greatest domestic security problems as militant unions, the IRA, and soccer rioting. She called for stiffer sentencing of thugs, set up a "war room" to monitor matches across the United Kingdom, and allocated five thousand police to handle soccer crowd control. Other sporting events, including rugger, were almost always peaceful.

I reported on the official inquiry that pointed to obvious problems: many stadiums were aged rattletraps where spectators were segregated by team loyalty that saw the most fanatical fans often squeezed into overcrowded concrete terraces at each end. The spectators were mostly young white males between sixteen and thirty, often liquored up, who sang, chanted, and cursed opposing fans, players, and police in a rising cacophony. Racial insults, including thrown banana peels at Black athletes, were common, while the soccer pitch might be bombarded by coins, bottles, firecrackers, and even darts. After the game, riots were generally organized by groups, called "firms," which went by monikers such as the Headhunters of Chelsea, Gooners of Arsenal, and Zulu Warriors of Birmingham City. Who were they? "Tanked-up yobs," as Thatcher's press officer called them, or angry, working-class, unemployed youth, desperate for a cause, letting out contempt for society? It turned out many had jobs, some even in banking, advertising, or the military.

No one seemed to understand the enigma of the League of Louts, as the UK media called them. A decade earlier, the film *A Clockwork Orange* had imagined a new culture of youth bullyboys seething with the thrill of intimidating others. I was struck more by the similarity to extremist political mobs of the 1930s, including the British fascist Blackshirts, and the newer versions of violent political mobs, both anarchist and extreme right, that were attracted to far-out doctrines covering anti-immigration, racial superiority, and hostility to elites. They were becoming more prominent in both the United Kingdom and across Europe.

Personally, the only tense moment I felt from soccer violence was in a posh hotel lobby in Brussels. I had flown in because the previous evening a match for the European Cup final in Brussels's Heysel Stadium between England's Liverpool team and Italy's Juventus ended in horrific televised disaster as unruly Liverpool fans poured into mainly Italian fan sections, pushing and chanting threats. Hundreds of Italians trying to flee were blocked by a concrete wall, and thirty-nine were trampled and crushed to death. English fan hooliganism, partially blamed for the disaster, had reached such a peak that the United Kingdom was soon banned from European soccer for five years. I went first to the stadium as they were still mopping up and disentangling the steel barriers where so many had died. It was shocking to see what the weight of mass bodies could do to even such hard metal. I then went to check in at the hotel, arriving just as many of the grieving, furious Italian fans were checking out. As I walked to the desk, I'd forgotten to ditch the copy of the London *Times* under my arm. Suddenly, I found myself flanked by Italians who looked ready to rip me to shreds. Realizing the risk, I whipped out my passport and cried, "I'm Canadian, *Canadese*." It was one of many times that document saved me from trouble.

I sensed I was becoming dispirited, even discombobulated by the stark contrasts in subjects I was covering. In just eight months I'd gone from Ethiopia, the heart of the greatest peacetime famine of modern history, to the tragic war in Lebanon, and then the miners' strike in England and raging soccer hooliganism. Over time such crisis fatigue is a common reaction among foreign correspondents who must catapult from one extreme to the other in their daily work.

As part of my beat, I also visited Northern Ireland (Ulster) during the IRA campaign to unite the North with the South (Eire), a war of icy terror waged against British security forces and Protestant militias determined to keep the North within the United Kingdom. I liked this area, the dark green and sea-lashed ancestral home of my Stewart family, and even grew fond of then gritty Belfast, a port city where the chill mists and distant ship foghorns reminded me of my Halifax youth. But I found the fanatical and self-romanticizing IRA and Protestant forces monotonous and the cold cruelty repugnant. The bombings, assassinations, and sniper murders were carried out on both sides with almost casual dispatch—thirty-seven hundred were killed, overwhelmingly civilians, and forty thousand injured, not counting the mental traumas of living so long with terror.

At that time, commenting on hopes for peace seemed dishonest. Reporting took on the grim predictability that clings to seemingly endless conflicts. Neither side had a knockout blow, and the British soldiers and spies could barely keep the high level of violence from getting worse. Thatcher refused to deal, and the hard men and women of the IRA and Protestant Unionists would not give up a struggle that both sides commemorated in slogans, songs, and gaudy wall paintings. Tragically, when the power-sharing Good Friday Agreement was finally enacted in 1998, it was something reasonable people could have devised twenty years earlier.

My spirits revived in the last week of April when I went on a routine assignment to Apeldoorn, in the Netherlands, to cover the fortieth anniversary of its liberation by Canadian troops from Nazi occupation. I was glad to go: the First Canadian Army's fight over eleven months from D-Day through northern France and Belgium, and the liberation of much of the Dutch nation—losing seventy-three hundred troops in these final months—was a triumph of will and courage. This virtually all-volunteer Canadian fighting force that played an outsized role in the allied freeing of Western Europe was shamefully underappreciated on the Continent—except for the Dutch, who were on the brink of famine when battle-weary Canadians units reached Apeldoorn on April 17 and took the surrender of all German troops in the Netherlands two weeks later. The Dutch told that story across generations: for decades their children laid flowers and miniature flags on local Canadian military graves; Canadian visitors, especially veterans, were warmly welcomed; and both countries felt emotionally bonded in a rare affection. In my youth, Canadian schoolchildren raised money, a nickel at a time, for victims of Dutch flooding in 1953.

Apeldoorn nurtured this affection as part of its culture. For the fortieth anniversary, Canadian veterans, most in their sixties and older, were invited to parade in honour through the main street. I expected to get some good scenes and moving interviews but didn't know what more we might find. On the morning when we showed up forty minutes before the parade, my heart sank. Only a thin, broken line of people were waiting along the kilometre-long route. Far off, I heard the sound of a military band, the 48th Highlanders of Toronto, announce the approach of the Canadian vets, which got me considering how to make the best of a modest showing. Then everything changed with astonishing speed: from side streets came tens of thousands of residents, including many families, to line the route, singing, cheering, waving flags of both nations. I'd never seen anything quite like it, a "love-in" of maybe two hundred thousand people, ten or twelve deep, that turned the parade into a vast spasm of gratitude which stunned the old soldiers.

Our team joined the marching ranks to film interviews, finding many too overcome to talk. "Kinda gets you—here. Difficult not to cry," a vet said between sobs. As open vehicles bearing vets who couldn't walk passed by, I saw parents rush forward with children to touch their gnarled and outstretched hands. A mother explained: "When my daughter grows up, I want her to be able to say she once saw those giants pass by, and even touched one." I talked to others who were throwing flowers to the startled vets. One said, "My life started when the fellows arrived. Before then, only darkness and fear—I owe them everything. Every year I go to their cemetery just to say, 'Thank you, guys.'" We got a last shot of the vets disappearing from view into the flag-waving multitude.

On returning to London, as Bob Geldof's giant Live Aid concert in Wembley Stadium grew nearer, I was moved by the remarkable groundswell in humanitarian concern for famine relief in Africa, particularly among young people. Friends urged me to attend, but I resisted and sought peace visiting family in Toronto. I had big assignments ahead: first to South Africa to cover the increasing violence of the security crisis over apartheid, and then back to Ethiopia for a third time to do a one-year-after appraisal of the famine relief efforts.

I also needed time away from news coverage to think about my future. It bothered me that I had no life plan or even a sense of what I wanted to do beyond my current London posting. My career was going well, I had the best of CBC's foreign positions, and I felt I was on a par with veteran CBC stars David Halton and Joe Schlesinger and some outstanding new correspondents such as Ann Medina. I was adequately paid and had few domestic expenses. Yet, for long stretches, I was far from happy. Something was off. With neither wish nor talent to move into management and no interest in high-profile TV studio work, my options were limited, except to move to another bureau such as Washington. I assumed I'd ride my youthful passion to be a foreign correspondent as long as I found it fulfilling and then switch to something else—maybe return to newspapers or join a humanitarian group. I also assumed, despite my uneven romantic history, that I'd discover the right person and get married, have a family.

These were my scattered thoughts as I lounged for a week in my dad's garden in the golden July of 1985.

The beauty of South Africa that summer could take your breath away—just as the towering evil of its apartheid system could too. No matter how much I'd read about it, I was taken aback by the all-embracing and suffocating lid of ultrasegregation clamped over the Black majority.

The system seemed not only grotesque and cruel but also quite dotty—a baffling, race-obsessed maze of laws that ensnared every aspect of life. They thought of everything, those architects of apartheid: regulating where Blacks could live, travel, and work; what kind of drink was permitted in their designated districts (light beer only); the sexual activity allowed (no race mingling); where they could or couldn't be entertained, educated, or allowed into sporting events; and, certainly, where they were totally barred—Parliament. Step outside such restrictions and a Black person could be arrested, whipped, and jailed. Most Black males I met had been thrown into a police cell at least overnight for being found without proper papers in a non-Black area. I found it hard to keep a straight face when South African officials denounced the CBC for calling their system "white minority government." Their defence was that while Parliament's dominant House of Assembly was all white, at least non-Blacks of mixed race or Indian backgrounds had separate legislatures for their own minority affairs. As a democracy, the South African system was a transparent sham.

I was there during July and August 1985, a period often viewed as the beginning of the end of apartheid. Violence was mounting, and a new state of emergency had been imposed over much of the country to try to clamp down on the protests, riots, and anti-apartheid guerrilla attacks. It was difficult to see how a South African bloodbath could be avoided. In a population of thirty-three million, twenty-eight million

(80 percent) were Black, and five million were white. This small minority had the country's massive military and security apparatus firmly in its grip. Whites were not totally united: English-speaking South Africans, descendants of the British, frequently advocated apartheid's end, while the greater number of Afrikaners, who spoke an offshoot of Dutch and whose ancestors were mainly Dutch and German settlers who'd arrived over three centuries before, were fired by a conviction of their duty to dominate the south of Africa. They rejected any comparison to more recent white colonists in other parts of Africa who had been forced to cede power or leave, and they were determined to fight anyone who tried to undermine their position.

I went there to compile a two-part documentary for *The Journal* called *The White Tribe of Africa*. It was meant to explain Afrikaners' insistence they were not European settlers who had stayed too long but by now were unshakably African. We travelled widely and spoke to a diverse range of people, from leading opponents of apartheid such as Bishop Desmond Tutu to liberals such as author Nadine Gordimer, as well as Afrikaner politicians, theologians, farmers, academics, and far-right local militants who were openly bracing for a coming war. In the Afrikaner heartland I was greeted with cool formality, even suspicion, because Canada's hostility to apartheid was well known. I questioned their belief that a rapid end to apartheid would throw the country into chaos with the observation that delaying reform had brought them endless states of emergency at home and isolation in the world. I got the sense some Afrikaners wished previous generations had never introduced apartheid, but they couldn't see how to dig themselves out of this inheritance.

While I was there, President P.W. Botha delivered his "Rubicon" speech, which stoked the crisis fires even higher. An enormous international audience watched the televised event because he was expected to announce that apartheid would begin to be dismantled and even that Nelson Mandela might be freed after more than two decades in prison. Astonishingly, he did the exact reverse, pouring scorn on those who had predicted reform and rejecting Mandela's release. He would not lead his people "into abdication and suicide," he roared; "we are today crossing the Rubicon. There can be no turning back." Foreign nations immediately increased sanctions, and South Africa became even more isolated, resulting in financial panic that threatened to cripple the economy.

This speech was a huge news story, not only for reasons of human rights but also because the Cold War stakes were high. South Africa's immense potential wealth and strategic position in Africa between the Atlantic and Indian Oceans caused the West to fear that any instability there would encourage Soviet meddling.

I hoped to stay longer for all the obvious reasons: big story, a roaring drama with unforeseeable twists and turns, a fascinating country, and a rich history to explain. I also welcomed the opportunity to work on my TV and documentary writing skills with one of the masters, the BBC's star reporter Michael Buerk, who was based in South Africa. I envied his ability to make a two-minute news grab stir emotions with a power almost equal to a half-hour documentary. I found him a cool and aloof British gentleman in person, but the warmth of his humanity and the craftsmanship in his prose shone powerfully in his work.

Too soon, however, South African officials had other ideas. I learned the embassy in Ottawa was seething over my crisis stories, protesting to the CBC and the Canadian government. Tony Burman had pulled every string he knew to get us in, but when he went to Pretoria to seek an extension of our time, the rejection was ringing. "Ah, you're Canadian," the official snorted. "Your visas are not being extended, and we would like your group to leave the country as soon as possible." Our pleas fell flat. "We have to suffer those American and British journalists because their countries invest heavily in South Africa," the official continued, "but why in God's name do we have to tolerate you Canadians? You are merely cheapskates and troublemakers."

I chuckled over the characterization but still had to pack and go.

Obviously, a Canadian passport wasn't always useful. This was my first of four foreign expulsions—my "orders of the boot."

In London I prepared for my return to Ethiopia. I ached to see the north and Tigray province again, so strong was the hold it had on me—both the land and its people's struggle to survive. I watched hours of our field tapes and studied every UN and NGO field report I could get on the progress of famine relief.

My apartment lease was up, and, because the CBC helped resettle overseas staff, I was driven to view several furnished apartments, quickly picked one, packed the few bags that held all my belongings, and moved, all within two days. I settled into a former Mayfair coach house on a lane near the US embassy on Grosvenor Square. The rented flats around seemed heavily populated by the protective staff of various embassies, and from my neighbours' garage would come a ceaseless babble of off-duty French bodyguards debating soccer teams and female film and music stars. Their burly presence meant I had little fear of break-ins, which was fortunate given my long absences abroad.

Back in Ethiopia, I retraced areas I had visited the previous year as well as some new ones, seeing how feeding centres and refugee camps were coping and how logistical efforts struggled to avoid disruptions. The refugee camps were vast, and the rate of disease and deaths remained shocking, but major progress had been made in supplying food and medicine. Aid teams, both Ethiopian and foreign, were cooperating far better with each other. The priority now was to keep the hungry rural population in their homes, meaning that supplies had to reach previously inaccessible regions, often by airdrops from large transport aircraft and runs by smaller planes and helicopters.

I took flights through enormous mountain canyons in small aircraft and landed in helicopters in areas I'd thought only mountain goats could reach. In one such ride we landed on a thin mountain pinnacle where no life seemed evident. "Just wait," the pilot explained. Within minutes at least a dozen sinewy farmers climbed to the site, pleading for food for their families. We promised we'd get word of their desperate need to a relief centre, the pilot took location notes, and we zoomed off to arrange a new airdrop. When it came, it was because other people in distant lands had helped make it happen.

Bob Geldof arrived in Addis Ababa while we were there, and our rooms were on the same floor in the hotel. We discussed how the enormous donations raised by the Live Aid concert might best be spent. He was extremely well informed, very astute, and dedicated, with an impressive ability to make swift decisions. He had been roasted by some of the UK media for not immediately arranging shipments of food but instead buying hundreds of large trucks to strengthen relief convoys. He was right: large backlogs of food were stuck in ports simply because of the shortage of trucks. Some of those in service were so old they were regularly breaking down along the hundreds of kilometres linking relief centres.

I almost lost my welcome with him early one morning when we were leaving on a shoot and our soundman seemed to be missing. I raced to what I thought was his door and pounded, yelling, "Get the hell up! We'll miss our flight!" I heard grunts, groans, and curses as the occupant approached the door and flung it open. There stood a dazed and sleepy Geldof. "Oh, excuse me, my mistake," I muttered, heading quickly down the hallway. The vocabulary of swearwords that pursued me was impressive even for an Irishman.

I kept hoping I could go deeper in my reporting, and I discussed how best to cover crises with relief officials. They all wanted our cameras there to validate their particular humanitarian efforts, but the far-sighted ones feared that our speed of satellite-assisted coverage of disasters and wars would have a corrosive effect on viewers. They recognized the danger of "compassion fatigue": people could grow inured to horrific images and exhausted by constant cries of help. A UN official put it bluntly: "The media are very skilled at covering a catastrophe, but not good at staying around to show how people recover, pull their societies back together, and rebuild lives," he said. "This leaves your viewers with a false notion that only horrible things happen in such poor areas; and so its people are seen as perpetually weak."

The criticism affected me deeply, and, whenever I was reporting in Ethiopia, I added more coverage of relief and rehabilitation efforts. We did stories of local people building small village dams to help through droughts and planting resistant crops and trees. We showed new health centres setting up in rural areas, even as hunger swept the plains and civil war flared in the mountains. Our news and *Journal* editors fully backed my efforts, and Canada's deep and broad response to African famine soon set an appetite for more public awareness of the complex challenges in foreign aid assistance.

As the CBC's international reputation rose significantly, our teams showed up in more places. At one stage *The Journal* alone had almost a dozen documentary units abroad. Our reports went to fifteen nations, and we shared resources and precious video field tapes with our main partners, BBC and NBC. As a result, American network scouts kept an eye on Canadian reporters. At least five CBC reporters had been hired away in just a few years. Friends within NBC told me my work in Ethiopia and Beirut had been noted in their New York headquarters. Always a sucker for flattery, I was pleased but did not give it much thought. Working for the Amnets was never a goal for me. But then the courtship began.

One afternoon in London, an NBC executive called me up. After brusquely introducing himself, he asked, "Have you got a contract?"

Not grasping his intent, I replied, "Well, I work for CBC full-time."

"Not what I meant," he shot back. "I mean, have you signed a legal contract?" slowly enunciating the sentence as if addressing a teenage nitwit.

When I said I had not, he suggested we have lunch to discuss matters of mutual benefit. Curious, I agreed. More pleasant in person, he explained that NBC had been watching my work and wanted to offer me a contract and a posting in Frankfurt, Germany, one of their main bureaus. I said I had no wish to leave the CBC, but he said I should find an agent, discuss terms with New York, and visit their headquarters. For weeks afterwards, I continued to decline the overture.

I cannot fully unravel my thoughts at that time. Was I even thinking clearly? The CBC reporters who moved to the Amnets, including my London office predecessor Mark Phillips, had been recruited for their experience, abilities, and mid-Atlantic accents, so similar to the American. They were valued also for their Canadian citizenship, which allowed them at times to go where US reporters might be barred. They all seemed to be thriving, but would I? Money wasn't a factor: the salary would be higher but not eye-popping. Certainly, there would be more foreign postings to aim for, along with the status of representing one of the giant US networks, and my reports would reach an audience of many millions. It all made a pretty good package, but I still couldn't work up serious enthusiasm.

I felt strong loyalty to the CBC and believed that, under the current management, its status would continue to rise. What should have concerned me more was my avoidance of making a decision one way or the other. I felt tired, listless, even drifting. I was probably depressed but didn't know it. I had accepted that psychic scar tissue went with my profession, but like most reporters then, I did not seek therapy. I thought that new adventures would shake me out of my becalmed state of mind—and, as ever, one wasn't long in coming.

Asia and the Philippines were far off my usual beat, but there I was at the end of February 1986, enjoying a drink by the sparkling moonlit bay in Manila as the nation celebrated a revolution. I couldn't imagine an image that epitomized more the old romantic notion of a foreign correspondent's life. I was covering the overthrow of the long and grisly dictatorship of Ferdinand Marcos, a tyrant who fled into exile accompanied by his infamously avaricious wife, Imelda. I had not expected to go, but there was a gap in reporters available.

Days earlier, on leave in Montreal, I was having a drink at Winnie's Bar with friend and author Mordecai Richler when a call came from the CBC asking me to fly immediately to Manila to cover the mass uprising. Richler, who liked nothing better than to talk news and travel, offered to help plan my last-minute flight connections—and in quick time I was booked, first class, on luxurious Thai Air out of London to Bangkok and on to Manila. I was airborne for a very long time and, at one point, high above Afghanistan, I could make out below the snow-clad mountain ranges where Soviet troops were ensnared in a losing war against Islamic guerrillas. I reached Manila super jet-lagged but just in time to see joyous crowds looting the presidential palace.

I had not been there during the years of the Marcos death squads, mass arrests, and torture, but here I was amid this wild, triumphant aftermath as people breathed free and democracy was lovingly restored. News at that time rarely got to cover crises that end in explosions of joy, but these national happy days were watched by the world. The mood was infectious, and I joined the news teams filing reports, covering the celebrations, and enjoying ourselves.

On one occasion I was sitting in the hotel lobby with some NBC friends, including family friend Tony Hillman, the former CBC producer. They knew I'd been offered a position with their network and quietly urged me to make the leap. That got me thinking, Why not? What had I to lose? And so, impulsively, I decided to accept. When I told them, they urged me to immediately call NBC's chief news editor, an impressive ex-Marine type I had met in New York. "You made my day, Brian," he enthused, "so glad you'll be joining our news family"—an obvious US-style exaggeration.

On the long flight home, however, I wondered about my reasoning: Had I made the choice to try something new or, rather, to flee from a life that seemed adrift?

10

My NBC Adventures

The leap from one network to a more promising position with a far larger news giant is, ostensibly, an occasion for bracing thoughts of success, even self-congratulation. While NBC appeared to welcome my arrival as their Frankfurt correspondent in the spring of 1986, it came at a time when I least valued my worth. I felt in a tailspin of disheartening emotions, my ambitions all askew.

Then things suddenly changed, sweeping me into the updraft I needed. Corny as it sounds, the transformation involved romance. One night when briefly in Toronto, I'd gone to a CBC get-together at a bar with my former Ottawa bureau colleague Mike Duffy. An instinctive meddler, Duffy took it upon himself to introduce me to producer Tina Srebotnjak—while quietly confiding to her I was the man she should marry. Dubious but amused, her interest was sparked, and more dates followed. Duffy had stuck me with the nickname Scoop in Ottawa, but this time it was his exclusive that proved flawless: almost forty years later, Tina and I are still happily married.

With my record, a promising courtship was no guarantee of ultimate success. The obstacles were formidable, and, as usual, my position as suitor bordered on the preposterous. I'd known of Tina by reputation—an attractive and strikingly witty rising star as a producer, first in radio and now television, already seen by many as the natural show host she was to become. We shared many interests, from love of books to films, but nothing could obscure the reality that her promising career lay in Canada, whereas mine was overseas, unpredictable, and at times hazardous. We decided to give a trans-atlantic relationship a good try. With my morale and energy revived, my start date with NBC arrived. I would need such bolstering more than I could imagine.

I'd already flown to New York for a single day of get-acquainted meetings at NBC's famous news headquarters in Rockefeller Center. There I marvelled at finding myself in the heart of Manhattan, media centre of the world, swept off to lunch by my new agent at the twenties-era glamour spot the Russian Tea Room. Next I was welcomed aboard by the chieftains of one of the world's premier news broadcasters, including the vice-president of news, John Lane, a compact ball of energy, and news anchor Tom Brokaw. I knew it was all the standard flattery shown a new hire, but I vowed to let myself revel just this once in the grand manner, up to and including the limo they had booked to whisk me back in style to the airport.

Except there was no limo. Instead, my day ended with a raging thunderstorm and one of the city's worst downpours of the year. Traffic was thrown into chaos, and after waiting as long as I dared, I gave up on my driver and set out walking in the storm, without an umbrella, and travelled, drenched, in the unfamiliar subway system. I made my flight barely in time. When I deplaned in Toronto, dishevelled and with sodden shoes squishing, I wondered if the deluge that had swept me out of the city like so much flotsam was a forewarning of things to come.

Fortunately, I'm not superstitious. On April 15 I was in an optimistic mood as I prepared for my official start at NBC, six weeks in New York on their tab to learn all the inner workings of the full news operation, including nightly news and the morning show. Best of all, Tina would join me when possible, and we thrilled at the thought of the cozy restaurants, art museums, and intimate piano bars nestled high above the twinkling lights of that great city at dusk. This wonderful dreamscape shattered in minutes when President Reagan suddenly decided to bomb Libya.

I'd been aware that escalating tension between the United States and Libya had hit a new high in the previous week after Libyan leader Muammar Gaddafi's agents bombed a favourite hangout for US soldiers in Berlin, La Belle nightclub, killing two of them and injuring dozens. Reagan, long steaming over Gaddafi's blatant sponsorship of terror groups, saw it as the right moment to take him out. The US raid at 2 a.m. on April 14 was short but heavy, hitting barracks and narrowly missing the leader's own compound near the capital, Tripoli. As I packed in Toronto for my flight to New York, I noted there was no footage of the raid, only dramatic live phone accounts by reporters as they waited in the darkened city for possible new attacks. I didn't worry that I'd be hurled into the story: I'd been promised those weeks in magical Manhattan learning how to thrive in NBC's ranks. I was thinking more of martinis than going on a mission.

A red message light on my phone glowed when I checked into my hotel, a short walk from NBC. The message directed me to call the secretary of the news chief immediately, and when she answered her words were folksy but no-nonsense: "He wants you to come in to see him." Inwardly, I swore. "Is this, umm, urgent?" I asked. "Let's say I'd put a spring in my step if I were you," she said, laughing. And so in no time I was in the newsroom being slapped on the back by Lane, a former Korean War officer with a certain into-battle charisma. "God damn, are we glad to see you," he enthused, followed with "We're gonna postpone your program here and get you right to Libya. Luckily, we have you booked on British Air to London and then to Tripoli."

While I was rushed to the business office to sign my insurance papers, he paced up and down in excitement. "These voice-only reports from the hotel roof while raids scream overhead are great moments—like Edward R. Murrow during the London Blitz. Just a day from now you may be up there as another attack comes in, broadcasting to millions! How's that for a start!" I forced myself to assume a wide-eyed and eager look.

The assignment was a frantic ending to the blissful reunions Tina and I had planned. When I called, she was disappointed, realizing we wouldn't meet for months, but, knowing the demands of news, unfazed. As I boarded my flight I wondered if I was setting some kind of media record for a new hire being shot off to a combat zone. I understood the reasons: I was going as backup to their superb reporter Steve Delaney, to help with the load and take over if something happened to him. Americans could be arrested or expelled in these circumstances, and my Canadian citizenship just might keep me in place, to stand atop the roof broadcasting as US fighter bombers ripped across the sky.

Landing in Tripoli, I lined up with other arriving reporters at passport control. We were immediately stripped of magazines and newspapers: "Reading hurts eyes," one officer said with a smirk. Two or three of us were diverted to another room, under armed guards. For further checking, I assumed, but instead to my astonishment we were told to grab our bags because we were leaving. "Leaving for where?" I demanded. The officer gave a who-gives-a-damn shrug and said, "You leave Libya. You go now!" No reason was given, and I was thrown out barely more than an hour after arriving. Two remarkably cheerful soldiers escorted me like proud doormen of an elite hotel to an Air Malta flight, where I had first to buy a first-class ticket to the island. Both NBC and Gaddafi's regime had sent me flying with near equal speed. Seeing Libya receding below me as we flew away, I tried to imagine the conversations in New York when they learned it was the Canadian chucked out, not their American.

I did not detect even dark humour in NBC's newsroom at this turn of events when I checked in with New York from Malta but was assured by editors they were pulling every lever they could to get me back into Tripoli. They leapt at my suggestion that, in the meantime, I provide analysis from Malta on the other aspect of the crisis—the real risk of a Cold War clash at sea. The enormous US carrier fleet that dominated the Mediterranean had blockaded Libya but was being shadowed closely by a growing Soviet force of cruisers and submarines. As during the Cuban Missile Crisis, a dangerous incident was all too possible. I had already studied the possibility of a Mediterranean naval clash while covering fleet operations off Beirut and had kept up with NATO and Soviet naval force deployments since. I was confident if an incident occurred, I could go live into their newscasts with context reports. Within two days the call came instructing me to fly back into Tripoli, where I arrived safely—although my luggage did not.

All the media were gathered—indeed, semi-confined—within the Al Kabir Hotel, where the US networks kept phone lines open night and day to New York. We could send out voice reports, but TV crews were forbidden movement except under tight regime escort for news conferences. Like the others, I was shadowed by very visible security when I went out to do basic information gathering, such as looking for signs of public unrest (none) or evidence of an economic crisis (plenty). Getting any valid appraisal of the public mood was futile because residents were understandably jumpy when approached by foreigners followed by state spies.

The NBC office was friendly, steady, and efficient, staffed by several veterans who'd covered multiple wars and crises. Someone slept all night by the open phone line, causing occasional complaints from the New York news desk that one of us snored like a bull elephant. I kept busy prepping to go live and, since we overlooked the harbour, I kept watch on a Soviet warship that had been trapped there after the US attack. There was nervous speculation in Washington that it might sail out to test the US blockade, which would have triggered the next level of international crisis. We were literally at the potential ground zero of a superpower game of chicken. One unavoidable aspect of joining a US network in tense times is that all reporting was assessed by intelligence services, especially those in Washington.

I imagined the White House receiving in its morning CIA briefing the item, "In Tripoli the NBC reporter sees faint steam coming from the ship's funnel but still notes crew members acting too casual to be ready to head to sea." I didn't expect Moscow would test the mighty US Seventh Fleet, but when superpowers are involved, the possibility of miscalculation is always taken seriously.

This whiff of John le Carré intrigue further enhanced my duties. The writer I dealt with at headquarters was the son of Humphrey Bogart and Lauren Bacall, Stephen. "Get me Bogart, please," I would ask, and when he came on we'd make my update sound like casual gossip: "This would be a great harbour to visit in your sailboat, Steve. Not a lot of traffic now, as nothing is stirring [hint hint], but a lovely exotic place, and lovely people."

Even waiting to cover a bombing raid can grow tedious as days pass, and the Al Kabir, with no bar, often no power, and in my case, no luggage either, could test patience. At one point, doubting my luggage would ever show up and knowing all stores were shut, the kindly bureau chief offered to lend me some of his underwear. "I doubt that will be quite necessary," I replied a bit too quickly, trying not to sound like a prissy Canadian. I was able, however, to help a colleague in need. When I passed though London, I had agreed to a CTV request to take some currency to their correspondent at the hotel, Philip Winslow, because they couldn't wire him funds. Winslow, an old friend I'd worked with at the *Montreal Gazette*, had been hanging on, though dead broke, for several days, so hard up he'd been reduced to prowling darkened hallways for what he called "corridor cuisine"—the uneaten buns and half sandwiches left out on room-service trays. We at least had a laugh when I noted we'd both risen to high points in our careers, he finding himself with no money, and I with no clothes. A few days later as the crisis was again heating up, my suitcase miraculously resurfaced.

As I was starting to feel proud to be part of such an elite team of journalists, however, the bureau got word that Libya wanted to throw me out again—my second expulsion in a week. Next thing I knew I was in a van to the airport, where I was greeted by an officer and soldiers who firmly walked me to the departure gate. Just as we approached, the intercom called me to an airport phone. A reprieve, I wondered? But it was a New York editor insisting that, whatever happened, "Do—not—leave! Too much is happening. Stay put!" I answered politely that although I agreed with the sentiment, the armed military detail marching me to my flight to Rome had other ideas. In such an absurd moment my Libyan adventure ended. Inwardly, I found the hardest part of this expulsion was to try to look disappointed.

When I contacted New York from Rome, we agreed I should monitor the potential naval conflict from Naples, where NATO maintained its Mediterranean headquarters as well as a large US naval base. I had scarcely started writing an overview report of potential conflict points when word came of another monster crisis in Europe, one that would profoundly shake even the USSR: Chernobyl, the largest nuclear accident in history. At 1:30 a.m. on April 26, one of four nuclear reactors of the Chernobyl plant in Ukraine exploded, causing a massive fire and the release of a hundred times more nuclear fallout than the total of the Hiroshima and Nagasaki bombs combined. A plume of radiation went northwest, affecting five million people as it drifted into parts of central Europe as far as Sweden and Wales, and causing a long-term death toll from radiation sickness over decades, ranging from four thousand to the tens of thousands—estimates are still debated by various international agencies. A KGB report two years earlier had warned that shoddy materials made a disaster at Chernobyl likely, and the Kremlin refused to publicly acknowledge the accident for several days. Incredibly, the first public indications surfaced two days later when an employee at a Swedish nuclear plant noticed high radiation levels coming off his shoes. A full scan quickly established the strength of the fallout and indicated it came from

Chernobyl, more than one thousand kilometres away. The entire continent of Europe then knew it was facing a historic crisis.

NBC called me in Italy with instructions to race to Sweden to "track down the fallout." For the first time I experienced how American networks spared no expenses at such moments: a private plane was booked through London and on to Stockholm, and three limousines awaited my crew and me at the airport, giving us the appearance of a royal procession as we raced north to confront the invisible monster—radiation. We had no equipment or protection gear, so we checked with medical centres, military posts, and local police but found no sign of panicky Swedes. Many farmers, however, worried about radiation effects on their crops and animals. The damage was serious, especially to farming in central Sweden, where the effects were felt for decades. Still, the absence of casualties or public panic left us with little visual story.

Curiously, I ran into the former world heavyweight boxing champion Floyd Patterson and his family touring Sweden, where he was a big favourite. He was shocked when I asked him about the nuclear accident. Not a regular news listener, he'd heard nothing about it, and no one bothered to warn him. He thanked me profusely but refused my interview request. The Chernobyl story, in the absence of visuals, was best handled with top-flight experts in our studio, backed up by maps of fallout cones, weather patterns, and the best open-source intelligence available on the nuclear system that had been affected. NBC was happy to receive field reports, however: the network liked to refer to the enormous scope of its team with lines such as "Our correspondent in northern Sweden has called in to report . . . "

I admired the high expectations set by NBC: correspondents were information generalists but needed to be exceptionally quick briefs, able to get up to speed on any subject within hours, not just to send in a story but also to appear solid and confident when going live into a major newscast. The possibility of instant demand, before millions, kept us sharp and studious, particularly in the days before instant online information. Still, the network's deep pockets kept reporters moving. In my extreme case, in less than three weeks I'd been flown twice into the Libyan bombing crisis and then covered part of the largest nuclear accident in history.

We knew that Chernobyl was a major blow to the Kremlin, especially given the ongoing disastrous Soviet invasion of Afghanistan. The whole suffocating crush of desperate state secrecy, corrupt management, faulty equipment, and substandard engineering seemed symbolic of a megastate that was profoundly unworkable at every level. Although we knew the story was enormous, almost no one comprehended just how close to the cliff edge the Soviet Union had staggered. Only in the wake of Chernobyl did General Secretary Mikhail Gorbachev realize that the old methods of punishing failure and commanding bureaucratic change would no longer work and that nothing less than perestroika—fundamental change and freedoms—must sweep Soviet Europe for it to survive. This daring last hope was already too late. The final ticking countdown had begun.

Immediately following my nuclear fallout chase, I was sent off on another quest—this one almost out of a movie script. In Berlin, Geneva, and Vienna, I was to search for shocking evidence of crimes committed during the Second World War by one of the world's most famous diplomats, Kurt Waldheim, who had been secretary-general of the United Nations for two terms and was now running to be president of Austria. This instant international scandal attracted a horde of world media and raised the question of how Waldheim could have hidden so dark a past for decades. Surely many governments would have scoured the background of the UN's top boss? Given my interest in human rights cases, I relished the search as I visited war crimes investigative bodies and experts, including meetings with Nazi-hunter Simon Weisenthal in Vienna.

Tall, lean, starched, and stuffy, Waldheim had joined the notorious

Sturmabteilung brownshirt movement shortly after Germany annexed Austria in 1938, and for much of the war he served as an army staff and intelligence officer in occupied Yugoslavia and Greece during periods of extreme atrocities when tens of thousands of civilians—Jews and non-Jews—were worked to death or shipped off to Nazi death camps. The German commander General Alexander Löhr, the "butcher of the Balkans," was hanged after the war, but Waldheim denied his military past until it was uncovered by investigative reporters. He then claimed he had never known of atrocities, but when I challenged him, he admitted he had known but could do nothing because "it was a horrible time."

I was pleased with our Waldheim stories. After he won the presidency in Austria, New York naturally wanted a "get"—an exclusive interview from a man now notoriously media shy. I used every argument I had while my supercharged bureau chief, Suzette Knittl, used even more, and we landed a bizarre form of scoop. His office curtly suggested if we set up with a single crew beside a nearby Vienna park at dawn, we would run into the president-elect on his morning walk. I argued that his ornate office would look more presidential, but it was a take it or leave it situation. At the time suggested, with little life stirring in the area, out of the parkside gloom strode the six-foot-four Waldheim and a single bodyguard. He stopped, giving me a sour semi-smile and a curt nod. I had time for four, perhaps five questions at most. He still insisted he had not helped with atrocities such as deportation of Jews and, turning the tables, criticized the unfair nature of such questions to a new president. With that, he left. There was not much meat, but NBC had its exclusive.

Years later accusations continued to swirl that even before Waldheim was elected UN leader, the United States, Britain, USSR, and Israel knew of his connection to war crimes, each preserving the secret to keep him on a useful string. The various powers deemed favours given at the UN well worth a blind eye. I am usually dismissive of conspiracy theories, but this one I'm inclined to believe.

I next flew to Poland to interview Lech Wałęsa, the squat and burly leader of the dissident Solidarity movement (see "Glitches and Greatness" interlude). He was already a world statesman of sorts though still officially a union leader/electrician at the grimy Gdansk shipyards. Three years earlier he had won the Nobel Peace Prize for courageously defending workers' rights in the face of Soviet power. In the early eighties, I had covered the beginnings of martial law in Poland and, except for two joyous occasions during papal tours, I witnessed the bleak, angry response to the economic semi-collapse as the miliary tried to end the turbulence. Army generals feared, if they did not act, that Moscow would invade to brutally crush resistance. There was much speculation that the Polish military would fight invaders, whatever the odds, but I tended to believe a Polish military expert who assured me, "Generals do not willingly lead their national armies to certain defeat."

Threatened, followed, detailed by secret police, and detailed for eleven months during the regime's martial law in 1982, Wałęsa was gruff, dismissive, and indomitable in return. I half expected he would have a "convenient accident" some night. Moscow feared his union movement would pollute the whole Soviet Union, and some reporters joked he was a dead man walking. Back at the time of his release, when I was still with CBC, Wałęsa had passed a group of reporters I was with as he strode into a church meeting. "Are you afraid?" one called out. "I am afraid of no man, and nothing—only God," he answered, smiling as he swept by. Three years later he was elected president.

By summer 1986, with some reforms taking root and Wałęsa and other resisters gaining strength, I would normally have felt energized. But instead, as soon as we had fed our story, I was scrambling to get back to Toronto with a very heavy heart. My father was in the final stages of terminal cancer.

I had learned of his diagnosis the previous December and had already flown back home several times to spend a few days with him. He was wonderfully looked after by my stepmother, Katherine, and relatively philosophical about his vanishing hopes. Only once had he fretted about my decision to leave CBC News, which he had regularly watched in some part, I felt, because he admired the ties I wore on camera. Like sons beyond number, I mourned that I had not known my father better. Though successful in his own career, he had never sought to discourage what must have seemed my own wild and risky wanderings abroad. My unrepayable debt to him added to my grief as the end approached.

Yet this heartache was not my only powerful emotion because, as my father was dying, I was simultaneously courting Tina. She had visited me in Frankfurt, and now in Toronto the struggle to handle the contradictory stresses of great sorrow and joy, of one relationship ending and another beginning, felt like it was tearing me apart. When I returned to Germany in early July, I believed my father might last until autumn, but he sank fast and, within two weeks, I abandoned a story about spying in Berlin to fly back for the funeral.

Whatever my personal mood, new adventures and exotic challenges awaited me. Within weeks I was helping refuel a private plane at a small jungle airstrip in Cameroon, West Africa, as we raced to cover a mysterious accident that seemed to be straight out of science fiction, one difficult even for scientists to explain. With no warning, a fatal mist of gas had suddenly risen from the modest-sized Lake Nyos in northwest Cameroon, spread quickly across a twenty-five-kilometre radius, then descended to kill seventeen hundred people, three thousand cattle, and innumerable birds and insects. Eerily, the dead showed no sign of trauma or struggle: they had simply collapsed, and their villages were undamaged. It sounded like the notorious US neutron bomb, designed to spare buildings but kill civilians. But in Cameroon? As news spread across the globe, speculation ranged from something of extraterrestrial origin to a top-secret US or Soviet chemical weapons experiment.

A clear explanation had yet to emerge as I raced to the area, along with reporters from around the world. Cameroon threw a security zone around the lake, making even getting near it a challenge, especially as major airlines shunned the whole area. After flying to Nairobi, Kenya, my producer found a bush pilot willing to fly us as close as possible, although his small plane's range was so limited we had to carry extra fuel drums squeezed inside with us, meaning we had to hand-pump the refill at a semi-abandoned airstrip. It was a madcap scheme, but we made it to the important camp of international scientists trying to fathom the mysterious mist. We were initially detained by authorities demanding to know how we'd flown so far in so small a plane, but the matter was soon dropped amid the confusion of far more pressing questions. Within a few days, the scientists agreed the likely cause of the disaster was a small eruption from an adjoining volcano that had released a gas cloud of three hundred thousand tons of magnetized carbon dioxide—a limnic eruption—which travelled fast before descending to quickly suffocate life.

We filmed burials and the treatment of survivors in hospital, but the lack of physical devastation, rather like the Chernobyl fallout, meant New York's attention soon waned. Because I was already in Africa, the news desk agreed to my suggestion that I go to southern Sudan on the way home, to file a report on a civil war there.

I'd already seen the beginnings of that war during my CBC trips to the Ethiopia and Sudan region and had tried to interest my new bosses in covering it seriously. Because we had no chance this time to prepare for an extensive shoot, we would be limited to a quick introduction to the killing fields of South Sudan. There the mainly Christian and animist populations were under siege by the Islamic government of the north. Private armed militias sent in as mass raiders by North Sudan were murdering civilians in large numbers, often kidnapping children as slaves and burning down villages. Resistance from the Southern Peoples Liberation Army (SPLA) was in its early stages and losing badly. Through contacts, we slipped into the country, reached newly raided villages, and filmed ruins and corpses. I did stand-ups explaining how this out-of-sight war was one of the most merciless on earth. We were all nervous and hugely relieved to get out without being killed or captured ourselves. The war was shockingly under-covered, and I considered we were "shining a light in the darkness"—work that my idealist side most valued.

Arriving back in Frankfurt, inexpressibly exhausted, I went to my new apartment to grab some sleep while the footage went to the office to be readied for editing some hours later. I'd lost my keys, so missed a precious hour of sleep waiting for a locksmith. I'd barely closed the door when the phone rang. "You better come in. Something's wrong with the video," the editor said in a half whisper. So instead of sleeping I raced in, only to discover that, unbeknownst to our cameraman, something within the camera had come ajar in Sudan. The footage was ruined—it looked like a 3D film viewed without the special glasses. Had we been in the field longer the flaw might have been discovered, but the rush made that impossible. New York had it flown over to see if top video labs could resuscitate it, but it remained non-airable, multicoloured mush. For me it was a major kick in the gut; to NBC, however, Sudan was not relevant to America's many hyperactive interests, so it was considered a minor mishap, quickly forgotten.

At a certain level, this attitude was understandable, given that the Cold War in Europe seemed to be approaching another intense period of East-West nuclear showdowns that might prove the most dangerous yet. I would continue to race out on stories to places like

Israel or Syria, but from Frankfurt my main beat was obviously Europe. I filed stories on the gigantic military forces deployed by NATO and the Warsaw Pact, and on the extensive diplomatic arm wrestling among Moscow, Washington, Bonn, Paris, and London. One of the big stories involved the widespread antinuclear demonstrations flaring across the continent as fears escalated of a war by design or accident. Another part of my effort was keeping tabs on dissident movements within the Soviet satellite nations of central Europe.

I appreciated this opportunity. I covered large-scale military exercises on land and in the air, and, following the strategic debates over a combined arms doctrine—the AirLand Battle plans to destroy a Soviet invasion—I hung around top diplomatic meetings. At the street level, I covered mass marches protesting US nukes in Europe, the most turbulent political debate in 1986–87. I had also to be ready to go live to New York to explain the latest twists in the superpower drama or personally brief senior NBC executives and visiting anchor personalities passing through the bureau. I was even asked to arrange a face-to-face meeting between the NBC news president and Chancellor Helmut Kohl of West Germany, which took days of maddening bowing and scraping to get a one-minute handshake and photo op.

I now possessed an extensive list of military and diplomatic contacts. Respect for Canada had opened many doors when I was with the CBC, but NBC's clout opened considerably more—in part because our reports played in Washington, DC, and in the White House. I enjoyed the status that went with my position. It was a great age for punditry, although in hindsight, when it came to the Cold War, no one seemed to know what the hell was happening. Although the turmoil, demonstrations, and doubts within NATO appeared to point to escalating dangers, the Cold War was instead approaching a surprising peaceful ending. The confusion was perhaps inevitable, given the difficulty of reading the two main protagonists, Reagan and Gorbachev. No one really knew what either man was thinking or doing. Both seemed guided by gut feelings, with flashes of remarkable insight, and they could suddenly change their core positions. Master diplomats, as well as fellow leaders like Margaret Thatcher, Kohl, and certainly Pierre Trudeau, were mystified by the lurch and wobble of events.

After the Helsinki Accords of the seventies, the Cold War appeared permanently frozen by the core East-West agreement not to challenge boundaries in Europe. That did not stop longtime Soviet leader Leonid Brezhnev, however, from supporting Communist uprisings elsewhere. His doctrine proclaimed the "irreversibility" of Communist gains, which clamped a heavy lid over desperately needed reforms throughout the USSR. At the same time, the Kremlin played up its military and especially nuclear arms strength, which caused many in the West to feel that NATO was on the defensive. In the eighties, Reagan concluded that Moscow had overplayed its hand and could not possibly afford the empire it had created. Ditching détente, he turned the contest on its head with his own doctrine, setting out to roll back Communism by supporting anti-Communist forces everywhere, from Poland to Islamic fundamentalists fighting Soviet troops in Afghanistan. Unfortunately, this policy of involvement would spawn many post–Cold War problems for the United States.

Reagan's other strategy, it seemed clear, in the expression of the time, was to spend the USSR to its knees by letting conservative hawks in his administration drive stunning increases in defence spending, including new fighter bombers and both intercontinental and intermediate-range nuclear missiles. Although the Kremlin could not match this outlay, Reagan upped the ante still more by heralding a Strategic Defense Initiative designed to block incoming intercontinental missiles—a challenge well beyond Soviet resources and technical capabilities. The power disparity in the Cold War was about to become apparent.

At the time, barely a handful of experts thought the USSR would collapse in the foreseeable future. Reagan, due to either another gut feeling or some geopolitical eureka moment, saw the end of what he called the "evil empire" fast approaching. Two moves in particular hastened this dénouement: the threat of the defence initiative in space and Reagan's move to put US intermediate-range (Pershing) missiles in Europe to counter Moscow's own SS-20 missiles already planted in satellite nations. Gorbachev hoped massive demonstrations across Europe against the US action would force governments to demand the Pershings' removal. They did not. Inside the Kremlin, battered by Afghanistan and Chernobyl, struggling with a bureaucracy that barely functioned, Gorbachev knew the great empire of Lenin and Stalin had lost its ability to intimidate Western Europe and that it barely had the economic resources to hang on to its satellites. He at least grasped that urgent reforms took precedence over an essentially unwinnable arms race.

Much opinion in the West, and most mainstream media, tended to agree with inside-Washington assessments that Reagan was an amiable dunce who delivered fine speeches, but he was far more complex than that. Unbeknownst to associates, he had developed a Bible-based conviction that all nuclear weapons must be abolished. At their Reykjavik Summit in October, Reagan and Gorbachev made a start on cutting back on missiles in Europe and briefly veered into discussing a ban on all nuclear weapons. When details emerged, other nuclear powers were furious: France, China, and the United Kingdom had no intention of giving up their own nukes. Thatcher, for one, said she felt "an earthquake under my feet."

If the superpower leaders were hard to read, so were the street protests. Almost all aimed at driving the US missiles out of Europe, without making much reference to similar Soviet missiles deployed in Eastern Europe. East Germany promoted major demonstrations against the US arms, and, ironically, many of the placard-waving citizens later merged with the dissident movement to help topple the same East German regime.

Despite the public nervousness, I often found it difficult to take some of the war scenarios seriously. Everything I was hearing about

Soviet forces in the east suggested corruption, logistical weakness, and demoralization. The threat of accidental conflict certainly had to be taken seriously, but a planned invasion of NATO territory seemed preposterous, as did the idea of any NATO aggression eastward.

One shoot at a top-secret US base in Germany epitomized for me a certain silliness in the air. We were promised an exclusive look at a new perimeter guard device "with an ancient pedigree." We noticed, but could not approach, several large mounds in the grounds because they were closely watched over by the distinctive guards of the US Department of Energy Security Police. I assumed they housed the nuclear warheads for the Pershing missiles. Then came the explanation: they were part of an experiment involving a highly sensitive guard force favoured by Roman armies—geese! On cue, a bored-looking soldier came around a corner shepherding a small flock of the goose-stepping, quaking birds. The Roman camps had found that geese possessed much better alerting senses than dogs. It did make for a funny story. New York loved it, possibility more than anything else I'd done, but I did wonder whether the Cold War, the greatest military standoff in history, was going to end in farce.

In any case, many aspects of my life were extremely enjoyable. Well-adapted to turbulent times, I was living a foreign correspondent's dream. I liked Germany and loved the sophistication and vigour of West Berlin, which I visited regularly, especially when Tina flew over to visit. I was comfortable in the NBC office, which was similar in many ways to the CBC London bureau, although better funded and incomparably more competitive. I can hardly overstate the difference: at CBC, when it came to foreign coverage, we rarely bothered to ask what our main competitors, CTV and Global, were up to. We were proud public broadcasters, unlike those private networks, and so we believed on different missions. The CBC even felt part of its purpose abroad, its *noblesse oblige*, was to shame the profit-hungry privates into setting up matching bureaus overseas for the greater good of Canadian journalism.

Among the commercial Amnets, however, competition was relentless. I admired aspects of it, even wished the CBC had more competitive fibre, but still, it had downsides. In Frankfurt it encouraged an air of subservient paranoia toward New York. Every day an embarrassing flurry of self-promoting messages appeared on an all-offices wire that bragged in detail of our "endeavours"—not just our actual stories but also those merely conceived of. Staff in other bureaus could read that Frankfurt was "endeavouring to book the US ambassador for the Morning show," as though we were struggling through blizzards with Captain Scott to reach the South Pole. These snippets were written by managers, not reporters, so balance was often missing. Other NBC bureaus played the same self-serving game, but Frankfurt outdid them, and I found it mortifying. My suggestion that my otherwise laudable manager tone down the self-glorification a smidge was dismissed as Canadian Protestant modesty, which was probably not entirely off the mark.

Overall, however, I was pampered by the bureau and had few complaints. But in quiet moments I sensed a strong kernel of dissatisfaction growing within me. By keeping my mind active on world affairs, I was avoiding my own personal issues. I had been putting off the hard realization that I was no longer satisfied in my life or fulfilled in my profession. Perhaps I was just burnt out, but I feared my malaise was more ominous. I was tired of rushing about and frustrated with always playing the role of media spectator, making me feel spiritually empty. The intense effort to get airtime at NBC meant short items, and I missed the opportunity the CBC had offered to do meaningful analysis and documentaries.

I was also tired of the single life, of my own nagging and unsettled company, of living in a series of furnished rentals. Describing me to friends, one London landlady had called me "a perfect renter, one that's rarely seen, like a ghost that pays his rent on time." Above all I wanted to settle down with Tina, which would require returning to Canada. I was an oddball contradiction—a homesick foreign correspondent.

At some point the notion of leaving took hold. Although I liked NBC a lot, I just couldn't see a long-term future with them, rushing from one crisis to another. Promotion did not seem likely nor even desirable. I had no ambition to work stateside or in a studio, and with no family obligations, my salary concerns were minimal. In fact, an inheritance from my father's estate now meant I could at least take a gap year off to ponder possibilities. I wondered about leaving TV and returning to my first journalistic love, newspapers, where I still had many contacts and a decent reputation. In those days, Canadian journalism was flourishing and had not yet begun the decades-long retreat it appears trapped in today.

One media contact was among my closest friends, Conrad Black, whom I had known since high school in Toronto. Although he had always been sure he was destined for extraordinary achievements and dramas in his life, I was often taken aback by his brilliant, convoluted, and stormy climb upward, a headline-grabbing saga of corporate conquests and controversies that had him profiled at thirty-eight as Canada's "Establishment Man" by historian Peter Newman. In fact, he was no fan of the establishment but found the guise useful in his corporate battlegrounds.

A boardroom warrior of astonishing daring, Conrad's primary interest was in growing his Canadian newspaper chain and, in 1986, he had startled London by acquiring the lofty *Daily Telegraph*, bastion of the Conservative Party, for only $30 million Canadian. Overnight, the deal gave him considerable influence in UK political circles, a gain so improbable it caused fellow publisher-tycoon Robert Maxwell to marvel, "Mr. Black has landed Britain's biggest fish with history's smallest hook."

Despite his wealth and new fame, or notoriety, our friendship had changed little. He was still the witty, insatiably curious, and history-obsessed mate I'd always known. We talked often and, as in the past, would debate world affairs, military history, strategy, and politics while he also waxed on about the latest fascinating people he had met. I have never encountered a more curious person or a memory so tenacious—we still continue conversations first started in the early 1960s. Since his late teens, he had dreamed of creating a newspaper empire because, as he later wrote, "This was a business that could offer commercial success, political influence, cultural and literary potential, and access to everything and everyone newsworthy in every field."

Conrad had offered me positions with his publishing chain before, but I made it a rule never to work for friends. Now, as I pondered my future, he called to tell me he was buying the Canadian general-interest magazine *Saturday Night* and wondered if I'd become its editor. Here was a job I was uniquely, even laughably, unqualified for, so I had no hesitation in declining. Also, Conrad, once a diehard liberal who harangued all who would listen about the glories of F. D. Roosevelt, had moved with his newspapers into increasingly strident conservative politics that I did not share. I'm most comfortable, personally and professionally, clinging to the centre. The political distance between us has since swelled to a galactic divide, but by setting up our own demilitarized zone around never-to-be-debated topics and personalities, our friendship remains unaffected.

As I debated my future, I felt a growing pull to leave journalism at least for a year or two to take on humanitarian work. I wanted to be useful and also to learn more about the complexities of aid, should I ever return to reporting. That idea inspired me, yet remained tantalizingly vague in my mind.

In the meantime, there was a job to do. I was in Damascus waiting for the release of US hostages taken in Lebanon when I firmed up my decision to leave NBC, although I kept it to myself for over a month because I was caught up in a wide range of stories that interested me. I was in West and East Berlin a lot and had spent a week filming the life of heroin addicts on the streets of Frankfurt and Hamburg. In May I rushed to Warsaw to cover the crash of a Polish LOT Ilyushin airliner on the outskirts of the capital, one of a series of air disasters within the Soviet sphere showing that aviation was as badly flawed as the rest of the Soviet infrastructure. Poland was embarrassed, so state security would not let us in sight of the crash, despite my persistent efforts. Too persistent, it seems: two days later I was summoned to the foreign office and, with exquisite good manners, told my visa was cancelled and I must leave. In fact, the meeting was so good-natured I told the translator on the way out I wasn't quite sure what it was all about. "Basically, he told you to piss off and go!" he explained. "Your visa isn't renewed. They did wonder why you kept smiling all the time." It was my fourth national expulsion.

With better timing, I was in Berlin in June for the city's 750th anniversary. Across the wall in the East, a muscular propaganda extravaganza presented massive citizen parades with happy banners and floats, impeccably impressive military march-pasts, and salutes to Moscow for its firm support, all meant to give every indication of a solid and permanent regime. In the West, Reagan was scheduled to address a crowd of only ten thousand near the Berlin Wall. Amid speculation about his speech, nothing earthshaking was expected. Again, the president had been underestimated.

Contrary to the wishes of his State Department, Reagan flung a direct challenge at Gorbachev that no other leader would have considered: "Mr. Gorbachev, tear down this wall!" The command was widely viewed as rude, simplistic, and fanciful, but once the idea was out there, there was no going back. That speech became one of the fundamental events in the ending of the Cold War.

By then I had informed NBC I planned to leave. The boisterous John Lane gushed, "You did everything we ever asked you to do," which I guessed was a compliment. The company asked if I'd go home via Seoul, South Korea, flying across the North Pole, to cover massive pro-democracy protests against the corrupt and brutal ruling government. I agreed, and the demonstrations went on for more than two weeks as security police in Darth Vader gear clashed with amazingly well-disciplined demonstrators. As I watched, never feeling threatened, skirmishes moved back and forth along high-end shopping streets and, later, I found not a single pane of glass had been broken. I was gassed several times but otherwise unharmed.

After I left Seoul, I had a stopover in Tokyo airport's first-class lounge. Few others were around, but in the couch opposite sat the most legendary of all US TV news anchors, Walter Cronkite of CBS. Would he be interested in comparing notes on the Seoul events? I wondered. Just then an earthquake shook the Tokyo region, and we caught each other's glance of half-concerned, half-amused anticipation. The moment passed, we were assured the damage was negligible, and we nodded politely to each other and went our separate ways. Not much of a drama to end my NBC career, but at least the company was grand.

11

Investigations and Liberations

For several weeks after arriving in Toronto, I was swept along in the rediscovered joys of domesticity, romantic stability, dinners with old friends, and, yes, the absence of crises and professional dramas to fret over. I moved directly in with Tina, in her nineteenth-floor apartment with its sweeping view of what to my misty eyes was a glorious city—lush greenery leading to gleaming downtown towers and the shining lake beyond. The city I once dismissed as the single most boring place on earth now seemed transfigured into an urban seductress with wonders to enjoy: from ethnic restaurants and plentiful cinemas to literary clubs and friendly pubs, all the way down to its well-built supermarket carts and flawless car washes. My morale was high.

The fact I was now jobless did not wreck my mood. It likely enhanced it: I had enough funds to explore options beyond journalism, the only work I'd ever known. In Frankfurt I had even written the first draft of a screenplay, "The Monterey Castle"—a fiction based on modern-day ocean piracy which I sold as a first treatment to a group in Los Angeles for US$8,000. The film was never made, nor will be, nor should be, but my musing on the possibility of writing and of snappy visits to LA for script discussions, along with parallel thoughts of creative writing for magazines, now helped glamorize long lunches with friends at the Roof Lounge of the old Park Plaza Hotel. I would toy with the olives in my martini glass, shrug, and say, "I may write." Quite possibly I was one of those wretches that enjoy the status of being an author more than the actual writing.

Such thoughts, however, were secondary to my main hope—to join a humanitarian group, an actual non-government organization, for a year, possibly much longer. I'd received some interest before leaving Germany from three Canadian groups that had heard of my desire to work with humanitarian causes, and they had invited me to meet with them when I returned. What I envisioned was a role based largely in Canada; I was realistic enough to acknowledge I would not initially join that inspiring foreign legion of NGO volunteers I had met all over Africa. Rather, I sought a blend of domestic and foreign work. I would train eagerly for relief projects, travel widely, and go on extended tours in crisis zones but not give up the happy home life I was determined to build with Tina. This vision came down to a complex concept of my value, but I soon discovered that the NGOs had more simple roles for me in mind: to raise money and boost their brands. When I finally met with them in Ottawa, it was clear my mission would be predominantly to solicit donors and lecture internationally to garner enthusiasm for their work—all activities I would flee from. Amid many pleasantries and much mutual flattery, I did.

I settled back for a rethink. Just then, however, an unexpected phone call arrived from my longtime foreign producer, Tony Burman, one that would lead me back to Ethiopia and have a profound impact on my future. Burman, now a senior figure in the CBC's premier current affairs show, *The Journal*, was setting up a special unit to look into the RCMP investigation of the Air India bombing two years earlier—the terrorist murder of 329 people, 268 of them Canadian. Would I come in as sole reporter? he wondered. Here was a monster story: a Canada-based Sikh terror group was suspected of having blown apart the airliner by a delayed-action suitcase bomb as it was flying high off the coast of Ireland headed to India. The bombing is still the largest mass murder in Canadian history, and it shocked the world for being the worst airline terror attack ever (before 9/11).

A section of a Sikh separatist movement operating openly in British Columbia was the main suspect. That meant great embarrassment for Ottawa because the Indian government was furious that Canada had not yet arrested the bombers, and Washington was alarmed that Ottawa's lax attitude to extremist movements left North America vulnerable to attack. Was there a major scandal to uncover? Despite promising leads, prosecutors lacked sufficient evidence to take anyone to court. There was no sign of progress but lots of intense secretiveness in Ottawa and rumours of infighting within the investigation. My task would be to investigate the investigators and, if there was a scandal, find it. How could I refuse?

"I bet within one week you'll have found the names of all the main suspects," said Mark Starowicz, the famed head of *The Journal*, stabbing with his unlit pipe to make the point when I visited his office. We'd known each other since our Montreal days, so he was familiar with my past investigations involving the Mounties. Our small special unit would work apart, as I preferred: one office, a whiteboard, and three researchers. We needed to be discreet, because the Air India bombing aroused deep, potentially violent passions within Canada's Indian and Sikh diasporas, passions that spilled over from dangerous ethnic turmoil within India itself.

For years, international Sikh communities had seen the growth of a "Khalistan" movement supporting Sikh separation of the Punjab district from India. One element, called Babbar Khalsa, became an armed faction, even more active after the Indian Army stormed the sacred Sikh Golden Temple in the Punjab, killing hundreds in 1984. Although banned in Europe and under extremely tight security watch in the United States, Babbar Khalsa was largely unrestricted in British Columbia, merely watched by the RCMP and the Canadian

Security Intelligence Service (CSIS). That's where the bombing was planned (as well as a second attack the same day, which struck an Air India airliner while at Tokyo Airport, killing two baggage handlers). Counterclaims were made by Sikh elements that India itself bombed its own planes to discredit Sikh separatism. Conspiracy theories abounded: India pointed to the likely involvement of its archenemy, Pakistan, but two public inquiries and years of investigations have since determined Babbar Khalsa's guilt.

Our own investigation faced more than normal hurdles. Questions arose of why the police were stalled and why our security agencies had failed to prevent the bombing in the first place. Scattered news reports, prodded by the investigations of victim's families, had found some indications of a monumental failure by the government to protect the airlines from a likely attack that should have been obvious. As usually happens when the harsh winds of scandal shake the bureaucratic limbs of Ottawa, ministers first obfuscate, then imply that media and opposition inquiries are reckless, and if questions persist, fall back on the timeless line of officialdom defence: "We cannot comment as long as there is an active RCMP investigation." That can fairly be translated as "Don't hold your breath."

Our reporting would follow trails to British Columbia, New York, and Ottawa, but the RCMP investigation was centred in Vancouver. That's where Burman and I headed on the early morning of October 19, 1987. As we flew across the great curve of Canada discussing our story strategy over drinks, we also decided to pursue my idea of returning to Ethiopia to find the missing Birhan Woldu (see chapter 1). We had no idea the world below was being jackhammered by the global stock market panic known as Black Monday. The 22 percent fall in Wall Street value was so spectacular it even surpassed the 1929 crash for one-day losses. We were on a planeload of innocents, except for the cockpit, which wisely did not alert passengers midflight that any investments we had would likely be unrecognizably thinner when we landed. I became aware that something was amiss only when the receptionist at my hotel handed me a message to call my broker in Toronto. When I got through to him, I heard considerable shouting in the background, and he was astonished I knew nothing of the tsunami of selling sweeping the world. His news, rough but not ruinous, served one useful purpose: it flushed any lingering thoughts of a gap year from my mind.

Frankly, I wasn't thinking of much then beside the riddles of the Air India investigation. As I strolled out to explore Vancouver's downtown, a city I'd visited only briefly before, I enjoyed the atmospherics—rain-swept streets and alleyways, mist overhanging the arc-lit harbour, occasional fog horns—all setting the right mood for intrigue. Investigative reporting needs special efforts to delve deeply on sensitive stories, because reporters lack the leverage of police or official legal inquiries: they have no power to seize documents, forcefully enter premises, make arrests, and, with the CBC, no possibility of paying informants. No one needs to talk to us, and the two easiest words in English are "no comment." Apart from essential investigative skills in research and connecting dots, we needed to locate confidential sources, or even rare whistleblowers, and be able to win their trust that we would never reveal their identity. It likely helped that the CBC was highly respected and that I had pulled off some high-profile stories on policing secrets without ever betraying a confidence.

I had kept up my interest in national security since my Ottawa days, so I started off with some reliable sources. I knew that bitter tension between the old RCMP and the brand-new CSIS were key factors in any botched operations. My exposés of lawless RCMP actions in the seventies had been part of a series of scandals that prompted the government of Pierre Trudeau to strip the RCMP of its security intelligence function and give the counterterrorism role to CSIS only one year before the bombing.

My sense for finding organizational fissures owned much to my experience at the CBC, an institution riven by intrigues and jealous divides of its own: between radio and TV realms, local and national newsrooms, news and cultural shows, and its English network and Radio-Canada in Quebec. The peppery atmosphere was rather fun at times, for journalists take to gossip like hippos to mud baths, but it would be a source of much internal grief in coming years.

In any case, we did find new sources who sketched out a shocking tale of missed chances to prevent the terrorism, bungled electronic surveillance, investigation reports overlooked or wrongly dismissed, and critical tipoffs lost in transit. It was not long before we knew the names of all the suspects in addition to the two known key targets: Talwinder Singh Parmar, the mastermind of the bombing, and Inderjit Singh Reyat, the bombmaker (the only one eventually convicted, on a mere manslaughter charge). All these Sikh militants had been considered dangerous months before the attack, but surveillance was wretched. I was directed to a site in a clump of woods where Parmar and Reyat had set off a test detonator weeks before the bombing. The CSIS team doing surveillance thought it a mere gunshot, did not stop the men to check their car, and took no pictures because they had not brought along a camera.

One source in particular was a font of inside knowledge. When I met him in a coffee shop he mentioned the "poison" between the Mounties and CSIS agents: "They were barely talking, it was a bitter personal atmosphere, so often they weren't sharing information."

"But you say they were wiretapping Parmar and Reyat and others for months," I replied, "so I assume there must be masses of files and those tapes from before and after the bombing. Any use there?"

He paused, sipping his coffee as his eyebrows pointedly rose. "Well, here's the problem at the centre of things—CSIS just erased lots of those tapes."

Although stunned, I tried to act cool. "The tapes before the bombing, or just after?"

"Both," he replied. "That's why there's panic in Ottawa—there's just no sane way to explain this. At first there were suggestions Sikh translators sabotaged tapes to protect Parmar, but that didn't hold up. Looks like CSIS simply didn't want them to get out."

I knew then we had a massive scandal to uncover, far bigger than expected. We raced to Ottawa and tried to get top government officials to talk about the missing tapes, which they clearly knew of but had kept secret. One put it down to an unimportant culling of material too bulky to store, an explanation that was ludicrous given the national and international importance of the investigation. Another minister insisted the evidence was likely irrelevant, but his face had that "Oh dear God, now what?" look that flashes when a hint of scandal invades official minds. I worried they would concoct some explanation before we got our exclusive to air, but they could not think of one, so kept mum.

We were, to our surprise, granted an exclusive interview with Parmar in his home, which had an almost spiritual status in the movement. He was living on a quiet street on which an unmarked RCMP surveillance van recorded all comings and goings. We were forewarned we'd need respectful head coverings and assured they would be supplied. They were not, and our interview nearly dissolved in low farce.

Shocked at finding us bareheaded, Parmar's sombre aides looked around frantically for substitutes before grabbing delicate lace doilies from armchairs. These were draped over our heads, which was not a problem except that Burman and I looked preposterous as they flowed well down our foreheads and covered our ears. When Parmar walked in, a figure of obvious toughness not without menace, I dared not glance at Burman for time cues lest we both break into uncontrollable laughter—a dangerous insult in the circumstances.

I began the interview discussing the Khalistan cause, the outrages of the Indian military against Sikhs, and Parmar's beefs about oppressive security outside his home. When I abruptly asked if he had "bombed Air India," he replied angrily and quickly terminated the interview. As we were rushed out the door, I almost forgot to hand back my doily.

Our story ("CSIS Erased Air-India Tapes") of the destroyed wiretaps and botched investigation made headlines when it ran in December. Government ministers and security officials tripped over each other in their scramble for cover. Predictably, the minister directly responsible, Solicitor General James Kelleher, said he would not prejudice the RCMP investigation by explaining "how many tapes were destroyed, when they were erased, or who gave the order." CSIS director Reid Morden suggested that the material might have been destroyed "because it was not worth keeping"—a ridiculous argument given that any suspects arrested would claim the destroyed material might have proven their innocence in court. The Mulroney government refused to appoint an official inquiry into the mess. This stonewalling merely convinced the opposition that a far greater scandal lay behind their refusal: "They're afraid that someday a royal commission will expose all the gross negligence and incompetence that occurred," Liberal John Nunziata insisted.

That day would come, but sadly not for a quarter century, which is why the Air India scandal left so dark a stain on modern Canadian history. It wasn't until 2010 that the commission of inquiry into the bombing concluded that a "cascade of errors" had resulted in the aerial massacre and botched investigation. There had been clear warnings that Air India would be attacked, and government failure to protect it was "inexcusable." The RCMP had failed to "identify, report, and share information." CSIS had destroyed 150 hours of wiretaps rather than give them to the RCMP because it refused to "collect evidence" for police—a stand that effectively sabotaged possible prosecutions. The commission found, too, that successive Liberal and Conservative governments had used the excuse of ongoing RCMP investigations for decades to avoid revelations and to reduce settlements offered to the families—even when only a single Mountie was working on the case!

Small wonder that many of the families believed the country didn't care because of racism, as most of the Canadians killed were of East Indian background. I put it down more to Ottawa's culture of excessive secrecy, encouraged by the Canadian public's chronic lack of engagement in security and defence matters. In a poll taken by Angus Reid in 2023, nine in ten people said they had little or no knowledge of the worst terror attack in Canada's history.

After the Air India story, I decided to stay on at *The Journal* because of the broad range of subjects I could cover in serious depth in forthcoming documentaries. Burman and I next set out to find Birhan Woldu and her family in Tigray, Ethiopia, and to make a documentary, *Life after Death*, on a people's brave recovery from famine.

From this saga amid the world's greatest poverty, we moved on to the summit of power: a three-part series, *The Reagan Years*, to mark the end of the president's two terms in office. This fascinating project took us across the United States at a point when the Cold War years were reaching their climax, and over to Europe, to record the broader reaction to the Reagan phenomenon. I followed massive tank manoeuvres in Germany, still training for possible invasion from a Soviet Empire no one yet believed was in rapid terminal decline. I had face-to-face interviews with some of the key historic figures of that period, including Henry Kissinger, Barry Goldwater, and Helmut Schmidt (the former chancellor of West Germany and one of the towering Western statesmen of his time), as well as former top officials such as the US secretary of state, General Alexander Haig. The series examined the highs, and lows, of this most influential president, from the wretched intervention in Latin American proxy wars, including the Iran-Contra affair, to his surprisingly positive relationship with Soviet president Mikhail Gorbachev as they helped speed the dramatic yet peaceful finale to the Cold War.

The workload was often heavy, but I had pleasant breaks at home while writing and editing the features—days of recovered normalcy. I proposed to Tina, successfully but with admitted lack of originality on St. Valentine's Day (we were married in September). Even in so pleasant a time, however, I found it impossible to duck disturbing flashbacks to my experiences in the field. I would suddenly be distracted by images of a vicious murder scene in El Salvador or a car-bombed street in Beirut strewn with body parts. On a country drive, the sight of smoke rising from a farmer's bonfire could provoke instant alarm—*mortar fire!* my mind would scream—gone in a second but still a jolt. Ethiopia thoughts struck hardest because there I'd witnessed the worst, I had recently been back, and I had now taken on personal responsibilities toward Birhan's family. I seemed more prone to feelings of vague guilt, for the more fortunate my new life became, the more unease I felt over its contrast with the depthless miseries continuing "back there." The fact that others in my profession struggled with similar doubts and aftershocks did not make it easier.

I didn't experience constant unease, for I was generally upbeat, but the very unpredictability of such thought-spasms made them especially jarring. I'd be in the middle of a laugh-filled dinner with friends when my mind might suddenly suck me back to those desperate feeding camps or the hyenas in the night pursuing victims along the famine refugee trails.

At a positive level, I'd also spent hours ruminating on my past coverage in Africa, thinking of other stories that badly needed media exposure—areas that were overlooked by the major US networks because they were not on the front burners of big power competition. In the eighties the CBC's wide-ranging investigations in Latin America, Africa, and the Middle East had carved out an internationally respected role for the network that coincided with a period of Canada's heightened interest in building influence abroad. When last in Ethiopia we'd heard rumours of another horror: some NGOs were struggling to rescue a growing stream of emaciated, terrified children fleeing from Sudan into Ethiopia in groups and alone. "What kind of bloody hell does a kid have to face before running to Ethiopia, of all places?" Burman asked succinctly. The answer made your skin crawl: from the slave trade. The centuries-old bondage nightmare was again alive in the wretched killing fields of war-torn Sudan.

I'd wanted to do a story on modern slavery for years. Some years before, I'd done a news item on the London headquarters of the Anti-Slavery Society, the world's oldest international NGO, founded in 1839 as an offshoot of the first abolition movement in the 1780s. They were now warning there was more slavery in the world today than in past centuries, in different guises, from indentured farm and factory workers to boy soldiers, oppressed house servants, and the sex trade. During the mid-eighties, wars and giant famines had dominated coverage. Now, however, exposing the extent of child slavery in Sudan was an opportunity to drive the issue home, despite the difficulty of pulling it off.

Sudan was chaotic, awash in arms yet desperately poor, gripped by famine, its population of roughly thirty million fractured along language, tribal, and religious lines as well as an exceptionally brutal six-year-long civil war between North and South. The scale was daunting: Sudan was then the largest country in Africa, a quarter the size of the United States (until South Sudan gained independence in 2011). The South, site of the main slavery problem, was so unsafe that several NGOs had pulled out. History offered little ground for hope: when Britain controlled Sudan in partnership with Egypt before independence in 1956, limited colonial development was concentrated in the strategically important, largely Arab North, which bordered the Red Sea and included both the Blue and White Niles. The non-Arab Christian and animist South was largely undeveloped, impoverished, and despised by the North. War was inevitable when the North embraced the conservative fundamentals of Sharia Islamic law and set out to convert the whole country; in 1983 the South rebelled behind the Southern People's Liberation Army (SPLA).

Although Sudan was one of the world's poorest nations, both sides had plenty of modern arms. Seeking influence, the United States and the Soviet Union had plied the government with billions of dollars' worth of weapons, while the SPLA was supplied by the Marxist government of neighbouring Ethiopia. What set this war apart were methods employed by Khartoum that encouraged slave raids as a weapon. Rather than rely on its weak military, the North armed Arab local militias in border regions to wage campaigns of pillage and terror against southern populations, mainly the Dinka and Nuer, to undercut the SPLA by depopulating large areas.

The most feared militias were Baggara Arabs, nomadic horse breeders and skilled riders, ancient enemies of the Dinka and Nuer small farmers and cattle breeders over control of grasslands and water rights. Without restraints from Khartoum, the raiders were free to destroy villages and crops, drive off livestock, and collect bounty, including people who were taken as slaves. The SPLA also committed atrocities, but the government-backed militia raiders fed the profitable slave trade, particularly with Dinka children. Captives were sold sometimes hundreds at a time in the North or abroad, fetching from thirty to sixty dollars; boys between six and twelve went for up to a hundred dollars. They had many uses: men worked on farms; women as house slaves, often as forced concubines; and children as cattle herders, house servants, and also in the sex trade.

I flew with the crew to East Africa to arrange passes from the rebel SPLA as well as a bush plane and ground transport, while Burman flew to London to wheedle visas and arrange for our later visit to the North. Within days I landed on a small rebel airstrip in Sudan's searingly hot South. Along with a local guide and van, I had an experienced crew, including one of the best television cameramen of his era, Michael Sweeney—brilliant, deeply sensitive, and remarkably good-humoured even in the most trying moments.

We arrived in the rolling savanna lands in the final stages of the dry season. The land was baked hard and heat waves rising from the yellow fields matched the overhead blast from the sun. The South also had thick forests and rivers, where we travelled just before the rainy season made the area virtually impassable, but mostly we filmed in more open cattle-breeding regions where slave raids were most common. In some camps of the pastoralist Nuer, the scene looked timeless, almost mystical in the smoke haze of campfires at the first light of dawn, with the long-horned cattle and young herders a ghostly white from the ash sprinkled over them to ward off insects. Sweeney captured this seemingly eternal beauty, but it was also eerie, for the people had little defence against militia raiders who might strike at any moment if SPLA protection faltered. Once again I found that when danger and fear are present, heat takes on a particular cloying heaviness.

We visited destroyed villages that had recently been raided by the northern horsemen, where some had been slaughtered but many women and children abducted. Those who resisted were killed on the spot. With great unease we also entered a militia-held village, still intact, where every vibe was hostile even though we'd been assured of safe passage. The local militia leader, lean in his flowing white cloak, stylish in dark sunglasses that gave him a Hollywood-tough image, had a taut and natural air of command. Aid workers had pinpointed him as a big wheel in the local slave trade, but when I raised the subject, he spat out his refusal to answer questions about such raids, insisting his was a purely defensive force to protect against Nuer or Dinka attacks. In a nearby courtyard, militia members were sorting small arms, and guards quickly motioned us away in a manner that left no doubt it was time to leave the village. We had no communication with the outside world when driving, the area was remote for hundreds of kilometres around, and we could easily go missing if we pressed our luck. We travelled mainly by dirt roads but also took some breathtaking flights into areas threatened by surrounding enemy forces (see "Suspense in the Air" interlude).

We followed the trail of fleeing children—an unimaginable but very real modern underground railway for teens and younger children.

Usually orphaned, they had to travel without adults, some for months, through thick forests that were virtually impassable in the rainy season and where many were drowned trying to cross strong rivers. Terror was constant, for they also had to fear wild dogs, lions, hyenas, crocodiles, and venomous cobras. They were too traumatized to trust elders. I was struck by how few children we saw in South Sudan; in some villages many had already died or been taken. Usually, when we'd visit a village anywhere in Africa, children would flock gleefully around to watch us and look at our equipment, but here when we saw them, they moved quickly away, like shadows.

We found a pathetic horde, however, on the Sudan-Ethiopian border, where we filmed a long line of hundreds of children, along with a few adult women, fording a shallow point in a wide river to get to a UN-organized relief camp. Those old enough carried bundles on their heads; they had few clothes, and those they had were torn. There were no smiles, just faces of desperation, and the only sound came from the nearby rushing water. Standing by an aid worker who looked too angry to speak, we wondered how the world could be so blind to what was happening here. The UN knew, countries knew, but there was no criticism of Khartoum.

The children's tales, after we managed to win their fragile trust, took us into a dark mental world hard to fathom. All kids may have nightmares, but these children had ones they could not awaken from.

"My parents were killed, so I had no one to look after me, so I ran away," said an eight-year-old. "I don't know where I am now and am just waiting for someone to lead me to where I am safe."

Another young girl saw her mother being dragged away, screaming, by militia. When her father tried to stop them, both were murdered, and her brother grabbed and taken away. "They wanted children, so I ran—we were attacked by lions—most children died in rivers—we lived on roots and leaves—here they say we will be safe. I never want to live in fear again."

The aid workers tried to ease the traumas, making efforts to let the children feel loved and safely protected. Classes had begun, and the teachers encouraged the children to play in groups, make toys, and join in traditional dances. Most of the supervisors were veteran relief workers who had witnessed many years of human suffering, but this level of pain was nearly incomprehensible. The UN camp director explained, "A lot of the children died of disease, starvation, were eaten by crocodiles, or died because they could not survive the sheer physical and mental exhaustion of such a nightmare."

The war was in the process of displacing two million southerners. The threat of famine grew as the fighting wrecked crops, devastated cattle herds, and made it virtually impossible to distribute food aid. Needing answers from the other side, we flew to Khartoum, where Burman had been setting up vital interviews, including, to my amazement given the official secrecy, with Prime Minister Sadiq al-Mahdi.

For my generation, Khartoum, near the edge of the Nubian desert, held a historically exotic fascination. The Blue and White Niles met here before merging as one into Egypt, and centuries of trade had flowed through the city's markets. In 1885, British general Charles Gordon had been defeated by a nationalist and religious uprising of Islamic fundamentalists under the mystic "Al Mahdi" (Muhammed Ahmad), an Arab-Sudanese rebel—so striking a figure that filmmakers cast leading British actor Laurence Olivier to play him in the movie *Khartoum*.

The intellectual Sadiq al-Mahdi, great-grandson of that historical Al Mahdi, was an Oxford University graduate who had twice been democratically elected as prime minister. He was also head of the Umma Party, a political and strictly Islamicist movement with an armed wing involved in the current war. I expected an icy meeting, but what I got was something very different.

In his flowing traditional dress, the prime minister moved smoothly toward our interview set-up, offering a cheerful greeting in rich, Oxford-tinged English. He was a charmer with such quiet charisma I had to remind myself his government permitted state-orchestrated militia terror in the South. We discussed the condition of Sudan, but when I raised slavery by northern militia, he denied that the government endorsed it in any way and argued that cattle raids and kidnappings between Muslim and non-Muslim populations were endemic in the South. Slavery existed, he conceded, but away from the law. I did not believe him; his government had unquestionably supported the worst militias. As for his Islamist passion, could that possibly coexist with a mainly Christian and animist South? He insisted it must, to achieve the peace Sudan and Africa desperately needed. He had recently approved peace talks with the SPLA, and he seemed sincere on this point: "The Sudan is Africa. Almost every African has a nationality problem like ours, and if Sudan should fail to unite itself through liberal diversity, then other parts of Africa will catch this internal war disease; that is the significance of the Sudanese case."

This warning was prescient, and this interview may have been his last with a foreign journalist, for in less than two months al-Mahdi was overthrown in a military coup that sought to block his peace overtures. He was replaced by General Omar al-Bashir, who ruled for decades over an even more brutal regime. The South achieved independence in 2010, but wars have raged in both North and South Sudan ever since, the fighting and related famines killing an estimated two million people. Some of the fighting revolves around land rights, slave trading, and the prospect of future oil fields.

Our two documentaries, *Children of Darkness* on slavery and *Rivers of Wars* on the conflict, were much praised by NGOs for bringing attention to the secret scourge of modern slavery and won both Canadian and global awards. They were widely shown abroad. We were proud of our work, but I was left with a sour taste as the flurry of attention over Sudan soon died out. Over the years, as I periodically read new exposés of Sudan's "unknown war," our disheartening ignorance seems permanent and surely willful.

Once firmly back in Toronto, I had my first experience of working inside the epicentre of CBC English news and current affairs, housed at that time in a jumble of buildings at Carlton and Jarvis Streets. *The National* and *The Journal*'s current affairs block shared a prime-time hour at 10 p.m. This news hour was so distinctive a creation that broadcasters from Europe, the United States, and Asia came to study it and poach staff when possible. Visitors could not, however, miss what a dump the CBC looked.

A few years later, we moved into a spanking new headquarters downtown, but for decades the various departments were shoe-horned into scores of dreary sites around Toronto, including a few mice-infested relics and likely fire hazards. Within those dingy hallways, the enthusiasm of radio and TV staff was impressive, as was their connection to their national audience. The threadbare setting only highlighted the achievements of Canada's public broadcaster in rising above increasingly tattered budgets to pull off great things.

The Journal was mostly housed in a large editorial room holding an overcrowded clutter of desks, a central bank of monitors, and a staff meeting room where story ideas flared into projects, were shelved, or got firmly dismissed. This space became the sanctum for all, cherished by some, resented by others. The staff came in all sorts, from brainy academic types, through rough-hewn former print correspondents, to intense arts and music specialists—a generally talented, very well-read, and competitive group. The show's driving power lay at one end of the floor, in the book-lined office-study of Mark Starowicz, who, in addition to being the show's creator, was CBC TV's leading broadcast intellectual. The other power centre was the separate studio realm of *The Journal*'s host and superstar, Barbara Frum, who was often absent because of a chronic illness, leukemia.

Today we'd say the show had swagger, even arrogance, but I saw it more as our pride in our unique mission to make Canadian public broadcasting excel—a quality that faced more hurdles in recent decades. Since the 1930s, the CBC's core mandate from Parliament has always been to protect Canadian sovereignty by defending its culture from outside (American) domination. That entailed reflecting our national identity across all regions and languages, providing a mirror for the country and a Canadian eye on the world that private stations either cannot or will not provide. Almost all advanced countries across the globe have a public broadcaster that is similarly set apart and seen as critical to social cohesion. The CBC stands out because of the extraordinary challenges it faces: it is required to broadcast radio and TV out of dozens of stations, English, French, and Indigenous, across the world's second-largest nation and covering a quarter of the world's time zones. What's more, it has to stand up to a daily barrage of programming from the world largest cultural influencer, the United States—a level of challenge unique to Canada's public broadcaster.

I found these days heady and appreciated the way *The Journal* took time to be the country's ideas exchange, exploring subjects in rare depth, from overseas conflicts to domestic politics, investigations, and arts and culture. Domestic and foreign awards poured in, and we had a global reach thanks to a consortium of public broadcasters that shared items—some *Journal* material went regularly out to as many as twenty nations.

To use a sports analogy, the CBC had reached the medals podium. For all this, however, I could sense trouble ahead. The high profile of the news hour, the unique mix of news and current affairs at 10 p.m., meant dangers were accumulating, especially for *The Journal*. Despite the flowery words from successive governments about the CBC's vital role in protecting Canadian sovereignty, the political reality was that parties in opposition favoured the CBC but quickly soured on it once in power. Governments regularly weakened the CBC through slash-and-burn budget cuts, and the Mulroney government launched a new round of cuts almost as soon as it took power in 1984. While the CBC was being required to perform miracles in so vast and diverse a nation, it was begrudged the necessary financing. Among the world's public broadcasters, Canada has ranked, then and now, near the bottom in funding per capita (currently around $33 CAD a head, well under half the global average of $88, and down at eighteenth out of twenty countries).

Inevitably, the money crunch exacerbated struggles within the CBC over who got what, and, not surprisingly, the relatively better-funded *Journal* rankled other departments, including News. As right-of-centre conservatives pressured the Mulroney government, *The Journal* was viewed with special venom as too liberal and progressive, while the prime minister was often rumoured to be furious about its coverage of national events. With hostility from above and infighting within, the 1990s promised to be rough for us, but few foresaw that the consequences in a couple of years would crush *The Journal* and weaken the news hour, leaving behind a residue of bitterness that has endured for decades.

I was certainly not wallowing in such forebodings in the last half of 1989 because I had too much else on my mind. After getting married in September, I was back travelling and, given the explosion of extraordinary stories, I was on the road for six months of our first married year. After the fall of the Berlin Wall in November, nine separate nations ended Communism in an unprecedented rolling tide of liberation, although the messy end of the Soviet Empire took almost two more years. My assignments kept expanding, but I was once again achieving my teenage dream to be in a ringside seat for the making of history. And what history! This time it was lifting spirits and elevating imaginations about the possibilities of human society.

I started out with a big theme project in late September, to make a two-part series on the New Europe, which examined the final countdown of twelve nations to found the European Union. Here was so bold a human enterprise that economists, historians, and global strategists strained to define its impact: "We are creating the world's most important superstate," Canada's senior diplomat, Allan Gotlieb, told us, "and the world will never be the same."

Given my recent experiences in Africa, I couldn't have asked for a greater contrast as I travelled with my crew and producer Robin Christmas to capture powerful images of Europe at what was seen as the conclusion of its long postwar period. I interviewed historians and economists, diplomats and union leaders. The weather was splendid, the food grand, and the core EU message tugged at emotions. The new European beginning was haunted, and properly so, by the unspeakable past of two great wars and the Holocaust. Nations united, knowing they could never survive such violent disunity again. The EU's message was clear: if so many here could rise above centuries of conflict and frequent wars, so could others worldwide. As students and workers paraded under the new EU flag, the European anthem rang out: the "Ode to Joy" from Beethoven's Ninth Symphony.

News from Eastern Europe got less attention. Measured reforms continued in Poland, Hungary, and the Soviet Union, and there were reports of street demonstrations in East Germany, but no one expected actual rebellion, let alone collapse. As the regimes fell, Gorbachev himself and the Western intelligence services were equally astonished. How to explain the biggest surprise of the twentieth century? There were many factors: the regimes were far weaker than anyone appreciated, while Gorbachev, sensing that the USSR was no longer willing or able to shore up so rickety an empire, suddenly declared that his military would not intervene in other countries' affairs. Still, the East European populations had shown no strong desire to rebel, and the dissident movements, except in Poland, were small minorities, strongly influenced by intellectuals and church groups, and strictly nonviolent. This very passivity gave state officials

A curious lad at eighteen months, I strike an adventurous pose in the arms of my father, Charles, in Montreal, 1943. I clearly want to explore the world.

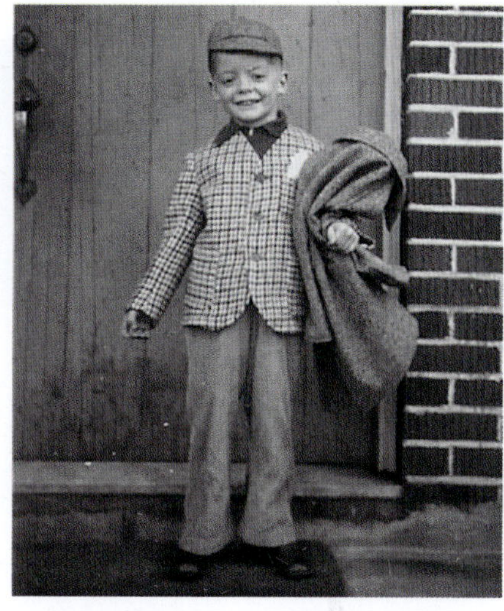

I had, it seems, a certain flair at age five in the bold new postwar era, proudly dressed in the latest fashion for the kindergarten boy.

The Stewarts at Christmas in Halifax, 1950, with the carefully groomed and orderly look of the new decade. Our Irish-Canadian mother, Mary Ellen, and father, Charles, with my brother David on the left, sister Heather in the middle, and me on the right. I still have that couch.

My short career as a goalie was as unimpressive as my equipment. Teams often picked their worst skater to guard the nets, but I was even worse at stopping pucks.

As a rookie newspaper reporter on the *Oshawa Times* in the mid-sixties—still a world of cigarette smoke, pounding typewriters, and ties. We had to be quick studies, writing on everything from city council to flower shows.

Montreal, 1969, and now with the *Gazette*, I shadow the visiting first NASA moon landers. That's Neil Armstrong, centre, with two tour officials.

Tense hours: at the height of the FLQ crisis in Quebec in 1970, I'm trying to learn from Montreal Mayor Jean Drapeau if troops are about to enter the city during the night. He knew but wouldn't give. I covered the crisis daily for almost two months.

Covering the civil war in Beirut, Lebanon, in 1984. Having achieved my goal to become a foreign correspondent, I faced my share of risk. Here I'm smiling, but they aren't, and I'm not sure if I'm being guarded or taken prisoner. They proved friendly.

The life had its adventures, including rugged bush flights to hard-to-reach crisis stories in Africa. In the foreground is my brilliant cameraman, Phillipe Billard.

Many destinations were grim, but not all of them. We occasionally passed through spectacular settings, such as this one in East Africa. I treasured these inspiring moments all the more, given the tension and sorrows we so often faced.

Waiting to take off to escape an approaching giant sandstorm in Sudan in 1985. The tension is evident; the flight was terrifying. In the background are cameraman Billard and sound technician Matti Lansoo.

Scrambling to cover what media were calling "The Worst Hell on Earth"—the great Ethiopian famine in 1984. Millions were uprooted, over one million died. Sound technician John Axelson and producer Tony Burman are with me.

In Tigray province, northern Ethiopia, the desperate flood of famine refugees was so large we sometimes had to work from the roof of our van. Billard is on camera; Axelson assisting.

Listening to the stories of refugees at a small relief centre one early morning in Tigray. It was to prove a fateful day for me.

Minutes later I saw this three-year-old child collapse, very close to death. This is the first image of Birhan Woldu, who would later be called the "face of famine" after our CBC video went global, which would have a powerful impact at the Live Aid Concert eight months later. Her despairing father, Woldu Menamano, looks on, helpless.

Birhan miraculously survived. I tried several times to find her and her family, but they were lost amid famine and war. Four years later, I was able to locate them and provide for their support and her education. I've remained friends with the family ever since.

The haunting image of Birhan's near death would go on to gain international fame, influence the Live Aid Concert, and raise record support for international famine relief. Here I'm visiting Birhan and her father, Woldu, in 1995, when she was thirteen.

I was based in London and Germany in the mid-eighties, and many of my stories were dominated by the Cold War, symbolized by the Berlin Wall behind me. The Soviet empire looked permanent, and stories often centred on diplomatic tension and arms talks. But humanitarian and human rights stories were rising in importance.

In the garden of Number 10 Downing Street, interviewing the formidable Margaret Thatcher. She loved her title "The Iron Lady." I worried she thought I was with another Canadian network—but I wasn't about to ask.

Sharing a laugh with Polish national hero Lech Wałęsa. As fearless leader of the Solidarity movement, he challenged Soviet control over Poland and was never cowed by threats. With him is his priest and bodyguard Father Henryk Jankowski.

The end of the Cold War did not bring peace. Here in the Gulf War, I'm with one of the advance US-led coalition units driving Iraqi troops from Kuwait City. Canadian reporters had to lobby hard to join frontline action as US and UK media dominated the reporting pools.

I vowed to avoid wars for a decade after my daughter, Kathleen Elizabeth (Katie), was born in 1993.

In studio with my friend Peter Mansbridge, long-time anchor of CBC's premier news show, *The National*. I did international affairs analysis pieces and increasingly worked in studio.

I was a frequent backup anchor on both news and, here, the famed current affairs show *The Journal* before it was unwisely ended in 1992. Outwardly confident on the anchor desk, inwardly my nerves rebelled. I hated it.

I also hosted a nightly current affairs show *The Magazine*, but I so disliked live studio work that I quit after eighteen months and asked to return to reporting.

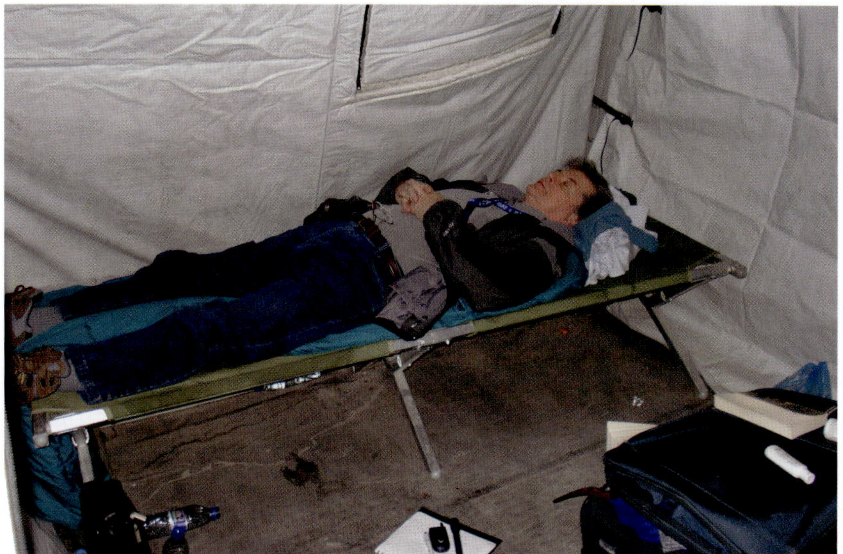

Back on the ground, an old man at war in my unglamourous quarters in Kandahar. I did many Afghanistan war stories, but reported only twice from there as, in my mid-sixties with knee replacements, I was no longer in adequate shape.

I felt ludicrous when donning the required armour before accompanying patrols. By 2010, the Canadian force there was weary, and even splendid troops sensed an air of futility as the Taliban grew stronger.

I retired when close to seventy. I still did foreign affairs analysis for CBC and was made senior fellow at what's now named The Munk School of Global Affairs & Public Policy at the University of Toronto. I loved this mix of work.

Above all I revelled in a peaceful life. Here I lunch with my wife, Tina Srebotnjak, and daughter, Katie.

I looked forwards to reunions with three Canadian TV news legends: Bill Cunningham on the left, Tony Burman, producer and news director, and Joe Schlesinger. Combining almost 200 years of news gathering among us, we had lots to talk about.

My old media passes evoke strong memories of times and places, some good, others dark—but all part of the career I chose.

Experiences in the Ethiopian famine deeply affected my life. I've backed efforts to expand rural schools in Tigray province, one of the worst-hit areas. Here on a private trip back, I'm shown new projects by Birhan and Bisrat Mesfin.

I've been back to visit the former site of Badingham College, which was my old school in England for four years in the fifties. Within its eighteenth-century premises, I first dreamed of a future as a foreign correspondent, on the ground to witness history made. The school is gone, and the space is now private offices.

In Rideau Hall, Ottawa, in 2024, with Tina and Katie after I received my Order of Canada.

and generals the confidence to give up the old order in the expectation, correct as it turned out, they would retain their careers in the new future.

The most stunning upheaval was East Germany, long regarded as among the toughest antireform states, but in October peaceful protests were gathering strength and, on November 9, the government stunned the world by declaring no restrictions on travel into West Germany. In Berlin, tens of thousands of people started pouring across the Berlin Wall, the sad, concrete symbol of everything menacing about the divided Europe and the Cold War. I managed to be there just as the wall fell, capturing the joy and doing items on Germany's reaction while also reshaping the documentaries I was writing. Like everyone there, I was caught up in a kaleidoscope of images: blazing lights of massed TV cameras; faces flushed with excitement, even tears of pure happiness; chipping out my own piece of the wall (now on my desk); and passing the once intimidating East German border guards, who watched us all flow by and transformed, polite to a fault—bullies suddenly robbed of a playground to terrorize.

Given the thousands of media on hand, I set out with my crew one afternoon to find a fresh angle by driving two hours east and stopping at a random village to see how life was playing out. Without contacts, I entered a local high school, sought out the English teacher as guide, and found a gem—a sensitive woman who took me through a few stores and the health clinic to introduce me around. Many people I met shared her determination not to join the surge to the west. "I never will desert my country," she said. "Rather, I'll work to make it a good place." Some poured scorn on local doctors who had been the first to leave. They took me around to see the lovely countryside under a soft autumn mist and, before leaving, I did a stand-up stressing that despite the attention on the human tide surging toward West Berlin, those who chose to stay should also be respected for making their choice. Most people did not leave, waiting instead for the two Germanys to unite in coming years.

On live TV appearances, I'd be asked, "What does this mean for the future of Europe?" I played it safe by stressing it would take months before the form of this new world took clear shape. I knew I would never see events like these again; I felt as though I were surfing atop a giant wave of rejoicing that was sweeping away corrupt regimes and healing the wound that had split Europe for over four decades.

Next, I flew into Prague, where a quarter of a million Czechs held rallies to gently will away Communist rule. It was called the Velvet Revolution because no life was lost, nor was there much verbal roughness. Yet in this country under the old regime, thousands of people had been imprisoned and tortured and hundreds killed by security services. I caught sight of one of the great civil rights leaders of the century, Václav Havel, an author and dissident leader who had been jailed frequently. His major philosophical work, *The Power of the Powerless*, had preached that if people under oppression live with truth, refusing to accept state lies, those who are governing will inevitably lose their authority. Here, now, the pinnacle of the government and the military had decided that their power wasn't even worth defending. Gandhi and Martin Luther King Jr. seemed here in spirit. The dissidents appeared to have minimal organization, yet historians have cited this revolution as likely the most disciplined and humane in history, all the more surprising because of the hard sacrifices made during the long oppression.

In sublime moments, the ridiculous always hovers nearby. News teams had grabbed all the media interpreters, so I was lucky to find a high school youth who was quite good as a translator and thrilled to be making a hundred US dollars a day. As we were about to head out to cover a speech by Havel, with a possible interview afterwards, his mother called to explain that he couldn't come. I asked why, concerned he might be ill. "Well, he's just got his first girlfriend and tonight will be his first date," she said proudly, startled by the long, heavy silence at my end. I hope the date was successful because it cost me my one chance to meet a real hero of mine—a very key player in the Czech and modern European story.

I entered 1990 scrambling to reshape my series of documentaries under the new title *Europe Unbound*, to include the amazing present—including the hot new issue for the continent to decide on, the unification of Germany. I'd soon be off to the USSR to help with coverage. The series incorporated both the EU and the end of a divided Europe. Days of hope and ambition lay ahead, and most of my interviews stressed the opportunities for trade and global relations. Flying home, though, I kept recalling the warning a trade expert gave me as we wrapped up taping: "The Cold War was a bandage covering the deepest wounds in our world, a superpower balance that held at least many conflicts in check. Now the bandage is ripped off, and we best fear what we're heading into."

INTERLUDE

Suspense in the Air

Our work in the field often took us into extreme circumstances, and some of my tensest moments came in the air. Usually I loved being aloft, living the *National Geographic* dream of seeing the splendours of Africa's forests, rolling plains, and glistening rivers spread out below. We flew in all kinds of craft, from cramped five-seaters to comfortable twin-engine prop planes, many piloted by aid volunteers and bush pilots. I preferred the small ones where I could see into the cockpit and know that the needles on the instruments were not spinning about in frenzied motion.

When our story involved a lot of charging around, I would clamber aboard one of the planes, sun-dazed in dirt and dust clouds or sweltering in relentless humidity, grateful to feel the air drafts from cabin vents. A plane was like a temporary oasis, where I was briefly free of the miseries below. If I didn't have a script to write, I could watch the spectacle of the land passing and the billowing clouds turning from purest white to pink and red if the sun was about to set. We learned which clouds should be avoided. A pilot once pointed and said: "If we fly into that upper layer, our wings will be ripped off!"

My most hair-raising moments occurred in 1985 in Sudan while flying at twelve thousand feet just above the worst Saharan sandstorm in twenty years. I was doing a series of stories on famine risk in Africa and wanted to show that the crisis had expanded to threaten some of the outermost populations. When my crew and I flew on our twin-engine hire from a remote regional airfield to the landing strip of a refugee camp well inside the desert, we thought we would miss the storm completely—and our Greek pilot agreed. But it advanced with a force that took everyone by surprise, and we were overtaken by a storm so broad and powerful it blew sand sixty-five hundred kilometres. On our return flight we found ourselves flying above what looked like a reddish-brown, flat curtain that stretched to all horizons. I'd never seen a true sand-and-dust storm before.

Sitting behind the pilot, I noticed sweat pouring down his neck as he kept fidgeting with his fuel gauges and radio controls. Alarmed by how jittery he had become, I leaned forward to ask if all was going well. "Not really," he replied. The radio beacon that was supposed to guide us back wasn't working: it turned out that the local operator, believing our flight cancelled, had switched off the direction finding beacon and gone home. With as much calm as I could muster, I asked, "And the fuel?" The pilot's voice betrayed concern: "I've switched to reserve tanks and we should be okay . . . if I can just find the town." With that he began banking the plane every minute or so to see if he could peer straight down to identify the terrain.

I sat back contemplating the possibility that we were lost and might have to crash-land almost blind in a desert sandstorm. My two crew were asleep, and I thought it pointless to awake them before it became necessary. Alone, I wondered if we'd survive or become the lost CBC crew of future legend, until our bleached remains were stumbled across decades hence. I started scribbling a farewell note just in case, while keeping a nervous eye on the fuel gauge.

Perhaps twenty minutes later, after I'd woken the crew to tell them, "We have a problem," the pilot suddenly yelled, "Got it! I see our town," and swung us into a tight corkscrew dive down through the sandstorm. Thrilled though I was, I still held my breath, remembering that a communication tower rose near the airport. Would we hit it? Swaying and bouncing in high winds as we descended, we finally landed, and I felt the overpowering sensation of being safe after all. As we settled in to stay the night, the pilot admitted he had to take the risk of hitting the communication tower. "If I had not found the airstrip," he said, "I would have had no choice but to try to belly land in a dried-out desert wadi."

On another flight in Sudan, I had a tense corkscrew landing, but this time our pilot was bizarrely jaunty rather than jittery, and we were over jungle, where the risk was not sand but anti-aircraft fire.

Civil war had erupted across South Sudan, where the Black African population, largely Christian, sought to secede from the strictly Islamist central government. The rebel army had captured most of the South and had surrounded Juba, a key government city and garrison in the tropical far south. The CBC had rare access to the war zone and, when we were offered a flight into besieged Juba, we leapt at it. This time the pilot of a twin-engine craft was a British adventurer type, eager to show off the circular aerobatics required to descend into the encircled city. That manoeuvre was the only way he could keep us clear of the machine-gun and 20 mm fire from the rebel positions in the jungle beyond. Inspired by the sense of drama, he agreed we could tape him pulling it off.

As we approached Juba and prepared to descend, he asked me to scan out the right side of the plane to spot any flashes of gunfire or tracers. The crew was busy taping him, so I was the lookout. We curled into the tightest bank I'd ever experienced as he began his corkscrew manoeuvre. It was quite exciting, actually, and, fortunately, I could spot no fire. As we circled down, the pilot kept up a running commentary filled with witticisms and the revelation that his wife in England had no idea he flew into dangerous areas. I wished he'd just concentrate on flying. He landed flawlessly, however, and we were greeted by the airport manager, delighted to have foreign visitors. He smiled broadly but gave us a dire warning: "Do not step on a mine: our hospital has run out of anesthetic and now amputates without using any." We got the siege footage we needed, and two days later our pilot circled us skyward in the same dramatic way. Again, no fire came from the treeline.

I never lost my love of these small, adventurous flights, even though, later, I heard that two of the very good pilots I'd flown with had died in crashes. One was caused by bird strikes; the other by a storm.

12

The Gulf War and Broadcast Battles

My first experience of the new post–Cold War world found me bouncing between the imploding Soviet Union and the exploding Middle East. Although spinning inside yet another vortex of runaway events, I wasn't ready to give up the fascinating vantage point I had on history as it unfolded.

In January 1991, when an enormous US-led alliance launched a UN-approved offensive to drive a massive Iraq invasion force out of oil-rich Kuwait, I was in the forward media position, the International Hotel in Dhahran, Saudi Arabia. Iraqi dictator Saddam Hussein had seized the tiny neighbouring Kuwait in August the previous year, and refused UN demands that he leave. Shortly after 2:30 a.m. on January 17 the alliance struck. The first departing waves of the US air assault screamed over my head and the Gulf War was on—the largest clash of arms since the Second World War.

Inside our media headquarters, alarms were blaring and air raid sirens whining as the hotel intercom beseeched guests to rush to a basement shelter that could be tightly sealed against biochemical weapons. Sound advice, but many reporters raced instead to the rooftop or balcony vantage points to begin phoning live coverage in to their networks. Most of us had covered ongoing wars before, but not the very start of one or one as massive—we had no clear idea how bad it would get or how long it would last. We carried around our gas masks and lightweight roll-up biochemical protection suits in nifty packs, for the risks of chemical or germ warfare were high and we were inside a prime Iraqi target. The hotel was close to the major US airbase, and Dhahran was stuffed with ammunition dumps, large petroleum containers, and key military and media communications. We were well within range of Iraq's most advanced missiles.

In those months, the Gulf War dominated world attention because the future of the whole Middle East and the global economy was at stake. A vast amount of the world's oil supply was within the conflict zone. I'd been prepping for the war since August, in Washington, New York, and London, and I'd covered the US construction of a remarkable forty-two nation coalition, including major Arab countries, to force Iraq out of Kuwait if Saddam didn't leave voluntarily by January 15. Such rare unity was due to the fact that Iraq had gone rogue by brazenly swallowing up Kuwait for its oil reserves. The coalition feared Iraq might next assault its longtime enemy Saudi Arabia by grabbing its oil fields, giving Saddam a stranglehold over the world's energy supply.

As the months passed, I was filled with more queasiness than I'd known before. I dreaded what the war might do to global stability and profoundly hoped it would not happen, though I was determined to cover the conflict if it came. Iraq had the world's fifth-largest military, with sophisticated weapons, and was well entrenched inside Kuwait, so victory would not be easy. The war-gaming military analysts I interviewed predicted weeks or even months of fighting and many tens of thousands of casualties before the Iraqis were defeated.

There was a painful irony in this combat for a world celebrating the end of the Cold War. The massive conventional US Army in Europe, which had spent two generations planning for a Soviet invasion, now shifted to the "lone and level sands" of the Saudi and Kuwait deserts. The coalition numbered close to one million troops, three thousand tanks, nearly two thousand aircraft, and two US naval task forces. Iraq boasted a million troops, five thousand tanks, and hundreds of missiles, including Soviet-built Scuds, and large stockpiles of chemical and germ weapons. Saddam was convinced that the United States, after Vietnam, was a paper tiger, unwilling to face casualties. Not for the first or the last time, this tyrant proved himself a master of miscalculation.

And so war came. On the second night, those trying to sleep were awakened by sirens and, suddenly, a blast nearby that shook the hotel. I threw on my gas mask and started running to the stairs leading to the roof, almost collapsing from lack of breath before I remembered that running in such a mask is not easy. I quickly checked out flashing emergency lights racing through Dhahran and ran down to my room to phone the Toronto desk, suggesting I be patched live into the News Special to report that Dhahran was under attack. I was told I'd have to wait several minutes until the current portion of the show could fit me in. Caught up in the egocentricity of a crisis moment, I gasped, "Why bloody delay?" "Well, Israel is also under missile attack, and that's more urgent" came the deflating reply.

Still, I was lucky to avoid the shelter—some who went there emerged traumatized. For nearly an hour they had stared at each other through claustrophobic gas masks while the hotel's British "defence consultant" told them, "This is a real air raid. If you have a chemical protection suit, use it." The thought of dying in extreme agony in a Saudi basement caused some occupants to leave the war immediately, including a young coalition soldier on our floor who suffered a severe panic attack and was rushed home. I knew I would not fare well in that shelter and never used it.

Over the surprisingly short six-week war, forty-four missiles were fired at Dhahran, most of them shot down in spectacular displays in the night sky. We grew blasé about the danger until one soared over our hotel and struck a nearby US barracks, killing twenty-nine GIs. The threat of biochemical weapons was taken seriously, however, as Saddam had used them in his recent war with Iran as well as on his own civilians to suppress rebellions. Near the end of the war he also set alight Kuwait's oil fields, sending darkly polluted clouds swirling across the battlefield—a form of environmental war that indicated how far he might go.

It was a heavily televised war, unlike any seen before. New satellite feeds gave coverage an unprecedented immediacy that was viewed around the world. Most who remember it recall the extraordinary live coverage by CNN of the waves of US bomb and missile attacks on Baghdad, which brought the war directly into their homes and offices. Two hotels were the epicentre of war reporting—the Al Rasheed in Baghdad and our Intercontinental in Dhahran. The journalists in Baghdad covered the more dangerous incoming fire, while we witnessed the outgoing attacks. Compared to our mission, the Al Rasheed duty seemed suicidal, but the top journalists there correctly decided that their hotel would be spared simply because the White House would never dare blast CNN's base. Those of us in Dhahran, however, thought that Saddam would gleefully take out all Western media if he could.

Our media centre was hotel glitzy but fiercely competitive as journalists from dozens of countries constantly competed for advantage by all means, fair or foul. The Intercontinental had none of that storied camaraderie of slightly seedy media hotels in past wars, such as the Caravelle in Vietnam or the Commodore in Beirut. There was little socializing, for starters, which the host country's ban on alcohol did little to improve. The bar tried to entice but its prize drink, a Kandana fizz—orange juice and nonalcoholic sparkling wine in a martini glass—failed to pack the joint.

There wasn't a lot of downtime in any case: the very availability of satellite feeds magnified the competitive pressure to send out more items, and chances to move around outside were strictly controlled by the all-powerful Pentagon media pool. Every day this pool sent out a few heavily supervised busloads of news teams to military sites to record stand-ups and interviews. The pool served only a small minority of the numbers clamouring to go along, but attempts by the CBC and others to sneak out on our own were invariably turned back with warnings that we risked losing our visas.

I understood the need for tight security, but what we non-US teams hated was the pool's overwhelming preference for US media, especially after leading American news superstars flew in to charm starstruck press officers. The grovelling for pool spaces was pitiful to see, especially when our own grovelling flamed out. Although Canada was the fourth-largest "Western co-belligerent," our media minders viewed us as peripheral. My producer, Bill Cobban, and I made frequent appeals that the CBC deserved better status because Canada had been among the first to join the coalition, with a fighter squadron and two destroyers. "I mean, what the hell does it take to get Canadians into a pool at the front?" I asked one cheerful Tennessean press officer. "Oh, I'd say one armoured brigade might do it," he drawled.

The system did have some benefits: all video shot by the networks as well as a good part of the military's own footage was shared, along with the latest news briefings from top commanders. We had a daily flood of images and information to harvest in the equipment-jammed room that served as the CBC TV field office. It helped that we had considerable experience in conflict: the legendary correspondent Joe Schlesinger handled the news stories, while I filed longer features and some news too. Schlesinger, then sixty-three and walking with a cane, always yearned to have the night's lead story, however short, while I preferred the longer, six-to-ten-minute "mini-docs." I considered him one of the best TV writers in the business, with a mesmerizing delivery, and he was generous in his comments on my work. Fortunately, we got on well, as he was a grouchy and unbeatably wily competitor when resources were at stake.

On days we both had stories, we each naturally wanted the best images for our own items, but news had first choice, and Schlesinger swooped in like a hawk to pluck up all the best scenes. He did get sleepy, however, around late afternoon when the main pool pictures were fed in, and sometimes he nodded off on the office couch—a habit I shamefully encouraged by feigning my own sleepiness with yawns, sighs, and drooping eyelids. When he seemed in dreamland, I'd lean forward, hoping he'd miss the video I most wanted, but the trick hardly ever worked. As a prize image flashed on the screen, his right eye would snap open and he'd bark "Mark that!" to the editor. After decades of covering crises, the best correspondents, like Schlesinger, developed bird-of-prey instincts, and his were the finest I ever saw.

Free of the hourly burden of news, I could concentrate on the tactical and even strategic analysis, subjects I'd been keen on since my teens. I had an advantage over many reporters because of my background covering US/NATO training in Europe for a massive all-arms campaign to defeat a Soviet invasion—the AirLand Battle doctrine that became the basis for the Gulf War's Operation Desert Storm. It required a highly sophisticated unity of effort involving land armies, along with air and naval power, to concentrate the full force on the enemy's vulnerabilities on a scale few militaries could even dream of achieving. The operation also required extraordinary command-and-control communications and logistical might that only the United States and its NATO allies possessed.

The ghost of the Vietnam defeat still haunted the United States, even though the Pentagon had spent the previous sixteen years overhauling its combat arms. Predictions of doom loomed over the operation. One pompous Middle East correspondent from Britain told me that the Yanks, compared with his countrymen, knew nothing of desert war and would end up hopelessly lost in the featureless sands (somehow, he had missed the recent arrival of GPS). I expected, however, that US airpower would devastate Iraqi units in Kuwait, and that US and UK divisions would be unstoppable. Armies cut off without air or land support in open deserts tend to surrender or flee en masse. We knew approximately where military units were positioned, so it was not difficult to speculate (as I did with hand-drawn maps faxed to Toronto) on the giant left-wing armoured hook operation that US general Norman Schwarzkopf planned. The big unknowns were the likely number of casualties and whether Iraq would use chemicals—and, if they did, what the US response might be.

In the final week before the assault, I saw much of the main attack force as it moved into positions behind the front line: thousands of tanks, armoured vehicles, and artillery pieces stretching out mile after mile beyond the horizon while, above, swarms of helicopters raced low over the troop assembly areas. I was able to get that far forward because I requested access to show off the amazing US logistical setup in the desert. One of the largest armed operations in history, the war required 576 cargo shipments and ten thousand aircraft, along with massive pre-positioned depots of food, ammunition, fuel, and water depots in largely traceless wastes. It was the pride of the pleasantly egocentric General Gus Pagonis, who I sensed was the real genius of both operations: Desert Shield, the defensive phase to block Iraqi advances, and Desert Storm, the attack to liberate Kuwait. When I scored an interview with him, the great assault and true test of his operation was only days ahead, and tension was building by the hour. He seemed flattered by our interest and gave us access to some of the forward areas. But what I really wanted was a position with the advance troops when the assault began. It was time to find unconventional means to get access.

I had already pleaded with CBC management to get our diplomats to lobby Washington directly to include us among the media positioned there. "Unless strong pressure is brought to bear, Canadian reporters will be entirely excluded from the greatest land battle since the Second World War," I warned in writing, adding, "I believe Canadians will regard this as an incomprehensible humiliation." I also suggested the solution: a special combat pool for left-behind nations, something I'd been agitating for among the other frustrated news teams.

I looked for help among the influential military analysts who'd joined our media base, many of whom I had previously interviewed. As long as you were relatively knowledgeable about esoteric theories on, say, proper tank deployment in desert warfare or the key imperatives of the AirLand Battle doctrine, it was possible to join a running seminar on how the war would or should be fought. Among these analysts, the most bizarre, outspoken, and daring was retired US Army colonel David Hackworth, a steel-hard, boisterous hero of countless rebellions against higher commands. He had lied to get into the army at fifteen, fought numerous battles in Korea and Vietnam, and won ninety-one medals in all, including ten Silver Stars for gallantry, an all-time record in any US service, and two Distinguished Service Crosses for "extreme heroism." Held in awe as a combat leader in Vietnam, he was said to have been the model for the charismatic, war-loving colonel played by Robert Duvall in *Apocalypse Now*. Unable to contain his combative nature or accept the rules, he was effectively dismissed by the military for denouncing the Vietnam operations of the high command. He was now a writer/analyst covering the war for *Newsweek*, and I found him personally warm, steeped in military insights, and a witty conversationalist. Though utterly dissimilar in personality, we nevertheless got on well.

Hackworth liked my idea of trying to skip around the media pool coverage and link up with the colourful French Foreign Legion regiments raring for action on the far edge of the coalition's left flank. "Perfect! What a plan!" he roared. "I believe the Legionnaires will likely be used to storm Baghdad if Saddam's rule appears to crumble. One van, with rations including a hell of a lot of water, and my clout, is all we'll need to get to the Legion." I felt the blood drain from my face; I wanted to do a colourful documentary, not skydive into a flaming Apocalypse Two. His use of "we" did not reassure me. Although I regarded the chance that France would take such risks for a US-run coalition as slim, his unquenchable love of action was sure to end in a wild firefight somewhere. I reminded myself his greatest fame came from his eight Purple Hearts, making him for a time the most often wounded soldier in US history. I could think of safer battlefield guides.

Fortunately, my big break came just as the land offensive into Kuwait began with rapid breakthroughs across Iraqi front lines. On the afternoon before the attack I'd got close enough to the front to see what seemed like a tidal wave of armour and troops pouring forward toward the battle. As the Iraqi collapse accelerated, American networks had crews in on the chase to be first to reach the capital, Kuwait City, as it was liberated. Our last shot was a scheme Cobban and I had worked on with several dozen journalists from Brazil, Italy, Australia, and other countries: to set up a spur-of-the-moment "world media coalition" or some such bafflegab.

We held a news conference in the lobby to demand access to the front. As intended, the ploy upset the carefully orchestrated media management plans of the Pentagon and White House. We also lobbied Saudi Arabia to "end US news domination." The next afternoon we were informed, rather sourly, that our "coalition, or whatever the hell it is" would get two buses to accompany a small joint unit of Kuwaiti and Saudi troops in action along the main road to Kuwait City. We were now a pool headed into the battle. Some grumbled about being saddled with a patched-up Arab unit a few thousand strong, but I recalled how the US Army had held itself back outside Paris in 1944 to give the Allied Free French division the honour of first entering the liberated city. Politics play a major role in coalitions, so I was fairly sure our midget force would be pushed into the lead in entering Kuwait City when the decisive moment came.

Before dawn, two rattling school buses filled with our multinational media force set off into battle. We'd drawn lots, and I'd won the sole seat allocated for Canadian TV, so with the help of a shared Brazilian cameraman, I'd have an exclusive if we made it into the capital—and back. Unlike US networks, the CBC had not provided us with the new satellite phone gear to file directly from the action, so I would ride 430 kilometers to Kuwait City, get to our advance unit, spend several hours covering the liberation, and then race back the same distance to Dhahran to edit and feed our file out early next morning.

We were an unlikely-looking contingent, a babble of many tongues, as we peered out at dark armoured shapes heading through dust clouds in the first feeble light of day, made dimmer by the ominous smoke from the burning oil fields. While Kuwait City was the objective, we had no clear idea what dangers lay ahead as we joined our small Arab unit.

By chance, I was seated next to a figure as extraordinary in literary circles as Colonel Hackworth was in military ranks: Oriana Fallaci, still striking at sixty-two, was Italy's most famous author-and-foreign correspondent. She was known internationally as the scourge of celebrity interviewees, revered and reviled for her sharp-witted, tough, venomous, and sometimes boorish comments. She'd run guns at age ten for the Italian wartime resistance, covered Vietnam, and was shot up so badly in a Mexican massacre that she'd been left for dead. Now she greeted my arrival as seatmate with a look that said, "Oh God, but I guess I could do worse." She perked up when she found me a good listener to her steady stream of cutting remarks about the bizarre bubble of fate we were in. "Do you notice how awful they smell?" she asked, referring to our fellow passengers. "Perhaps it's fear," I offered. "No, filth!" she declared. I complimented Fallaci for her celebrated profile of Henry Kissinger in 1972, when she got him to describe himself ridiculously as "the cowboy who leads the wagon train by riding ahead alone on his horse." She chuckled. "Men try to impress me and often say very stupid things."

After joining the advancing armoured column, our route took us through abandoned Iraqi defences across a countryside littered with the debris of war. We were passing other coalition units, confirming my view we were the chosen first liberators of the capital. Several times we stopped so the soldiers could be photographed celebrating atop knocked-out tanks. On one site an officer screamed at several TV crews they were standing in a minefield, causing a quick scramble back into the buses. Excitement was building, and soon we were on the outskirts of Kuwait City, which was surprisingly intact because the only heavy fighting had occurred around the airport.

I felt I was in an old newsreel of liberation: as we charged forward, the streets were filled with flag-waving civilians, many weeping and jumping for joy. I heard heavy firing all around because those with captured Iraqi weapons followed their celebratory custom of blazing skyward, with no thought of where their bullets might land or who they might injure or kill.

Several of us made our way into the royal palace, the scene of a fierce battle with Iraqi invaders but now looted and vacant. I walked through its deserted corridors with two or three others in an increasingly desperate search for a washroom. Outside, I was surprised when two US commandos roared up in a desert buggy. They had been out in the desert ahead of advancing troops, and one of their tasks had been to check that our small media unit was not headed into an Iraqi ambush. Much amused by the whole liberation spectacle, they looked as relaxed as if they were lolling on a beach in California.

Everywhere were wild and tearfully emotional scenes. Clearly, the inhabitants had been living in deep fear of Iraq's notorious security service. I captured lots of the drama on video, and, after several hours, I jumped on the first returning media bus for the race back across the desert to Dhahran to get my exclusive out. It was an adventurous dash, past the blazing oil wells in the night, eerily heightened by the flickering explosions of detonating ammunition dumps. At the Saudi border crossing, we passed a small knot of reporters angrily demanding entry to the war zone, led by the irrepressible, cane-wagging Joe Schlesinger, furious to be missing the climactic moments of the offensive.

The bloody mop-up stage of the war was still underway. As we passed the US airbase in Dharan, two secretive F-117 Nighthawk stealth attack jets screamed off into the predawn sky to join in the aerial demolition of Hussein's invasion force. The black silhouettes with their swept-back wings gave them the fearsome look of aerial predators: I thought of a line in *Macbeth*: "night's black agents to their prey do rouse."

Hours later, my story sent, I was exhausted but pleased to have experienced again the rush of high-stakes news coverage of an historic event. The land war ended in a hundred hours with a total coalition victory, and President George Bush wisely refused to follow the urgings of hyped-up war hawks in Washington to charge into Iraq and topple Saddam Hussein. With Iraq evicted from Kuwait, he would go no further than the UN had authorized, in part because he believed weakening Iraq would only boost Iran as a regional superpower. This degree of wisdom was missing a dozen years later when his son, President George W. Bush, found the lure of taking Baghdad irresistible.

The Gulf War was a seminal moment in modern history, and its aftershocks are still rumbling today. There were many lessons. For me, the aftermath underscored the danger of triumphalism in global affairs. The startlingly quick US victory, coming on the heels of the historic "win" over Communism in Europe, ditched the national depression over Vietnam and sprouted an intoxicating worldview among policy makers that the United States had a duty to mould the course of history in pursuit of democratic capitalism. Regime change was in. *Time* magazine that March captured the new vision as "the birth of a new American century—the onset of a unipolar world, with America at the center of it."

But out of triumphalism came many of today's woes. Horrified to see the US army inside the Muslim world, a Saudi Islamic radical named Osama bin Laden began mobilizing al-Qaeda, an international pan-Islamist guerrilla force to fight infidels. An era of heightened global terrorism helped trigger both the Iraq and the Afghanistan wars. While the UN-backed liberation of Kuwait was justifiable and skillfully executed, the United States miscalculated the rapid collapse of the isolated Iraqi force in Kuwait, cut off in an open desert without air support, as proof that Iraqis would not strongly resist an invasion to overthrow Saddam Hussein. A new breed of neoconservative super war hawks, profoundly overconfident in America's ability to work military miracles, contemptuous of foreign foes and of overly cautious friends, and inspired by the chance to spread free-market doctrines everywhere, pushed the nation and its allies into a labyrinth of deadly military adventures.

My last view of the old Soviet Army as the Cold War faded out and Communism went into its death spiral was of hundreds of its young soldiers forced to pick potatoes in muddy fields outside Moscow to meet a national food emergency. I was doing a documentary on the general crisis in Russia, which seemed bottomless at the time. As we filmed the soldiers, civilians were casually siphoning fuel out of their army trucks, having easily bribed a bored sergeant to look the other way—a half farcical image of a superpower's fading authority even at home.

I visited Russia several times between 1990 and 1992, during the fast-moving fall of the Soviet Union, to try and capture the fallout of historic events no one had fully predicted because they were so unimaginable. After Eastern Europe fled from the Kremlin's grip, Mikhail Gorbachev tried to save the Soviet Union through measured political and economic reforms. But they satisfied few Russians because they coincided with a widespread economic crisis. A hero in the West, but not at home, Gorbachev was caught in a vise between diametrically opposed populist demands, led by Boris Yeltsin, and calls for a return to the old order, led by hardcore Communists. An armed coup in August 1991 by Communists and some army units was beaten back by a populist uprising under Yeltsin's leadership—sealing the fate of the Soviet Union. By December Gorbachev was gone, Yeltsin took control, and all Russia remained in a state of upheaval.

Foreign capitals were nervous. Contrary to later Russian myth, the West, and certainly the United States, were not eager to see a humbling collapse of government in Russia. The question of who would control its nuclear arsenal, the world's largest, was paramount. My feature stories dealt with the social unrest, the economic crisis, and, most importantly, the nuclear threat. Fortunately, the CBC news correspondent in Moscow, Don Murray, was a highly gifted interpreter of the wild and complex drama across the political arena, so I was able to concentrate on my own work.

I was in Moscow just after the red Soviet flag at the Kremlin was lowered for the last time and the new Russian tricolour raised. Since my earliest memories of cinema newsreels, the Kremlin, the flag, and images of Stalin and his successors taking military salutes in Red Square had been projected as the centre of the world's most threatening force of evil. Now I was struck once more by the way, in a major world crisis, the eye of the hurricane can look surprising calm. My travel diary records, "Drove by the Kremlin this afternoon. Although the winter clouds were piling up in grey ranks behind the sharp towers, for the first time the once-forbidding heart seemed almost tame. Red flags gone, only the Russian colours to droop in the winter clamminess. No one home save the weird Yeltsin."

As a history buff, I was haunted by the spectre of the early Weimer period after Germany lost the First World War. The similarities were scary: an old order shattered, all certainty erased, a deepening depression with hyperinflation and the currency in ruins, a population close to panic and feeling betrayed, and a military elite bitter at loss of status. Social dysfunction complicated the heralded arrival of democratic parties while also opening rich horizons for corruption and gangsterism to flourish. Out of despair came growing acceptance that only a strong presidency with near dictatorial powers could safely manage the state. That would soon come.

I felt great sympathy for average Russians, who saw all hope for the future demolished and now had to sell their possessions, or themselves, for enough to eat. Because unemployment had been denied under the Soviet order, there were insufficient services to help the millions in severe distress. People lined up for hours at food shops, but the shelves were often empty. Black markets became scenes of mass desperation, as in Berlin in 1923. Some of the elderly were reduced to selling off meagre possessions for a pittance. I talked to one old lady trying to sell a few faded dolls: "I have nothing left," she said. "I hope my daughter will help, but she has three kids and many problems." A veteran with war medals was selling eight plastic water bottles. "You can do lots with them," he assured me, "fill them with water, or booze. Let your kids play with them. Juggle." In the same open market, a new hierarchy of thugs was also boastfully evident. When our crew approached a few stalls surprisingly filled with Western tech goods, watches, leather jackets, and boutique handbags, we got swift warnings to vanish fast, or else.

Even the iron-fisted Soviet security system seemed confused about the new rules. Once the old ones were relaxed, everything seemed negotiable. Reporters seeking interviews easily entered the long-dreaded offices of state oppression. A few officials demanded payments of a laptop to get an exclusive, but usually "side tips" were cheaper. One day I attended a news conference inside the gilded Kremlin hall in the morning and, in the afternoon, spent hours with a pig farmer in the country. That day, he was trying to convince the local Communist bureaucrats to let him sell spare land from a collective farm to increase his food production—the kind of privatization Russia desperately needed—but they quickly slapped him down. I sensed they relished showing us Western media that their power still existed and had determined to completely humiliate him before us.

In St. Petersburg, I was excited to get an interview with the mayor,

Anatoly Sobchak, the rising political star who some saw as a future president. As co-author of the new constitution, he was courted by Western diplomats and financers. I was impressed by his top aides, who with cool efficiency made us feel comfortable and important. Regrettably, I did not note their names, for his executive assistant was a former KGB officer, Vladimir Putin. It annoys me that I can't swear I met Putin, known in political circles as "the man with no face."

I loved St. Petersburg, with its grand imperial past laid out along canals and the Neva River, which I was fortunate to see under the full moon of a crisp winter's night. Near the Fontanka Embankment, I paid homage to the Fountain House apartment of one of my favourite poets, Anna Akhmatova. But you never knew what bizarre turns were waiting. One night I went to interview an economist on the social malaise. Most of the building's lights were out as her gloomy teenage son led us wordlessly up back stairs to her flat. After we set up in her library office, I was struck by the dim candle lighting, and I assumed she was saving on electricity. She was friendly, but seconds into the interview I was started to see, barely off camera, a large number of satanic goat-headed statues placed among her books. Nonplussed, I managed to throw in a few questions about the need for new social benefits. I should, though, have asked her to guide us through the Satanic movement in post-Soviet Russia, to see how everything connected. Was Stalin perhaps revered by them?

Increasingly, my diary notes mention fatigue to the point of bone weariness. CBC travel budgets were always tight, so when we went abroad we hit the ground running, cramming our days with work. My two-part series on fears about Russia's nuclear security had me travelling among Moscow, Washington, New York, and London for interviews. After a day gathering material, I needed to study at night to keep up with developments, but I was frequently too tired. That was my dilemma: I was ecstatic about my dream role in journalism but also finding the life ever more demanding.

With my higher public profile, strangers often came up to chat. On a flight to Moscow, an Air Canada steward said, "When I see all the glamorous places you are in and the exciting stories you do, I give way to real envy." A few nights later in Moscow, however, I wrote, "Almost groggy. Tired of this kind of travel . . . the dreary half-life of hotels and airports and dead-tired dinners with weary crews and producers."

Still, every morning I'd be revived by the excitement of being in Russia, the fascination of the story, and by long talks with remarkable characters emerging from the shadows of the Cold War. The nuclear story throbbed with real-life dramas worthy of espionage novels. I talked with a retired KGB agent about mutual concerns he'd shared with the CIA and MI6 about the safety of Russian nuclear secrets, and with a revered physicist who had escaped Stalin's purges because he worked on the USSR's first atomic bomb, and who warned me that nuclear materials were inadequately guarded.

Most memorable was a meeting on a park bench with a genial factory retiree whose job had been to place individual bombs inside the multiwarhead ballistic missiles. "They were small, a bit smaller than a volleyball, and they were always warm from the nuclear material inside," he said. Each bomb represented enough nuclear megatons to wipe out a major capital region; six might kill tens of millions of people. "Were you ever nervous?" I asked. "Not at all," he replied. "At our end they were perfectly safe. Without being triggered, they wouldn't go off." When I inquired whether he thought about the countless civilians who would die if his work was ever fired and triggered, he said, "I never thought there'd be war. It would mean suicide for all. So it was a good job."

Our series on Russia's nuclear dangers fit the mood of international nervousness over the Kremlin's control of its own weapons. This frightening spectre persuaded the United States to give hundreds of millions of dollars to its old foe to tighten security at its nuclear sites and to ensure that its seven thousand weapons scientists were paid sufficiently to resist the temptation to sell secrets abroad.

As I continued my travels to crisis spots, my profile on *The Journal* was increasing, and so was my workload. In the spring of 1992 I was nominated for the Best Overall Journalist award (the Gordon Sinclair) in Canada's prestigious Geminis, but in my diary, pride is overshadowed by complaints of wear and tear. Flying back from Russia, I found, "I could hardly walk off the plane my knee was so sore and have been hobbling ever since. This has added to my generally low spirits. I have a deep worry I could be, temporarily at least, wearing out as a foreign correspondent . . . a sense I don't have the fortitude I once had, nor the same willingness to put up with the drudgeries of the road."

Barely home, still jetlagged, I was asked to put aside the editing of my Russia series and fly immediately to South Africa to cover the historic referendum on March 17, 1992, to see whether the white population would support the end of apartheid. The vote would be a key step toward ending not just modern apartheid but the all-white rule that had endured over three centuries. Barbara Frum had been scheduled to host two episodes of *The Journal* live from the country but was too ill to travel, and I was asked to take her place. Despite my exhaustion, I was enthralled by the thought that in three years I'd have covered the fall of Communism in Europe, the fall of the Soviet Empire in Russia, and now, almost certainly, the end of apartheid.

The moment was deeply moving: although only white people voted, they overwhelmingly accepted that apartheid was indefensible and that there should be no more all-white elections. This result meant that the long and courageous resistance to oppression by the Black population and their white allies had triumphed, and it was celebrated around the world. Apartheid had employed all the brutal tactics of police states—mass arrests, beatings, and targeted assassinations—with the added twist of profound social humiliation. As with segregation in the US South, the greatest wounds were likely to children who had to witness parents and grandparents denied entry to white areas, forced to give way to so-called superiors, and treated as third-class citizens while they in turn were denied basic rights.

The mood of the moment was upbeat. It was fascinating to talk to a broad section of South Africans, from those inside the all-Black Soweto to political factions from the African National Congress (ANC) to white liberals who had also faced hostility and threats for opposing apartheid. I travelled to meet with hard-line elements of the Conservative Party who fought tooth and nail to block such reforms to the bitter end. I held panels, wrote stories, and got my wish to discuss the struggle in my interview with Nelson Mandela (see "Glitches and Greatness" interlude). I love examining various elements at play whenever historic change comes to fruition: here you had the fall of Communism (which stripped white politicians in South Africa of their excuse to reject negotiations with the ANC because it was "Communist inspired and aided"), along with the growing opposition of foreign nations to apartheid (with Canada in the forefront under Brian Mulroney) and, above all, the incalculable power and resilience of the Black resistance epitomized in legend and fact by Mandela.

I was home only a few days before I was told I'd be hosting a *Journal* special on the upcoming British election from London, where I'd also edit my series on the Russian nuclear danger. I was still absorbing this news when *The Journal* was shaken to its core by the death from leukemia of its powerful and beloved host Barbara Frum. I was told to fly immediately to Washington to do an interview that had been set up for Frum in top secrecy with author Salman Rushdie, still in hiding from an Iranian death sentence for alleged blasphemy against Islam in his novel *The Satanic Verses*. Rushdie, a British citizen, had been guarded around the clock in secret UK safe houses for four years and had been flown by the RAF to Washington to try to stir up more Western protests against Iran's aggressive actions. *The Journal*'s interview was one of only a handful scheduled by British security and the FBI.

I was directed to show up with my crew at the parking lot of a hotel in suburban Virginia. Several vans with tinted windows drove slowly past, clearly checking us out, before one pulled over, scooped us up, and dropped us in the hotel's underground parking space, where a freight elevator rushed us to an upper floor sealed off by security. Little was spoken: no one was taking the Iranian threat lightly. Once we had set up, a cheerful Rushdie seemed to burst into the room, every bit the gregarious socializer he'd been famous as before his days in hiding. The long interview went well. We talked about his life with a bounty on his head ("socially rather inconvenient") and about the need for free societies to stand against such threats from both ideological and theological tyrannies. The moment the interview ended, his bodyguards swept him out, and we grabbed our tape and raced back to Toronto for the evening show.

The pall of gloom following Frum's death continued to hang over *The Journal*. "Very emotional day in the office," I wrote, "with feelings that an era had ended. Perhaps *The Journal* will fall too." My foreboding was realized just six months later when, suddenly, the most creative current affairs show in Canada's English TV history was snuffed out. This brutal obliteration was conducted by upper CBC management, with the eager agreement of the corporation's Ottawa masters.

To add to the upheaval, *The National/Journal* hour was dragged from its 10 p.m. perch and thrown, with the new moniker *Prime Time News* (*PTN*), into the 9 p.m. competitive cauldron of US-produced police and sitcom shows. The changes were all made under the corporate super slogan of the time, "repositioning," but rushed into service. The original hour had been carefully planned over eighteen months; its successor was thrown together in three. Ill thought out, amid chaos and internal rancour, the new show became one of the crowning fiascos of Canadian TV history. It suffered a 17 percent drop in ratings while gifting the opposition CTV news at 11 p.m. a 40 percent jump. People clearly wanted entertainment in prime time and serious journalism later. *PTN*'s ignominious retreat back to 10 p.m. was soon inevitable, and much of the coming decade was spent trying to repair the damage.

For years, "Who killed *The Journal*?" was a long-playing mystery within CBC ranks. Whatever the intrigues behind the corporate mayhem, it says much about the perverse relationship between government and public broadcasting in Canada. Even as CBC struggled to gear up for the new internet age and the growing competition from what was then called "the World Wide Web," efforts to downsize public broadcasting seemed addictive in Ottawa. The more the CBC appeared threatened, the more the government wanted to slash its budget—a mindset suggesting that political payback was part of the mix. As media scholars Christopher Waddell and David Taras wrote, "Whichever party was in power viewed the CBC through the lens of what it could do for them or, more frequently, how it could hurt them."

Prime Minister Mulroney, an intense watcher of newscasts, shared this narrow view and saw the CBC as an active threat to his efforts to save national unity. *The Journal* alarmed him the most, not only because it frequently gave lengthy coverage to his critics but because its audiences at 10 p.m. included academics, teachers, executives, politicians, journalists, activists, and other influential people. To bring order to the CBC, he had chosen Gérard Veilleux, the head of the Treasury Board, who had a reputation for tough budget cutting, to become its president, despite his limited knowledge of broadcasting. Brainy, hard-charging, and with a notoriously fiery temper when displeased, Veilleux was known to demand quick obedience to his directives. The priority order from Mulroney's office was to make major budget cuts. The prime minister also chose like-minded members of the CBC's Board of Directors, including the voluble John Crispo, possibly the most verbally extreme anti-CBC voice in the country, who had openly declared his contempt for it and damned *The Journal* as "lousy." Senior CBC officials had no doubt which show was the number-one target—along with its independent-minded executive producer, Mark Starowicz.

"*The National* was never seen to be as contrary as *The Journal*," Trina McQueen, vice president of News and Current Affairs, told Knowlton Nash. "They didn't want a current affairs presence; they wanted straight news." A longtime defender of *The Journal*, McQueen was abruptly shoved out of her roll in June 1992 and shifted off to head regional broadcasting just before *The Journal*'s doom was made official. (She soon left to become a major corporate star in private broadcasting.)

Ironically, my own standing rose despite the chaos. I was made chief correspondent just as *The Journal* died, and was soon retitled as senior correspondent by its successor, *PTN*. After Frum's death, I acted as on-air host for weeks at a time in the studio. On the one hand this role was flattering, but on other it threw me against those same internal demons I'd secretly borne in Montreal when I first entered TV. "May 6: Can still only face these ordeals, for such they are, on valium or lorazepam, which build confidence. No way to live for long periods." "May 9: Finished my three weeks stint as The Journal Host last night . . . utterly exhausted. Night after night seeming to drain every last bit of nervous energy out of me."

Why didn't I simply refuse to host? In part ambition, given the importance of visibility in TV, but also to please my employers. I belonged to a generation that felt an obligation to take on any assignment. Hosting was also interesting work, especially the interviews, and I persisted in hoping that one day I might conquer those demons. It wouldn't be an easy struggle.

13

"A Wound to the Soul"

As the senior correspondent in the new *Prime Time News*, I had more responsibility. I was also reunited with my old friend Tony Burman, whom the "change agents" had appointed as executive producer—the indispensable saviour of the storm-wracked ship. He asked me to be part of an urgent inner cabinet devising "the way ahead." I leapt at the chance, sending him a confidential six-page memo recommending ideas to shake up command, improve quality, and make the show "zesty, unpredictable, controversial, and novel." I called for "more investigative drive and conflict stories—a new aggressiveness." I look back on my strident advocacy of prioritizing combative programming with some regret. It was the zeitgeist of the times in news gathering, but in coming years I came to regard modern journalism's overemphasis on conflict stories and easy "gotcha" political reporting as partly responsible for the growing cynicism in society toward almost all institutions and a weariness with mainstream journalism.

Essentially, though, I remained what I was most suited to be: a reporter, with no wish or aptitude to become part of management. I was mainly focused on foreign affairs, with frequent globe hopping, but based in Toronto. A month in India for a documentary *Tides of Peril* on growing Hindu-Muslim-Sikh tensions was followed by coverage of the Northern Ireland conflict—back to gritty, divided Belfast with its surly gangs and aggressive street marches. Then came a special on Nelson Mandela, in which producer Robin Benger, originally South African, arranged for us to shadow the great man during the run-up to the country's first truly free national election.

It was deeply moving to see this remarkable figure, only four years freed after twenty-seven years as a political prisoner, hold vast rallies where he preached not only an end to oppression but a need to avoid thoughts of revenge and think of the future, not the past. He sang with them, even danced a little, but also seemed tired at later rallies, fighting to keep his eyelids open. I worried about his safety as security seemed thin, imagining the bloodbath that would be unleashed if he were gunned down—a violent reaction strong enough to change the course of history. I felt the same when I met two other leaders of vast movements who became presidents, Lech Wałęsa in Poland and Lula in Brazil. Like them, Mandela appeared unshakably serene, unbreakable (see "Glitches and Greatness" interlude).

After the *Prime Time News* hour was stabilized at 10 p.m., its news and current affairs journalists continued to do excellent work. The quality of staff, including reporters and editors, was high, and Burman's management team strove to restore standards and morale. Our foreign coverage won international awards, and CBC's very presence abroad forced commercial competitors CTV and Global to keep up their coverage too. We knew, however, that our "world-class" status was receding as Ottawa's budget cuts reduced our ability to travel and adequately support foreign bureaus. With declining parliamentary funding, the CBC was forced to rely increasingly on advertising, which meant siphoning ever larger sums from the news budget to produce more ad friendly dramas and comedies. Burman estimated that 40 percent of news funding was lost to entertainment in the years after repositioning.

For me, ironically, the more strained our news service, the busier my own niche became. When not abroad myself, I functioned as an interpreter of foreign news in our Toronto headquarters, which meant assembling, sometimes with only a few hours' notice, an analysis or background item for that night's newscast. That became easier as major advances in TV technology allowed the rapid editing of tapes from abroad, more two-way remote interviews, and the creation of more compelling graphics. I shaped, wrote, and fronted the pieces, and skilled producers and editors made it all happen. On the best nights we'd have pieces fed in directly from our overseas correspondents in the field, accompanied by a longer analysis piece.

I maintained a fair balance between home and abroad, with fewer trips into the field but for longer periods on documentary series. I witnessed many situations of explosive hatred and intense human suffering. On my India trip, I went north into the Kashmir region, disputed by India and Pakistan since 1947, and followed patrols of Indian soldiers looking for Muslim guerrillas. Then we drove by van into the Punjab to explore Sikh separatist resistance. We'd been warned about ambush by Sikh underground units on the road from New Delhi to Amritsar, and, when we pulled into a truck stop at 3 a.m., drivers regaled me with stories of recent kidnappings and torture. My diary notes: "I slept not at all . . . when we finally left, we had an extremely tense drive through the mist, with only one other truck ahead of us . . . perfect ambush situation. When we got to the hotel, I had a bottle of beer before collapsing into bed for one hour's sleep before starting the full day."

At home, I gorged myself on domesticity, gaining weight on regular meals, drinking red wine, and going soft. Now entering my fifties, I appreciated showers and clean sheets, shelves full of books, and quiet moments devoid of anxiety. Tina's career was flourishing as she took over as co-host of CBC's *Midday* show, a one-hour Canada-wide program that mixed straight news and current affairs with human-interest items and humorous stories. Tina, knowledgeable about our literature, arts, and regional issues, filled me in on Canadiana.

The day before I left for India, we learned we were going to have a child. I was ecstatic. On October 22, 1993, Kathleen (Katie) Elizabeth Stewart was born, and I flung myself into my new life as a parent.

I vowed not to cover another war until Katie was at least ten years old. I would still report on human catastrophes and work in crisis zones until the shooting began, but would skip the fighting. Fortunately, others were eager for field assignments, including a remarkable wave of female foreign correspondents—among them Ann Medina, Anna Maria Tremonti, Susan Ormiston, Gillian Findlay, Sheila MacVicar, Nahlah Ayed, and Adrienne Arsenault—who would have shone in any period of Canadian journalism.

I wanted to do more investigative analysis of foreign conflicts, to peel back the layers of government, diplomatic, and military decision making during crises and unearth the vital paper trails that go unseen until future historians pick through the archives. This led to the perfect story: the Somalia affair, a national scandal in 1993 of racist brutality, killings, command failure among our military, and duplicity by some leaders in Ottawa. The events would shock the nation, cause the disbandment of our elite parachute regiment, and damage our military at the core while darkening Canada's pristine peacekeeping image. Our challenge was how to make watchable TV out of a probe into such a dark maze of deceit and denials. I worked again with producer Robin Benger, a witty and captivating talker who could charm almost anyone into a revealing conversation.

Prime Minister Mulroney had volunteered to send the Canadian Airborne Regiment as part of a fourteen-hundred-strong Canadian contribution to a US-led UN peacekeeping force in Somalia, one of the world's poorest countries, wracked by a famine and civil war between heavily armed militias. The motive was lofty, for Mulroney felt Canada should be a lead player, as it had been in Ethiopia. The problems, however, appeared early: some in senior command worried the much-vaunted Airborne was the wrong regiment to send. Trained to be a hard-hitting assault force, it was a mix of the good and the very dubious. A macho cult in at least one unit brought disciplinary problems from a far-right racist element. The regiment's commander warned that one unit had gone rogue and should not be sent overseas, but he was replaced and they were all sent—a fatal miscalculation.

Wise commanders know such tightly wired combat units should not be left in monotonous camps with too little to do. The paratroopers were based in a dreary semi-desert region they knew almost nothing about, with little local order, and surrounded by a very malnourished population. At times, teenagers snuck through the surrounding camp wire to steal food. Private video recordings later showed that many in the Airborne despised the locals and looked for opportunities to intimidate them. Before long, many locals saw the Canadians as brutal bullies who held back relief supplies. Rocks were thrown, and soldiers fired back. Somalis who were caught trying to steal food were bound, blindfolded, and left to sit in the burning sun for hours. One who fled at night was shot and, according to a doctor's report, possibly finished off with a final bullet to the head. Later reports suggested that some paratroopers, looking for kills, set out supplies to lure youths to attempt thefts—the term was upgraded to "sabotage" to permit easier rules for firing.

The most gruesome crimes occurred when a sixteen-year-old, Shidane Arone, was dragged into a storeroom, beaten, waterboarded, burnt with cigarettes, raped with a broom handle, and tortured to death. His agony continued over so many hours that his captors took beer breaks to discuss how far to go. As many as eighty personnel heard screams and howls, even the youth's cry for mercy: "Canada, Canada, Canada." No one intervened or raced to report what was happening to superiors, suggesting both a widespread moral malaise and a climate of fear of the rogue paratroopers. In all, nine members of the regiment were arrested, but eventually seven of them were acquitted or let off with reprimands. One of the torturers, when arrested, tried to committee suicide, which the base command attempted to cover up. As word of the Somalia affair began to break, Ottawa felt forced to order a high-level investigation—which dragged on so long the government demanded an end date although many questions were still unanswered.

We felt the Somalia crimes were being covered up—and CBC Radio's Michael McAuliffe was able to uncover the paper trail that left no doubt. Our report profiled a regiment that had been inadequately officered and was ill-prepared for a mission that required "peace enforcement." Eventually, what doomed the regiment irrevocably in the public's eyes was a series of violent videos we obtained from military writer Scott Taylor showing soldiers celebrating racist attitudes and engaging in gut-wrenching hazing rituals. Shaken by the scandal and the unending barrage of revelations, the new Liberal government disbanded the whole regiment, a controversial move that aroused the fury of the military. I was surprised, for the Airborne had a proud history and still had many fine members. It was one of those cases where the media, having pursued leads as far as they could go, found themselves overtaken by far greater consequences than they expected.

While videos shown during the Somalia affair proved more explosive than any written revelations, the challenge for our two-part series *Rwanda: Autopsy of a Genocide* in November 1994 was to move beyond the atrocity images that had horrified the world when they first appeared in April. The same gory video of machete gangs slaughtering civilians had been shown over and over, and the footage fed into the widespread false narrative that the bloodbath was just another example of African tribal savagery. The truth was far darker: Rwanda's horror—the murder by the dominant Hutu majority of up to six hundred thousand of the minority Tutsi population in a hundred days—was a well-rehearsed genocide, planned over several years. Hutu extremists in the government and the military set out to liquidate their historic ethnic Tutsi rivals using trained kill squads from a youthful militia known as the Interahamwe. Our goal, however, was to follow the paper trail of advance warnings that proved the UN and major Western nations had ignored clear warnings that genocide was being planned and chose not to act. The genocide became the worst and most shameful disaster in UN history—and Roméo Dallaire, the Canadian commander of the peacekeeping mission, was left isolated to take most of the blame.

For our series, Benger and I sought out evidence in Western capitals, at the UN, and from human rights groups showing that all the steps toward genocide had been evident for years: the demonization of Tutsis as subhuman "cockroaches"; requirements that they carry internal passports for easy identification; and several massacres of hundreds of Tutsis by the Interahamwe that informants identified as practice to see how quickly the slaughter could be carried out.

I had an exclusive TV interview with Dallaire after his return. I thought of him as a victim, betrayed by the UN, which had sent him with a shockingly anemic force of peacekeepers. Unquestionably brave, he had saved thousands, but could not stop the worst. I assumed his inner agony was severe but was unaware of his post-traumatic stress disorder, which would lead to a failed suicide attempt in coming years. Calm in appearance and tightly self-disciplined, when I laid out some of the advance warnings we had identified, he grimly rubbed his hands, saying, "No one is able to play Pontius Pilate on this one."

When I pressed further, he fell back on professional caution and misled us, insisting the UN had no "intelligence service" that might have revealed the plotting. But in testimony at a Rwanda inquiry years later, he revealed that a high-placed Interahamwe official had fed him warnings of the coming wave of killings. He had boldly faxed

New York for permission to intervene and seize the weapons but was refused. Nations in the UN simply did not view his mission as a priority or General Dallaire as worthy of a full hearing.

We had uncovered a trail of documents from many sources to prove advance warnings. I was disappointed in how easy it had been to compile so much evidence that, if listened to at the time, might have deterred the extermination. I cannot believe such warnings in a European country would have been so dismissed. In the same decade, major UN and NATO action was untaken to prevent "ethnic cleansing" in the former Yugoslavia.

In journalism, as in other professions, rewards are important both for the honour bestowed and for persuading management to keep backing your efforts; the falsely modest pretend they don't count for much, but they do. I was lucky at this time: in 1993 came the Canadian Association of Journalists Award for Investigative Reporting; the following year, Benger and I won Canada's Gemini Award for TV's Best Information Segment for our Rwanda investigation; and two years later I won the prized Gemini as Best Overall Broadcast Journalist (the Gordon Sinclair Award). I was invited to make more speeches, moderate debates, even give interviews to local media.

Still socially on the awkward side, I rather liked being somewhat "prominent." It helped break the ice. I enjoyed being approached by strangers when waiting for luggage at an airport or shopping in my neighbourhood. They'd ask about news items they'd seen, my views on ending a war, or when we'd cover their favourite issue. I was touched when asked how I could stand seeing the scenes I did, or asked whether I saw hopeful ones as well ("I do, and many of them," I'd reply). Many people asked, "Whatever happened to that little girl in Ethiopia?" (meaning Birhan Woldu, in chapter 1). I am immune to the boredom bug, and usually found that everyone had interesting stories to tell.

At home I found parenting great fun and endlessly fascinating, and Katie was an easy child to enjoy time with. Physically, however, the signs of wear and tear were mounting: my knees were giving out, my weight was soaring, and my usually disciplined control of drinking was slipping. I was dreading an event I'd long looked forward to, returning to Ethiopia for the tenth anniversary of the famine. I knew how rough some of the travel could be, and I also worried about those flashbacks to the horrors of 1984–85. They'd become less frequent in recent years, but would they now be revived in full force?

Sometimes you can't win: I left for Ethiopia determined to avoid any risk of food poisoning but let my guard down when passing through London, dined on a friend's "very well-aged pheasant," and was violently sick on the overnight flight from London. My first stop in Addis Ababa was the hospital, followed by twenty-four hours in my hotel bed shaking with fever. When conscious I was bathed in sweat and ignoble self-pity as I wrote in my travel diary: "I am now deeply depressed: if it's not my knees, it's pneumonia, or heart murmurs [false alarm], or falls, and now food poisoning . . . Tina agrees this has to stop . . . I'm wrecking my prospects of a decent fifties by just letting myself go."

We often said in the documentary field that the best trips begin badly—"the documentary god demanding a sacrifice," crews said. But I continued in a low state of mind as we flew north to the former famine epicentre in Tigray. Looking down on those mountaintops and high plains that I'd first seen as a drought-blasted dustbowl a decade earlier, I was ashamed, for I could think of no place on earth where self-indulgence is less appropriate. Still, in those first days I seemed in mental crisis: "I'm in no shape to think reflectively about Ethiopia . . . just feel rotten; defeatist . . . I keep thinking of how many times I've been shivering under hotel bedsheets, yearning for home while this 'glamourous life' goes on. Perhaps just sick of it all."

I had always felt a highly charged atmosphere of spirituality in this northern region, the ancient host to one of the oldest branches of Christianity, and now of so many humanitarian shelters and church schools. I was still immune, however, to the comforts of such conviction: "So utterly depressed and sick tonight I reached for the hotel Bible and tried to get some solace. Still all beyond me."

Fortunately, I'm not given to prolonged depressions, and I could only be inspired by Tigray's recovery. I encountered some images and sensations that I feared would ignite flashbacks of the famine: the tin emergency huts that still stood and the smell of wood fires, and the burial grounds for so many victims.. Now, however, the changes inspired such hope. The huts, once empty of their last relief supplies as thousands of starving refugees clustered in their shadows, were packed with stockpiled emergency food and medical supplies in case of another crisis. The smell of smoking fires came not from vast camps that could, at best, cook only one small meal for those lucky enough to be closest to the meagre food lines, but from busy food stalls in villages and family dinners on small farm plots after a decent harvest. The streets teemed with life and, rather than eerie silence, we heard the cries and songs of children playing games. My producer, Sue Dando, and cameraman, Brian Kelly, were wonderfully creative in capturing from my memories the striking contrasts between the years of pain and these days of hope.

Ethiopia now had a democratic government that poured reconstruction aid into Tigray and worked closely with outside agencies to strengthen agriculture. Driving across the countryside, I hardly recognized large sections that blazed in green or gold, where before only a dun-coloured wasteland had stretched out to the horizons. I remembered how thousands of villagers had laboured by hand in exchange for food rations to build regional dams to help in future droughts, and I saw them now filled with water, sparkling in the sun. We passed new government medical clinics in the countryside where farm families were treated and closely examined for signs of malnutrition. And we visited colleges where classes were filled with nursing students and the latest computer technology.

I met up with some of the giants I had encountered during the famine. Among them was Sister Jean Harris, who still worked at the relief centre where I first saw Birhan Woldu and her father. She wept only when she watched some of our footage from 1984 but assured me she now felt only joy "because of all [the Tigrayans] have done since." She perfectly understood my passion for the place and its people.

Before leaving, I set up more permanent support for the Woldu family and ensured future education for Birhan and her siblings. On the afternoon of the day we left, the crew went to an area that had been suffering terrible droughts. As always, we drew a crowd and, just as we were setting up for a final stand-up at dusk, the wind quickened and the sky, thick with clouds, began to drop the first rain seen in months. The joy was electric as children played happily in the downpour's growing puddles. It was the perfect closing shot to cap our upbeat report on northern Ethiopia.

Back at home, my efforts to balance a happy home life with an exciting but demanding career were strained by my neglected physical state. After two failed knee surgeries, I finally had a successful full replacement in the summer of 1998. More ominously, deeper signs of severe nervous strain were building. Sudden anxiety attacks came with dizziness, tingling in hands and face, sweating, and an inability to speak clearly. Though debilitating, they were soon followed by a full, head-clearing recovery. Foolishly, I kept the increasing number of attacks to myself, hoping less stress, better sleep, and more judicious use of alcohol would steady me. I never thought I was experiencing the opening salvoes of what my generation had called a nervous breakdown.

The all-out assault started one night in the fall: I began to feel sweaty and panicky at a teacher-parent night at Katie's school. Hoping for the usual comeback, we went afterwards for a lobster dinner. There the uncontrolled fear began again, with tingling, dizziness, and bouts of incoherence. I refused to go to an emergency room, confident I'd wake up with a clear head. But in the morning my brain felt heavy, my hands were uncoordinated, and my vision was disjointed by flickering auras. Tina, fearing I was having a stroke, raced me to Sunnybrook Medical Centre, where the doctors ordered CT scans and other tests along with close observation. I felt bizarrely calm despite my inability to identify even a fork by name. The possibility that my brain might not recover never occurred to me. The neurology staff were puzzled: tests showed no abnormality or sign of stroke. They kept me overnight for further tests, comfortably bedded down. I remember thinking in a fleeting bout of clarity that the sheets were pleasantly crisp and the pillow just right. My mental life, long absorbed by global affairs, had shrunk to the most picayune of concerns.

The moment I awoke, I felt a curious revival underway. My brain was functioning far more clearly, and my body was escaping from numbness in odd stages: first from my feet to my knees, then up to my hips. In under an hour, I started making phone calls to family and friends, assuring them in NASA-speak that "all systems are go!" I startled an editor I called to explain I would not be in, adding cheerfully, "I may have had a stroke!" Later that morning, five or six neurologists and interns gathered around my bed, expecting I'd still be incoherent. Instead I was sitting up, broadly smiling, and bragging of my total recovery. "I was flabbergasted," one of the team told me later. At my insistence I was soon discharged, heading home in almost euphoric spirits.

My confidence was absurd; these demons were not about to give up easily. A few weeks later I was rushed back to emergency with another debilitating attack, although this time I recovered more quickly. A long list of tests of my brain and heart came back with the comment "no abnormalities found." The problem was not physical but psychological.

I worried I might have to quit television journalism, but, oddly, I seemed able to handle high-stress situations. The attacks struck in the calm moments. Then, on January 10, 1999, my nephew Ian Stewart, who had been inspired years earlier by my Ethiopian reports to become a foreign correspondent, was shot in the head during a streetside ambush in Sierra Leone and was close to death. At thirty-two, he was bureau chief for Associated Press in West Africa. He had been covering the drive of a notoriously vicious insurgent army to take Sierra Leone's capital, Freetown. The rebels, reinforced by thousands of child soldiers, were feared by all. A car carrying Ian and two AP colleagues ran into a squad of them, teens with assault weapons. One of them, wearing a bowler hat, fired a burst that instantly killed Ian's friend Myles Tierney and hit Ian in the middle of his forehead.

Communications were in chaos, and it was hours before my brother, Dave, called me with scarce details: after the gunman was shot dead by soldiers, a small band of rescuers, carrying Ian strapped to a door, had struggled to a small army base where an aged helicopter flew him to the airport for a medevac to a foreign hospital. His chances of survival were slim. I called Canada's Foreign Affairs hotline, which activated a Crisis Watch, contacting diplomats and aid groups to see if they could help and assisting the family to liaise with AP in New York. For days there was little sleep.

Eventually, a series of flights got Ian to one of the world's leading clinics for head injuries in London. There, skilled surgery and extraordinary luck saved him: the bullet had shot straight down the pathway between the two hemispheres of his brain without destroying either. Years of physical and psychological therapy were needed before he could fully walk again and handle the post-traumatic stress disorder (PTSD) and survivor's guilt he suffered from. His career in journalism was over, but with remarkable resilience he went on to build a fulfilling life with family and as an author and lecturer in international studies at the University of New Mexico.

In those early weeks after Ian's near-death experience, I could not escape the thought he had followed me into a profession that seemed increasingly under assault. The number of journalists killed, and wounded physically and mentally, had surged through the nineties and seemed certain to keep growing as numerous smaller conflicts fed on the chaos of the times and an endless supply of youthful warriors and lethal weapons. My mood wasn't elevated when, weeks later, I went to Baghdad to check on a virtual war-in-waiting between Iraq and the United States. US overflights searching for potential Iraqi weapons of mass destruction and increasingly severe UN-imposed sanctions had much of the country gripped by fear over the threat of war and the terror of Saddam Hussein's secret police. Indeed, Iraq seemed caught between two nightmare possibilities: a major war of devastating consequences or the continuation of Saddam Hussein's suffocating rule.

Once home, I was again hit by sudden flashbacks to scenes of suffering civilians in wars and famines. I made an appointment with Dr. Anthony Feinstein, a neuropsychiatrist at Sunnybrook who, with other specialists, had puzzled over my strange crash-and-recovery breakdowns the previous winter. Through him, I became patient zero in a landmark international study, the first ever to investigate the trauma and psychological damage risked by foreign correspondents due to the hazards they run and the horrors they cover.

When I first saw Feinstein, he was head of the hospital's neuropsychiatric unit treating people with multiple sclerosis. His side interest in war and trauma originated in personal experience. Born in South Africa, as a young doctor he'd been conscripted to serve as medical officer in the country's counterinsurgency war in Namibia, where he experienced the stress of firefights between the army and guerrillas as well as the human costs of war.

In our early sessions, I found Feinstein could relate to my memories of high-risk situations: the feeling of experiencing life vividly and to the full after coming through dangers; the intense appreciation for nature when living on the edge; and the cloying sense of fear that seemed stronger in muggy tropical heat. As I related my experiences in conflicts, from El Salvador to Sudan and Lebanon, I told him I'd often felt high anxiety and saw myself as anything but gung-ho—rather, as the last of the cowardly correspondents. I strongly disliked wars, but they were part of the career I'd always wanted, covering foreign news, which required me to understand the patterns and dynamics of modern conflicts. Later, I was disturbed less by memories of violent events than by the flashbacks that invaded my mind, sometimes daily, with vivid pictures of human suffering I'd witnessed: mothers holding out a child near death to appeal for my help; the faces of starving people wondering why I did not help anyone but instead only watched.

Feinstein was confident I did not suffer from PTSD but from conversion disorder, a condition that reroutes (converts) emotional distress into physical symptoms. That would explain my loss of clear speech, scrambled thoughts, inability to control limbs, and spreading numbness. It would also account for the calmness, even casualness, that had later baffled me: at the depths of my hospital emergencies, I'd found pleasure in the smooth ride of the gurney and the subdued hospital hubbub. Those with conversion disorder often show *la belle indifférence* (the beautiful ignorance) during attacks. Fortunately, with therapy, a clear understanding of my problem, modest medication, and a healthier lifestyle, he said the attacks would recede—and he was right.

Intrigued by my case, Feinstein continued his research into trauma in journalists who covered wars and other catastrophes. He wanted to know more about the people who chased these stories "with a tenacity that was both impressive and alarming." What motivated them? How did they react psychologically to the high stresses and dangers of their work? PTSD had been studied extensively among soldiers, police, assault victims, and war refugees, but there was no research on foreign correspondents, which was surprising given they saw so much trauma in reporting the turbulent events they witnessed to the world. The gap seemed ominous, suggesting that most news organizations neglected to provide or even consider the psychological welfare of their war reporters—and the correspondents were complicit in the silence as well.

When Feinstein asked me to suggest someone in the field who could help him contact major news organizations, I recommended my former CBC colleague John Owen, a US-Canadian citizen who was then European director of Freedom Forum, a nonprofit organization dedicated to expanding free media across the globe. He immediately arranged funding from the forum's Washington headquarters and opened doors at many of the biggest news organizations in the United Kingdom, United States, and Canada to get their help in providing questionnaires to their foreign correspondents, along with scores of interviews.

Many reporters were glad to speak out, but the strongest resistance came from CBC correspondents. I was not surprised. I remembered how, at a public forum back in 1983 soon after Clark Todd was killed in Lebanon, I critiqued our profession as the only one that failed to prepare those it sent to war zones with even basic first-aid skills, let alone a few days' survival know-how in hostile environments. Several colleagues brushed aside my concern, culminating in the guffaw-inducing pronouncement of the great Joe Schlesinger: "The real requirement for a job like that—you've got to be a little crazy!"

Feinstein published his findings in a major medical study in 2002, followed by his book *Journalists under Fire: The Psychological Hazards of Covering War* in 2006. His work made an immediate impact by forcing the profession to take seriously the mental health of its members at risk. Feinstein later collaborated with Canadian director Martyn Burke in making the acclaimed documentary *Under Fire: Journalists in Combat,* which was shortlisted for an Oscar in 2012. The reality finally acknowledged is that many who covered conflicts abroad suffered, even long after their return, from severe depression, melancholy, loss of pleasure in normal life, and feelings of emotional pain including guilt. Alcohol and substance abuse was also a risk.

The situation was complex, however: while up to a third suffered from PTSD, many, like myself, did not. This variation suggests, Feinstein wrote, "a self-selection process is at work, ensuring that most journalists who chose conflict as their area enjoy what they do, are very good at it, and keep life-threatening hazards from undermining their psychological heath." However, further studies by Feinstein and others revealed that those who escape PTSD often suffer what came to be called "moral injury," involving prolonged emotional distress, including nightmares and flashbacks. The two maladies can involve similar symptoms, but PTSD is a mental illness arising when someone experiences extreme stress and personal danger, while moral injury is an emotional reaction triggered by feelings of shame, anger, and guilt. The pain of moral injury is extraordinarily deep, for those who witness morally outrageous scenes, such as massacres or famine, can suffer, Dr. Feinstein says, "a wound to the soul, an affront to your moral compass based on your own behavior and the things that you have failed to do."

In my experience, foreign correspondents are a mixed lot. Many struck me as remarkable, deeply committed professionals who, at personal risk, were bearing witness to history in the making. Some were attracted to risk, but others were timid, studious types who loathed the dangers. Some were loners who dodged the news pack; others fed on sharing information with fellow reporters. Some appeared superficial in their reports, but others were better judges of the dynamics of conflicts than embassy diplomats. In Feinstein's study I was relieved to find others like myself, who, though fearful of risks, were driven by the wish to cover momentous events and tell large audiences their stories.

Despite being better prepared than we were, those covering wars and catastrophes will always face risks to mind and spirit. Fortunately, world media now can consult the Toronto Moral Injury Scale for Journalists, which identifies possible signs and encourages "discussion of an overlooked condition." It came out of joint studies headed by Feinstein's research group at Sunnybrook and the *Globe and Mail* newspaper.

I'm proud to have played a role in the earlier studies that helped lead to this progress, and most grateful for the guidance I received on my way back to a healthier life.

INTERLUDE

Glitches and Greatness

A chance to interview a major historical figure on camera at the height of a political drama comes with tensions. You pray there won't be technical glitches because you know that your subject will be tightly scheduled, be preoccupied with other concerns, and want this meeting over as swiftly as possible.

But there will be glitches. I found that, in TV, you had best count on them. Before you roll, lights will need to be adjusted, camera angle shifted, sound problems corrected, and tape wires fixed. This could all take seconds or consume minutes, and you'll be left dangling, having to engage Greatness in small talk. Since that's not my forte, I always prepared reserve topics to lighten the mood.

When Nelson Mandela walked onto our small interview site in South Africa, the whole country was nervous; it was the eve of the historic referendum to end all-white voting, which would spell apartheid's doom. His leadership of the campaign made him the global man of the hour: a symbol everywhere of courage and conscience but also a potential target of white anti-reform assassins. As always, he looked incredibly serene, showing no hint of the inner pressures that must have been enormous.

I had my chat theme ready. I knew Mandela had a passion for boxing and had been an amateur fighter in the fifties (not a great one, but about as skilled in the ring as I was in hockey nets). He loved the training, self-discipline, and endurance he gained in the boxing ring that prepared him for almost three decades as a political prisoner.

I'd heard that to learn all he could about the "sweet science," he had devoured copies of *Ring* magazine, the boxing bible at the time. Here, at least we had something to connect us: as a young teen, I too was fascinated by boxing, followed fights on the radio, and even collected old copies of *Ring*. We would have followed the same champions in what was a golden age of boxing.

As soon as I heard a vague scurrying among the crew, the sure sign of a glitch being fixed, I leaned forward and said, "Sir, we'll roll in seconds, but I understand we both loved *Ring* magazine in the 1950s." I caught a sudden glint in his eyes. "Why yes, they were wonderful fighters then. Perhaps the best."

"Giants!" I confirmed. "I'd listen to the fights every Friday night. What legends they were—Sugar Ray Robinson, Archie Moore, Willie Pep, Marciano, LaMotta, Joey Giardello."

He threw in some names, and I noticed that Mandela had almost imperceptibly started the muscle-memory twitch boxers and fans often get when talking fights: hands curled into half fists moving tiny jabs with right and left. I found it stirring, seeing him clearly free for a moment from the heavy weight of world expectations. After a few more seconds of mutual recall, the signal to roll came, and we settled into a serious interview about the hopes for racial peace and progress in South Africa.

In the eighties, the equivalent hero reformer of towering world fame was Lech Wałęsa, a dockyard electrician and leader of Poland's Solidarity union movement. In defying Moscow's rule, Solidarity sent shockwaves through the Soviet Union and helped bring on the collapse of Communism.

I had long expected that Wałęsa would be bumped off or imprisoned, but when I interviewed him for NBC in 1986, he was on his way to becoming Poland's head of state. I didn't look forward to trying to fill time with him if we had a glitch because he seemed tightly wound and could be snarky with media.

But I need not have worried. Wałęsa loved glitches—electronic ones at least. When we were told we'd face "a slight delay," he peered around and noticed our soundman fiddling with a wall socket and various wires. In a flash he was out of his chair and kneeling beside the problem. "What the hell you trying, man?" he said gruffly. "You need to connect this to that one. Let me try." He was in his old element, enjoying the moment, impressing us with his deft fingers. I think he was showing off a bit.

When all was fixed and ready to roll, his mood seemed lighter, younger.

I almost joked, "Do you do house calls too?" but refrained.

14

Boots Away and Happy Endings

Back in Toronto, my anxiety under control, I accepted an offer to host *The Magazine*—the current affairs half of the news hour. It was a big deal: I even got a local newspaper headline announcing "Paul Stewart the New Host"! It was interesting work, with lots of interviews, panel discussions, and some of my own analysis of foreign stories. With a more stable schedule, I could plan to share time with old friends such as Gavin Weightman, my *Richmond Times* buddy and now a writer. Our families shared a holiday villa in Provence, France, every few years for over two decades.

In London I'd meet up with my always astonishing friend Conrad Black, now Lord Black of Crossharbour, the wealthy owner of international newspapers including the *London Telegraph* and the *Jerusalem Post*. I'd been a witness at his wedding to political columnist Barbara Amiel and had dinner afterwards at their small celebration at the exclusive Annabel's club in Mayfair, along with the Thatchers and the Rothchilds—definitely not our set! Denis Thatcher told Tina, "We like your man Brian."

"Oh, I didn't know you knew my husband," she said.

Startled, dismayed even, Denis replied, "Not your *husband*, your prime minister!"

It was bizarre seeing my old chum and his wife pursued by London's paparazzi, a glamourous in-couple known for their wit and glittering parties. Yet in private he and I spent long hours in gabfests just like old times, about politics, military history, and friends.

Although I never shared his interest in wealth and social status, and our politics grew very wide apart, we've stayed firm friends for over sixty years. For decades his public career was marked by spectacular achievements, often followed by wild controversies and setbacks, which he took with remarkable calm. I once asked him if he ever felt vertigo given his swift rise to celebrity on two continents. "Never. I feel I'm competent at these heights," he said, "and will see how far I can go."

As it happened, we had lunch in the ornate House of Lords dining room, and years later in the bland visitors' room of Coleman federal prison, Florida, where he resided for three years after his internationally headlined conviction for various corporate-world crimes (several of which were later overturned by the US Supreme Court). His enemies predicted fellow prisoners would destroy him, but he flourished inside: his naturally courtly manners, confident calmness, and real interest in anyone he met made him a popular figure among convicts. On one visit I saw him quickly defuse a simmering row between two inmates with some courteous refereeing. We'd eat his favourite coin-machine burgers off cardboard plates while he told me how much he enjoyed mentoring the mainly Black inmates to pass school exams and lecturing to both prisoners and guards on American history. He took piano lessons from a fellow inmate and spent long hours writing political columns and his memoirs. Convinced he was an innocent victim of US justice, he grew ever more bitter in his political views until, after his release, he became a supporter of Donald Trump. Since then, to honour our friendship, we have maintained a verbal demilitarized zone where all mention of the T-word is banned.

After two years in my studio role, I missed reporting and asked to return to being senior correspondent, working on documentaries and foreign analysis pieces. I benefited from highly skilled producers, including Carmen Merrifield, who showed me how I could better use new technology, subtle music, and lighting effects to enhance the mood of a documentary. I also took on the host role for the weekly foreign affairs show *Our World*, produced by Jennifer Clibbon and shaped by studio maestro Fred Parker. In addition, I wrote a foreign affairs column for the CBC website, an enjoyable reminder of my newspaper days in Montreal in the sixties.

My own satisfaction in the busy hub of TV journalism did not dull me to the steady erosion of the public broadcaster's strength. All around me programs were being axed and employees laid off as the dire Mulroney cutbacks were succeeded by equally deep slashes to funding from Liberal government. Pressed to the wall by declining revenue, management spoke of "re-engineering" while they closed down long-standing regional stations and eliminated or weakened local news stations, to the fury of staff and viewers.

Fortunately, enough strength remained in our operations to excel in big moments, such as elections, referendums, and crisis moments including 9/11, the Balkan conflict, and the Afghanistan War. There were still occasional blockbusters, including the most-watched documentary series in Canadian TV history, *Canada: A People's History*, the seventeen-part series, in French and English, produced by Mark Starowicz, now head of documentaries. I was able to do in-depth studies ranging from Canada's changing role at the UN, the global consequences of emerging food shortages, and the mounting pressures of more than seventy million homeless migrants. As early as 2003, we spent time looking at ominous signs of a new, deeply disaffected, and divided trend in US politics—a foreshadowing of decades of seemingly intractable turmoil and divisions to come.

One subject that concerned me most was the seeming inability of governments to cope with the swirling complexities of the world as the hectic pace of urgent problems and crises picked up. The endless tsunami of information swamping power centres and bureaucracies had no precedent. As the pressure of constant media demands kept expanding, so did the impatience of the public for quick solutions to issues. No government dared admit it, but the problem of overload, exhaustion, and confusion was now systemic—and dangerous. The public and media were right to point out failures by government, but we didn't really grasp just how much more difficult governing had become over the past four decades.

When I discussed this problem with senior diplomats, foreign affairs scholars, and modern historians, I found wide agreement: even the best-informed government power centres showed signs of being overwhelmed. Madeleine Albright, who was US secretary of state under President Bill Clinton, noted that since we had both graduated in 1964, the world's population had increased by five billion, the number of governments had grown from 64 to 194, and now even the smallest crisis could not be ignored for fear of nasty surprises. That's not all, for countless activist groups and NGOs now poured their own urgent demands into the mix, so that "the pounding for attention never ceases," she said. Zbigniew Brzezinski, the former White House national security advisor, growled that along with overload, there was constant pressure to prep for committee meetings and "shape the narrative" for the insistent media—at a time when much of the population had little sense of geography. In Canada and other Western capitals, that narrative shaping often led to simplistic slogans and empty pledges of future priority action.

The faster communications sped up, the more frantic became our search for answers, and even the best intelligence services not only failed to foresee giant events like the fall of Communism and the financial crisis of 2007–8 but often predicted conflicts that failed to arise. Extensive studies of the misfires of "big thinkers" by US political scientist Philip Tetlock found a curious dilemma: "We normally expect knowledge to promote accuracy, so it was surprising to discover how quickly we reach a point of diminishing returns."

Since the 1980s, I'd come to think of modern TV journalism, particularly in foreign coverage, as a massive vortex sucking us deeper into a swirl of blindingly complex events. The media's push for continuous breaking news heightened the public's sense of rudderless impermanence. As a reporter, I had been thrilled to be riding the wave of so many fast-paced historic events; as a citizen, I worried about the ability of societies to adapt to the anxieties and frictions of such nervous change. How can democratic systems, shaped in the nineteenth century, maintain public trust in increasingly cynical and impatient times? I am not trying to defend governments, but those of us on the outside fail to appreciate the frustrations of those in office, constantly besieged by rising public demands for action, the nonstop criticism of the opposition, and the "indignation machine of the modern media," as Michael Ignatieff called it.

Many factors are involved in growing public mistrust of government institutions, including the arrival of social media and the spread of political cynicism and conspiracy theories. However, the shift emerged decades ago and was so profound that it alarmed scholars, including the US senator and public intellectual Daniel P. Moynihan, who, in March 1971, in a widely debated essay in *Commentary* magazine, warned of a growing "bias towards negativity" led by the media's "adversary culture" and its "almost feckless hostility to power." The arrival of "gotcha journalism," with its aggressive questioning of public figures, further heightened the combative nature of the media. I am certainly not opposed to hard investigative reporting, which I did a good deal of in my time, but a widespread problem arises when the media covers almost exclusively the easy-to-reap negative stories of conflict, cynicism, and the stench of government failure while neglecting to report the complex challenges facing those in government—and even their occasional successes. The theatrics of political combat encourages posturing and overhyped anger and incivility in arenas such as the televised Question Period. In television it became more common from the eighties on for editorial meetings to dodge subjects that we sneeringly called "process stories"—those with a lot of context and detail meant to show how the governing systems really worked, sometimes successfully.

This adversarial trend had a worrisome impact on the functioning of government: instead of greater transparency, we got more attempts to control the news. Ministries, fearful of revealing anything that would fire up new controversies, became more insular, while the flow of information was centralized around the Prime Minister's Office. In Ottawa and other layers of government, an inordinate amount of time was now spent fine-tuning press releases and debating media strategies. Government departments operate more defensively and centralize information flow to avoid criticism that helps the opposition. Donald Savoie, one of Canada's leading scholars on government, warns that this extreme caution leaves government "with a crippling overload problem, creating bottlenecks at the centre of government." He notes, "Accountability in government does not have much of a chance in this environment, and, when accountability goes, trust is never far behind."

Clearly, distrust has become rampant throughout Canadian society, affecting not just politicians but many key institutions, including the media, which has sunk to a meagre 38 percent trust level (down from 55 percent in 2016) according to a 2024 report of the Reuters Institute for the Study of Journalism. Generalized distrust fosters not just divisions but also loathing: it was estimated by the early 2020s, that up to 3 million Canadians did not vote because they feel that no candidate can be trusted. In this already highly cynical era, the spread of falsehoods and conspiracies on digital media challenges our notions of reality, to the point where it becomes harder to separate fact from fiction, or even downright fantasy. It is no solution for media to run an occasional good-news item, the usual minimal concession to criticism. What's needed is a steady emphasis on more nuanced, context-rich stories, domestic as well as foreign. Some print media is showing promise in this area, but TV needs a greater commitment to balanced and deeply researched coverage that is less addicted to the theatrics of political conflict. Change won't be easy, given the ongoing thinning out of newsroom staff, but at least journalists have never had more resources for solid research at hand—online and among academics, NGOs, and various activist groups and think tanks.

In the winter of 2007, I squeezed uncomfortably inside a Canadian light armoured vehicle (LAV) in Afghanistan heading out on a morning patrol to check on Taliban activity in Kandahar Province, the notorious heartland of the radical Islamist Taliban movement. I can't say I was anxious to find the guerrillas. Rumbling across the dun-coloured, starkly rugged terrain, at age sixty-five I was an improbable-looking figure in my helmet and protective vest.

Three years later, when I returned for a second round of reports, limping from knee pain, I looked even less appropriate to the soldiers who'd need to rush me to safety in an ambush. They were a fun lot and friendly, and as they travelled, they played their rock and country music over the LAV intercom. One asked me, "So who's your favourite—early Sinatra?"

I wasn't in Afghanistan because I yearned for excitement. Friends at the CBC, including Peter Mansbridge, had urged me not to go, given my age and the fact I had nothing to prove. I went simply because there were key details of the war I needed to check on, including the reason why Canadians were receiving such restricted, often misleading information on the campaign. I was heading *Inside the Mission*, an ongoing CBC series that tried to show how each stage of Canada's role in the NATO/UN-mandated campaign was devised, planned, controlled, and played out in the field. While rotating CBC reporters covered the troops, I was focused on the command side, on the struggles of the military to meet the often-confusing directives of politicians to "sell the war" to an increasingly dubious public. The challenge was interesting, given how little war information Canadians got compared to the coverage people in allied nations received, especially in the United Kingdom and the United States. Our political and military leaders released so little intelligence that I found it easier to sense how the campaign was really going, or failing, by speaking to military and diplomatic sources in foreign capitals.

This limited awareness had two causes. Both the Liberal and the Conservative governments, and even some opposition parties, tried to avoid open debate on the war and to say as little as possible about it to avoid any possible public backlash. And, although we had some first-rate, military-savvy reporters in Afghanistan, there were never enough. Canada, unlike the United States and the United Kingdom, had an extraordinary shortage of journalists who knew anything about military affairs. The military could pump out a diet of superficial, relentlessly upbeat media handouts that the combat-experienced British and US news corps would have eviscerated. This political/military manipulation of information behind "support our troops" sloganeering encouraged a willful self-deception. While Ottawa and the Canadian base outside Kandahar City bragged of victories over the Taliban and of prestige won among allies, British and American military opinion concluded early on that our twenty-eight-hundred-member battle force was understrength, underarmed, and incapable of pursuing Taliban forces aggressively enough.

As I continued to dig into command decisions, I was amazed to learn how little our politicians and military commands knew about the Taliban phenomenon when they recklessly volunteered for the Kandahar mission, which was launched in mid-2005. The continuing ignorance of decision makers five years later was especially shocking because a secret report I later learned of had been given to NATO command back in early 2005 by a senior Canadian staff officer, Colonel George Petrolekas. It starkly warned that the allied alliance knew alarmingly little about even normal intelligence basics: Taliban command structure, central plans, internal alliances, strength, tactics, and its culture and religious fundamentals. The report was a prescient warning of a core problem that bedevilled the whole allied campaign. "Without clearly knowing why the Taliban does things confounds our ability to defeat it," Petrolekas concluded, for "the enemy is far more sophisticated, politically conscious and strategic in its conduct of operations than we have previous credited."

When I first arrived in 2007 at the sprawling Canadian base outside Kandahar City, the provincial capital, I found commanders still baffled by the elusive Taliban. I'd barely put my bag down when a rocket screamed over my head to explode near the airstrip. The guerrillas were nearby. Yet only months earlier in two rare hard-fought, conventional-style battles (Operation Medusa and Panjwaii), more than a thousand Canadian Forces personnel claimed victories that their ground commanders claimed had "broken the back of the Taliban." The Taliban had wisely withdrawn to winter sanctuaries, including in neighbouring Pakistan, where they regrouped and abandoned conventional tactics in favour of guerrilla-style insurgency. The Canadians were left scrambling to adopt a counterinsurgency doctrine, totally new to them, at which they were doomed to fail in this large and complex theatre of operations.

I thought the regular units and most of the officers were highly committed professionals, while the reservists won steady praise from allies. Yet the force floundered from the start, despite occasional successes, because their numbers (even after the initial twenty-eight hundred troops were boosted by another thousand) were ridiculously puny for counterinsurgency. (The British in much smaller Helmand Province, with nine thousand personnel, were still dangerously overstretched.) In this type of conflict, winning requires separating the population from the insurgents, then staying among the population to protect it and gain support. These operations are critical to gathering intelligence and weakening the insurgents. The Canadian units could at most temporarily clear villages of the Taliban but weren't strong enough to stay. They also didn't have enough reliable local forces to do much of the work for them.

The situation steadily deteriorated from 2007 on, when increasing guerrilla attacks forced the Canadians, under pressure from Ottawa, to limit casualties. They had to look to their own safety by staying mainly inside defensive positions. US reporters were shocked to find that it was rare for six to eight hundred personnel to be sent outside the heavily guarded base at any time. Those numbers were not enough to secure significant numbers of tribal villages or even much of urban Kandahar City itself.

I'll leave full coverage of the war to historians. Personally, my experiences there varied from frustrating to farcical. The media operated under heavy restrictions: we were unable to cite the number of rockets slamming into the base, film wounded soldiers, or report on a firefight unless a soldier was killed. I argued with a base commander that this policy gave Canada a sanitized version of the war which suited Ottawa's wish to downplay it altogether. He merely shrugged in response as if to indicate "it is what it is."

When I was out with troops, there was always some tension as they assumed they might encounter roadside bombs, ambushes, or sniper attacks. On both trips I ran into mishaps that seemed symbolic of a well-meaning but floundering mission. I was taken once in a small convoy to visit a Canadian aid project in Kandahar City. When they parked the LAV and the others piled out, I found the back doors were jammed. A sergeant yanked and pulled at the rear exit without success. The thought flashed through my mind of being slowly roasted inside if the Taliban set the vehicle ablaze. Eventually, my group had to pry me out through an exit in the roof, which caused great consternation to the squad leaders but considerable amusement to local Afghans.

On another outing, I was taken with a crew to see a grade school that Canada was funding as part of its large aid program. As we were about to enter, a barrage of rocks came over the wall, hurled by the boys in the playground, who found that stoning their foreign benefactors was hilarious fun. We taped the soldiers dodging the rocks and bellowing back at the kids to stop. In microcosm, this incident seemed to say something about the wearisome disappointments of the mission.

During my second trip, in 2010, I found the tension far greater as the Taliban advanced on many fronts. The allies were desperate to train national police and army recruits, but the guerrillas were infiltrating training units and killing foreign instructors. One day I covered a session of police training by a retired Texas Ranger with gun and holster on his hips. As the stone-faced recruits found their seats, I asked him, "Are you worried a few may be Taliban?" "Sure, but I'm betting I'm a faster draw than they are," he drawled in reply.

Since the guerrillas were now installed within Kandahar City, my fellow reporter Andrew Potter of *Maclean's* magazine and I staged a media mutiny and refused to join a patrol we thought utterly mad. It was approaching dusk, the most dangerous time for snipers, and our government media minder said he had arranged for a couple of LAVs to take us see the central marketplace. Potter, normally a jolly philosopher type, and I fumed that it would put everyone—troops, bystanders, and us—at serious risk of attack when all we could film was people buying fruit. After much grumbling, the patrol was scrapped.

Next morning, we joined another patrol, but one that seemed haphazardly planned. I noticed that the soldiers acted more intense than usual as we drove down one country road. We suddenly stopped and they poured out to check on a farmer with a shovel who had been digging beside the road—perhaps to prepare a bomb site. "Why don't we just take him out?" someone asked without conviction. After several long minutes, the drama passed. Years later, Potter told me he'd run into someone who had attended an angry debriefing session following the patrol. The senior officer wanted to know why the route was planned on such a dangerous stretch of road. "You almost got

Brian Stewart blown up!" he roared. It was news to me, but I can't deny feeling rather flattered by the concern.

Various assessment teams of allies have concluded that Kandahar was the main point of failure in Afghanistan. Canada had volunteered to take it on hoping for miliary and diplomatic prestige, but allies grew tired of Canadian "boosterism" for their war, as British ambassador to Afghanistan Sherard Cowper-Coles called it. The head of the NATO and allied alliance in southern Afghanistan in 2006–7, British general David Richards, argued that the weak Canadian force should never have been given so vital a mission as Kandahar. The Americans, who had handed the province over to Canada in 2005, had to send heavy forces of Marines back into Kandahar in 2010 to stabilize the ground war there.

A year later the Harper government, ending the combat role sooner than expected, brought the troops home. Canada lost 158 troops in Afghanistan and many thousands more were wounded physically and mentally. Canada's sense of itself and its foreign capabilities has not yet fully recovered. But it's clear now that even if Canada had doubled or even quadrupled its commitment, the outcome would likely not have been significantly different. Unless the Afghan population rose to block the Taliban, there were always limits to what outsiders could achieve, especially as the insurgents had sanctuaries in neighbouring Pakistan. A detained Taliban soldier put it neatly to an American captor: "You have the watches, but we have the time."

The Afghanistan tour marked the end of my roving reporting career. When our group stopped overnight at the Forces' Camp Mirage airbase in Dubai, I didn't join them for dinner in the sparkling city. Instead, I spent quiet hours reflecting on travels past, content to decide those days were over. My last act before hitting my army bed was to remove my dusty hiking boots and drop them ceremoniously into the refuse bin outside my door.

The boots were the first thing the surprised group saw when they returned, and next morning they asked if anything was wrong. Quite the opposite, I said: this was my way of celebrating that my days in the field were done.

Back home, I'd retired, but the process was very gradual. The CBC wanted me to continue on contract to do special reports for *The National* and serve as news analyst when needed. On my last official day, they asked me to host *The National*, which turned out to be a moving goodbye. They even aired a documentary on my career. I went on to present a wide range of stories, so many that someone wrote in to complain: "I keep hearing Stewart is going, or is gone, and then he's back again . . . will he ever please just go?"

I was thrilled to have a more reflective life. I'd been made a distinguished senior fellow at the Munk School of Global Affairs & Public Policy, an idyllic role for me as I got to attend lectures, moderate debates, sit in on discussions with diplomats and scholars, and read position papers to my heart's content, all without a news deadline hanging over me. I was particularly interested in helping to devise courses on crisis management and strategy, along with the school's director, Janice Stein, who has an outstanding global reputation in these areas.

At fourteen I'd dreamed of seeing history being made. Now, ambition satisfied, I thrive on the calmness of days, enjoying the feeling of life slowing down as it was meant to do. I am fully a homebody with Tina, surrounded by my books and living close to our daughter, Katie, a psychologist. I remain profoundly grateful to journalism, and especially the CBC, for all the fascinating experiences I've had and the people I've met. Although I'm still prone to some moral injury symptoms, they have diminished with time.

A question I still get asked a lot is whether I ever wish I were out there covering the world. I do not. I'm happy to be beyond that swirl of events that I now watch only from afar. A history buff, I delve as much into the past as I do the present and feel enriched by the soft twilight glow of nostalgia.

Acknowledgements

When I began this memoir, I was fortunate in having a good long-term memory and, what's more, I loved to revisit those long past decades I had lived through. I soon found, however, that being a hopeless nostalgic does not make writing much easier when you're dealing with a vast arc of time that stretches back to Second World War victory gardens, newsreels in cinemas, pre-plastic toys, and Canada before TV existed—not to mention the many revolutions that have swept my world of journalism.

Inevitably, I needed a lot of help in tackling such a span, just as I needed family, friends, and a superb editor to bear with me during long months of my moaning, groaning, and bellyaching over the hard task I had taken on.

I owe debts of gratitude to a number of my former CBC colleagues and friends who helped check my memories of great events we had covered together as well as the often rocky times our Crown corporation endured: Peter Mansbridge, Tony Burman, Mark Starowicz, John Owen, Ann Medina, Lara Chatterjee, Robin Benger, Carmen Merrifield, Margaret Davidson, Jennifer Clibbon, and Sandra Clemenson. Sadly, several of the great cameramen I worked with are no longer living, but Brian Kelly in London was generous in helping me relive dramatic times together in the field. Friends from the early times in Montreal and Ottawa who helped my recall included Leigh Beauchamp, Terry Haig, Patrick Oliver, and Sandra Davies.

On the Ethiopian famine, David MacDonald, Canada's emergency coordinator for African famine in 1985, gave unstintingly of his time, as did my friend Bisrat Mesfin, who in Makelle, Tigray, Northern Ethiopia, is chairman of the Ethiopian Youth Educational Support (EYES) charity. My four-decade friendship with the family of Birhan Woldu, also in Tigray, so resilient across the years, has been a constant source of inspiration to me.

Tim Draimin, one of Canada's leaders in struggling for human rights in Latin America in the 1980s, helped me recall the wars of El Salvador and Nicaragua, while Janice Stein, founder and head of the Munk School of Global Affairs & Public Policy at the University of Toronto, was insightful, as always, in discussing the turbulent years of the twenty-first century so far. Author/philosopher Andrew Potter, now a program director at the Max Bell School of Public Policy, McGill University, was a witty companion on my media tour to Afghanistan and helped me recall some of our more bizarre experiences there.

At every stage of drafting this memoir, my wife, Tina Srebotnjak, proved not only a marvel of patience but a wise counsellor on writing decisions and a reliable confidence supporter. My daughter, Katie Stewart, another morale booster, rescued me from innumerable computer meltdowns (mine, not the equipment's). My sister, Heather, shared her literary judgments as well as vivid memories of our distant youth together.

Kevin Hanson, former president and publisher of Simon & Schuster Canada, convinced me to write this memoir. I cannot say enough for the publisher, the many examples I've received of its encouragement, and the solid professionalism from Grace O'Connell and the whole team.

Of all the breaks I have received, the greatest is to have worked with editor Rosemary Shipton, a legend in Canadian publishing.

Having worked with editors all my career and long valued the creative abilities of the best, I was fascinated to observe how Rosemary lived up to her star billing, invariably improving my text by surgical cutting and by so often calmly offering wise guidance on the way forward.

Sources

Chapter One: The Child in the Ethiopian Famine

Clay, Jason W., and Bonny Holcomb. *Politics and the Ethiopian Famine 1984–84*. Milton Park, UK: Routledge, 1986.

Hampson, Fen Osler. *Master of Persuasion: Brian Mulroney's Global Legacy*. Toronto: Penguin Random House, 2018, especially ch. 3.

Hancock, Graham. *Ethiopia: The Challenge of Hunger*. London: Victor Gollancz, 1985.

Harvey, Oliver. *Feed the World: Birhan Woldu and Live Aid*. London: New Holland, 2011.

Jansen, Kurt, Michael Harris, and Angela Penrose. *The Ethiopian Famine: The Story of the Emergency Relief Operations*. London: Zed Books, 1985.

Plaut, Martin, and Sarah Vaughan. *Understanding Ethiopia's Tigray War*. London: Hurst, 2023.

Solomon, Nassisse. *"Tears Are Not Enough": Canadian Political and Social Mobilization for Famine Relief in Ethiopia, 1984–85*. Beyond Boundaries Series. Calgary: University of Calgary Press, 2019, ch. 10.

Chapter Two: Radio Free Brian

Hennessy, Peter. *Britain in the Fifties*. London: Penguin, 2007.

Kynaston, David. *Family Britain 1951–57*. London: Bloomsbury, 2009.

Chapter Three: Toronto the Good and the Swinging Sixties

Black, Conrad. *A Life in Progress*. Toronto: Key Porter, 1993.

Bothwell, Robert. *The Penguin History of Canada*. Toronto: Penguin Canada 2006, ch. 14.

Henderson, Stuart. *Making the Scene: Yorkville and Hip Toronto*. Toronto: University of Toronto Press, 2011.

Sandbrook, Dominic. *Never Had It So Good: A History of Britain From Suez to the Beatles*. London: Abacus/Little Brown, 2005.

Bray, Christopher. *1965: The Year Modern Britain Was Born*. London: Simon & Schuster, 2015.

Wiseman, Nelson. *1950s Canada: Politics and Public Affairs*. Toronto: University of Toronto Press, 2022.

Chapter Four: Passionate Montreal in Years of Ferment

Bothwell, Robert. *The Penguin History of Canada*. Toronto: Penguin Canada, 2006.

Bothwell, Robert, Ian Drummond, and John English. *Canada Since 1945: Power, Politics, and Provincialism*. Toronto: University of Toronto Press, 2001.

Clarkson, Stephen, and Christina McCall. *Trudeau and Our Times*. Vol. 1, *The Magnificent Obsession*. Toronto: McClelland & Stewart, 1991, pp. 95–129.

English, John. *Just Watch Me: The Life of Pierre Trudeau*. Toronto: Knopf Canada, 2009, pp. 1–98.

Gravenor, Kristian. *Montreal 375: Tales of Eating, Drinking, Living and Loving*. Montreal: Megaforcemedia, 2017.

Jenish, D'Arcy. *The Making of the October Crisis*. Toronto: Penguin Random House, 2018.

Mills, Sean. *The Empire Within: Postcolonial Thought and Political Activism in Sixties Montreal*. Montreal: McGill-Queen's University Press, 2010.

Purcell, Susan, and Brian McKenna. *Jean Drapeau*. Toronto, Clark Irwin, 1980.

Chapter Five: TV Times

Nash, Knowlton. *The Microphone Wars: A History of Triumph and Betrayal at the CBC*. Toronto: McCelland & Stewart, 1994.

Brazil. *Truth Commission Report*. 2010.

Canada. Privy Council Office. *Commission of Inquiry into Certain Activities of the Royal Canadian Mounted Police*. Ottawa: 1981.

Eckel, Jan, and Samuel Moyn. *The Breakthrough: Human Rights in the 1970s*. Philadelphia: University of Pennsylvania Press, 2015.

Eulich, Whitney. "Ten Economic Protests That Changed History." *Christian Science Monitor*. November 5, 2011.

Franklin, James C. *Human Rights in Latin America*. Oxford: Oxford University Press, 2023.

Nash, Knowlton. *The Microphone Wars: A History of Triumph and Betrayal at the CBC*. Toronto: McClelland & Stewart, 1994.

New York Times. "Canada Says the Mounted Police Opened and Copied Mail Illegally." November 10, 1977.

Riding, Alan. "The Pope's Visit to Mexico." *New York Times*, January 20, 1979.

Shenon, Philip. "US Releases Files on Abuses in Pinochet Era." *New York Times*, July 1, 1999.

Valenzuela, Arturo, and Pamela Constable. *Nation of Enemies: Chile Under Pinochet.* W.W. Norton: New York, 1993.

Chapter Six: Horror in Latin America

Allison, Mike. "El Salvador's Brutal Civil War: What We Still Don't Know." Aljazeera, March 1, 2012.

Amnesty International Report. *El Salvador: Peace can only be achieved with justice.* April 4. 2001. Index Number AMR 29/001/2001. Peac 2001.

Didion, Joan. *Salvador.* New York: Simon & Shuster, 1983.

El Salvador: War, Peace, and Human Rights, 1980–1994. Microfiche collection of US documentation, National Security Archive, George Washington University, Washington, DC.

Forche, Carolyn. *What You Have Heard Is True: A Memoir of Witness and Resistance.* New York: Penguin Random House, 2019.

Jenkins, Anthony, Eduardo Galeano, and Lou Dematteis, *Nicaragua: A Decade of Revolution.* New York: W.W. Norton, 1991.

Sierakowski, Robert J. *Sandinistas: A Moral History.* Notre Dame, IN: Notre Dame Press, 2019.

United Nations. *Report of the UN Truth Commission on El Salvador.* Report to the Security Council, New York, 1993.

Chapter Seven: Thatcher Years and the London Bureau

Cannadine, David, *History in Our Time.* New Haven, CT: Yale University Press, 1998.

Hastings, Max, and Simon Jenkins. *The Battle for the Falklands.* London: W.W. Norton, 1984.

Judt, Tony. *Postwar: A History of Europe Since 1945.* New York: Penguin, 2005, ch. 17.

Vinen, Richard. *A History in Fragments: Europe in the Twentieth Century.* London: Time Warner Books UK, 2000.

———. *Thatcher's Britain: Politics and Social Upheaval of the 1980s.* London: Simon & Schuster UK, 2010.

Jenkins, Simon. *England's Thousand Best Churches.* London: Penguin Books, 2009, pp. 479–80.

Chapter Eight: Beirut Furies and Fascination

Fisk, Robert. *Pity the Nation: The Abduction of Lebanon.* Oxford, UK: Oxford University Press, 1991

Geraghty, Timothy J. *Peacekeepers at War: Beirut 1983.* Washington, DC: Potomac Books, 2009.

Glass, Charles. *Money for Old Rope*. London: Pan Books, 1992.

Kassir, Samir. *Beirut: A War Memoir.* Oakland: University of California Press, 2011.

Mackey, Sandra. *Lebanon: Death of a Nation*. New York: Congdon & Weed, 1989.

Makdisi, Jean Said. *Beirut Fragments*. New York: Persea Books, 1990.

Randal, Jonathan. *The Tragedy of Lebanon*. London: Hogarth Press, 1983.

Tueni, Nadia. *Lebanon: Poems of Love and War*. Syracuse, NY: Syracuse University Press, 2006.

Chapter Nine: Greed, Grievance, and Generosity

Beynon, Huw, and Ray Hudson. *The Shadow of the Mine: Coal and the End of Industrial Britain*. London: UK: Verso/New Left Books, 2021.

Geldof, Bob. *Is That It?* Oxford, UK: Sidgwick & Jackson, 1985.

Judt, Tony. *Postwar: A History of Europe Since 1945*. New York: Penguin, 2005.

Laqueur, Walter. *Europe in Our Time: A History 1945–1992*. New York: Penguin, 1993.

Stewart, Graham. *Bang! A History of Britain in the 1980s*. London: Atlantic Books, 2013.

Towns, David, ed. *Health in Humanitarian Emergencies: Principles and Practice for Public Health and Healthcare Practitioners*. Cambridge, UK: Cambridge University Press, 2018, ch. 2.

Chapter Ten: My NBC Adventures

Friedman, Norman. *The Cold War: Threat, Paranoia and Obsession*. London: Andre Deutsch/Carlton Publishing Group, 2009.

Leebaert, Derek. *The Fifty-Year Wound: The True Price of America's Cold War Victory*. Back Bay Books, 2003.

Sayle, Timothy Andrews. *Enduring Alliance: A History of NATO and the Postwar Global Order*. Ithaca, NY: Cornell University Press, 2019.

"US Raid Haunts Libya." *Middle East Report* 141 (July/August 1986).

Black, Conrad. *My Life In Progress*. Toronto: Key Porter Books, 1993.

Vinen, Richard. *A History in Fragments: Europe in the Twentieth Century*. London: Time Warner Books UK, 2000.

Weinraub, Bernard. "U.S. Jets Hit Terrorist Centers in Libya; Reagan Warns of New Attacks If Needed." *New York Times*, April 15, 1986.

Chapter Eleven: Investigations and Liberations

Hitchcock, Willian L. *The Struggle for Europe: The Turbulent History of a Divided Continent—1945 to the Present*. New York: Anchor Books, 2004.

Hobsbawm, Eric. *Age of Extremes: The Short Twentieth Century*. London: Penguin, 1994.

Human Rights Watch. *Sudan* 10, no. 4A (August 1998). *Global Trade, Local Impact: Arms Transfers to All Sides in the Civil War in Sudan*, ch. 2. https://www.hrw.org/legacy/reports98/sudan/Sudarm988-03.htm.

Human Rights Watch, International Rescue Committee Report. *The Lost Boys of Sudan*. October 2014, https://www.rescue.org/article/lost-boys-sudan.

Judt, Tony. *Postwar: A History of Europe Since 1945*. New York: Penguin, 2005, pp. 585–633.

Service, Robert. *The End of the Cold War*. Oakland: University of California Press, 1997.

Sixsmith, Martin. *The War of Nerves: Inside the Cold War Mind*. New York: Pegasus Books, 2022.

The Air India Flight 182 Archive. Faculty of Humanities, McMaster University, Hamilton, ON. https://airindiaflight182.humanities.mcmaster.ca/.

Chapter Twelve: The Gulf War and Broadcast Battles

Freedman, Lawrence and Efraim Karsh. *The Gulf Conflict 1990–1991*. London: Faber & Faber, 1993.

Nash, Knowlton. *The Microphone Wars: A History of Triumph and Betrayal at the CBC*. Toronto: McClelland & Stewart, 1994, ch. 21.

Taras, David, and Christopher Waddell. *The End of the CBC?* Toronto: University of Toronto Press, 2020.

Chapter Thirteen: "A Wound to the Soul"

Canada. Commission of Inquiry into the Deployment of Canadian Forces to Somalia. *Dishonoured Legacy: The Lessons of the Somalia Affair*. Ottawa, 1997. http://publications.gc.ca/pub?id=9.700365&sl=0.

Dallaire, Roméo. *Shake Hands with the Devil*. Toronto: Penguin Canada, 2004.

Feinstein, Anthony. "In the Face of Moral Challenges, Journalists Need Help." *Globe and Mail*, October 22, 2022.

——. *Journalists Under Fire: The Psychological Hazards of Covering War*. Baltimore, MD: Johns Hopkins University Press, 2003.

Human Rights Watch. *The Rwandan Genocide: How It Was Prepared*. Briefing paper no. 1, April 2006. https://www.hrw.org/legacy/backgrounder/africa/rwanda0406/.

Stewart, Ian. *Freetown Ambush*. Toronto: Penguin Canada, 2002.

Chapter Fourteen: Boots Away and Happy Endings

Boucher, Jean-Christophe, and Kim Richard Nossal. *The Politics of War: Canada's Afghanistan Mission 2001–14*. Vancouver: UBC Press, 2017.

Brewster, Murray. *The Savage War: The Untold Battles of Afghanistan*. Toronto: John Wiley & Sons Canada. 2011.

Ignatieff, Michael. "Why Are We in Iraq? And Liberia? And Afghanistan?" *New York Times*, September 7, 2003.

Petrolekas, George. Report of the Canadian Liaison Officer to NATO Joint Forces Command. Allied Joint Force Command Brunssum, the Netherlands. Dec 4 January 2005.

Savoie, Donald J. *Government: Have Presidents and Prime Ministers Misdiagnosed the Patient?* Montreal: McGill-Queen's University Press, 2022.

Stein, Janice Gross, and Eugene Lang. *The Unexpected War: Canada in Kandahar*. Toronto: Viking Canada, 2007.

Tetlock, Philip E., and Dan Gardner. *Superforecasting: The Art and Science of Predicting*. Oxford, UK: Signal Books, 2015.

Whitlock, Craig. *The Afghanistan Papers: A Secret History of the War*. New York: Simon & Schuster, 2021.

Index

About the Author

Brian Stewart was for decades one of the Canada's most prominent television journalists, and was acclaimed for his foreign coverage for both CBC's *The National* and *The Journal.* Born in Montreal, and originally a newspaper reporter, Stewart went on to become a foreign correspondent for CBC in London and NBC in Frankfurt. He worked in ten war zones, hosted the CBC foreign affairs show *Worldview*, and interviewed many of the historic figures of his time, including Nelson Mandela, Margaret Thatcher, Salman Rushdie, and Henry Kissinger. After retiring, he was appointed Senior Fellow of the Munk School of Global Affairs & Public Policy, University of Toronto. Stewart is a recipient of the Order of Ontario, the Queen's Jubilee Medal, and the Order of Canada.